RENEGADE POETICS

CONTEMPORARY NORTH AMERICAN POETRY SERIES

Series Editors Alan Golding, Lynn Keller, and Adalaide Morris

Renegade Poetics

Black Aesthetics and Formal Innovation in African American Poetry

EVIE SHOCKLEY

UNIVERSITY OF IOWA PRESS
Iowa City

University of Iowa Press, Iowa City 52242
Copyright © 2011 by the University of Iowa Press
www.uiowapress.org
Printed in the United States of America

Design by Teresa W. Wingfield

The University of Iowa Press is a member of Green Press Initiative and is committed to preserving natural resources.

Printed on acid-free paper

Library of Congress Cataloging-in-Publication Data
Shockley, Evie, 1965–
Renegade poetics: black aesthetics and formal innovation in
African American poetry / Evie Shockley.
    p.   cm.—(Contemporary North American poetry series)
Includes bibliographical references and index.
ISBN-13: 978-1-60938-058-8, ISBN-10: 1-60938-058-4 (pbk.)
1. American poetry—African American authors—History and criticism.   2. African American aesthetics.   3. African Americans in literature.   I. Title.
PS310.N4S56 2011
811.009'896073—dc22   2011007473

In Memory of

Anne Spencer and Gwendolyn Brooks,

and for

Ed Roberson,

Sonia Sanchez,

Will Alexander,

and

Harryette Mullen,

Renegades, All

CONTENTS

ACKNOWLEDGMENTS

I USED TO WONDER WHY the acknowledgments for academic books were so incredibly long; now, at the end of my own journey from project proposal to published monograph, I wonder only that they aren't even longer. In the interest of space, many people I mention in only one context below might well have been thanked in two or three others. My apologies at the outset for the omissions that, like any mistakes or missteps within the body of this text, are all the more lamentable for being inevitable in connection with a project of this size.

The bulk of first books by academics begin as dissertations. This one did not, but I still cannot pass up the opportunity to thank the members of my dissertation committee, Wahneema Lubiano, Barbara Herrnstein Smith, and Irene Tucker, for their example, their teaching, and their support of my graduate work. Despite the differences between the focus of my dissertation ("gothic homelessness" in British Victorian and twentieth-century African American prose) and the project of this book, so much that I learned from them in working on that text proved indispensable to me in producing this one. My dissertation director and tireless mentor, Karla F. C. Holloway, deserves thanks for all these things and many more; she is the embodiment of grace (and professionalism) under pressure.

This book began, instead, as a conference paper, as did most of the chapters herein. In that light, I'd like to thank Dorothy Wang for organizing the panel on Experimental Minority Poetry for the 2002 MLA Convention and, along with her, my co-panelists Aldon Nielsen and Timothy Yu for a conversation that helped transform an interest into an intellectual passion strong enough to sustain this project. Memorably, Lorenzo Thomas was in the audience of that panel; his comments that day were both challenging and encouraging, and he remains, even after his transition, one of my most important interlocutors. I am grateful as well to the rest of the chairs, conveners, panelists, respondents, and audience members at whose invitation, in whose company, and with whose help I worked out bits and pieces of this book in the years since, including Charles Bernstein, Joseph Donohue, Erica Edwards, J. Martin Favor, Tonya Foster, Jacqueline Goldsby, John Keene, Lovalerie King, Keith Leonard, Julie Patton, Marjorie Perloff, and Juliana Spahr, among many others. My thanks to Rutgers colleague Mary Hawkesworth for the kind invitation to give a research briefing to members of the Women's and Gender Studies department. And a special thank-you to my former colleague, David Eng, for being the first to say that it wasn't crazy for me to undertake this project, rather than a revision of my dissertation, as my "tenure book" (though, in retrospect, it may have been!).

I am happy for the opportunity to thank the editors and publications that first brought parts of this project, in earlier forms, to print. In *Mixed Blood*, C. S. Giscombe published my first attempt to articulate my dissatisfaction with the constructions of black aesthetics in the wake of the Black Arts Movement ("Post-Black-Aesthetic Poetry: Postscripts and Postmarks"); and Brent Hayes Edwards included in a special section of *Callaloo* devoted to the work of Ed Roberson a version of the essay that became chapter 5 herein ("On the Nature of Ed Roberson's Poetics"). Along a different angle, I'd like to thank my coeditors at *jubilat*: Cathy Park Hong, for thinking aloud with me about the marginalization of poets of color from discussions of innovative poetics, and Rob Casper, for not only talking with me about my project through most of a three-hour road trip, but also providing enthusiastic support (and publication) for the "Experimental African American Poetry Forum" that Terrance Hayes and I organized and edited. Conversations with these poets and many others who approach poetry from a more writerly than scholarly perspective were invaluable for helping me ensure that *Renegade Poetics* addresses the broadest possible audience. And, of course, these thank-yous to editors and publishers could not be complete without my grateful appreciation to the University of Iowa Press, especially my editor, Joseph Parsons, who met nearly every concern I raised with a calm "no problem," and the editors of the Contemporary North American Poetry series, Alan Golding, Lynn Keller, and Adalaide Morris, whose repeated expressions of interest in and engagement with the project over the years of its writing were ever so encouraging. This is also the place to thank my anonymous readers, whose thoughtful, detailed feedback greatly improved the book.

Without the time to write and the access to necessary bibliographic and archival resources I was afforded, *Renegade Poetics* would still be a work-in-progress. I would thus like to acknowledge the fellowship support I received from the American Council of Learned Societies (ACLS) and, via a Scholars-in-Residence Fellowship at the Schomburg Center for Research in Black Culture, from the National Endowment for the

Humanities. My gratitude goes as well to Williams College, particularly the Africana Studies Program, for the office, library privileges, and collegiality extended to me during my year as a research associate there. For assisting me with access to archives that were invaluable to my chapter on Anne Spencer, I would like to thank Edward Gaynor and Sharon Defibaugh at the University of Virginia's Albert and Shirley Small Special Collections Library and Nancy Kuhl at Yale University's Beinecke Rare Book and Manuscript Library. Special thanks to Ms. Shaun Spencer Hester, Anne Spencer's granddaughter, who gave me a personal tour of Spencer's home, restored garden, and writing studio, and to the Anne Spencer House and Garden Museum, Inc., for its work in preserving the poet's legacy.

The Schomburg Center deserves another few words, because in addition to providing me with an office, access to its collections, the assistance of its fabulous librarians—especially Diana Lachatanere and Steven Fullwood—and staff, and a research assistant (Peter Hobbs—thanks!), the Scholars-in-Residence Fellowship put me in connection with a brilliant and generous group of scholars whose feedback helped me understand things about my research that it would have taken me triple the time to figure out on my own. I am grateful to all of the 2007–08 and 2008–09 Scholars, but particularly to our fearless leader, Colin Palmer, who stuck with us despite the multiple trials he confronted during those two years, and to Nicole Fleetwood, Anthony Foy, Carter Mathes, and Laurie Woodard, with whom the conversations begun at the Schomburg continued afterward long enough to get me within sight of the finish line.

To my colleagues in the English department at Rutgers University–New Brunswick, who cheerfully worked around my absence when I was on leave and demonstrated their support in innumerable other ways, I am very grateful. In particular, for generous advice, endless encouragement, and critical feedback, I'd like to thank Harriet Davidson, Brad Evans, Meredith McGill, Richard Miller, Barry Qualls, Carolyn Williams, and Edlie Wong. Brent Edwards, with whom I had the pleasure of working for a few of the years that I've known him, deserves more thanks than I can express for treating me like a peer while teaching and advising me at every turn. Carter Mathes remained "on the hook" as an ideal reader until the manuscript was completely done; I thank him for keeping the bar high, even when my efforts fell short. My thanks to the graduate students in my fall 2006 course, "The Long Poem in African American Poetry," and my fall 2009 course, "Black Aesthetics in Theory and in Practice," for the patience and insightfulness with which they entertained and engaged ideas I was working through for this study. And these thanks hardly begin to express my enormous debt of gratitude to Cheryl Wall: consummate mentor, brilliant interlocutor, and cherished friend.

To George Elliott Clarke, who first modeled for me the path of the "poet-scholar": *merci bien*! To my friends and former colleagues in the English department at Wake Forest University, notably Janis Caldwell, Mary DeShazer, Dean Franco, Michael Hill, and Jessica Richards: my gratitude for the supportive intellectual space in which I first began to develop these ideas and work on poetics. To my various poetry communities (especially Cave Canem), including the growing community of poet-scholars who refuse to choose (particularly Elizabeth Alexander), I give thanks for the many conversations that have inspired and taught me so much. To Candice Jenkins, for seeing me every step of the way; to Rebecca Wanzo, for reading drafts and telling me what I'd written; and to Mendi Lewis Obadike, for reminding me at precisely the right times that I had to finish the book so she could read it: my love and undying friendship. To Meta DuEwa Jones, compatriot, for believing that this book does important work and for nurturing it with invaluable conversations and incisive written feedback: my deepest appreciation and admiration. To Aldon Nielsen, for calling me Professor Shockley, for being an endless fount of advice and good humor, for eloquently ignoring the duller conventions of academic writing, and for practicing what so many simply preach: my highest esteem and my hope that he will take pride in this book, which would have been a much lesser thing without his example and support.

I love my family, all of whom have believed in my ability to do this, without always knowing precisely what "this" was. Heartfelt gratitude to my parents, Foster and Leatha Shockley, who have sacrificed much for my sake; my sister, Teresa Shockley, and my brother-in-law, Thomas Hotes; my twin nieces, Alicia and Olivia Hotes, whose birth reminded me that there are things more important than research; my mother-in-love, Aline Robolin; and the whole network of my relations, by blood or commitment, who make me the person I am, upon whom the scholar I am depends.

Finally, there is no one who deserves more thanks or to whom I feel more gratitude than my partner, Stéphane Robolin. I counted on him to read the roughest drafts, to give me the most honest feedback, to make innumerable cups of coffee, and—hardest of all—to live with me through the stresses and frustrations, as well as through the joys and triumphs, of the writing process. His time, his intellect, and his faith in me have made all the difference again and again. *Merci mille fois, mon amour.*

RENEGADE POETICS

INTRODUCTION
Renegade Poetics (Or, Would Black Aesthetics by An[y] Other Name Be More Innovative?)

Though Maroons, who were unruly Africans, not loose horses or lazy sailors, were called renegades in Spanish, will I turn any blacker if I renege on this deal? —"DENIGRATION," HARRYETTE MULLEN

marronerons-nous Depestre marronerons-nous?
(Shall we turn maroon, Depestre, shall we turn maroon?)
—"LE VERBE MARRONNER," AIMÉ CÉSAIRE

To speak of a Black literature, a Black aesthetic, or a Black state, is to engage in racial chauvinism, separatist bias, and Black fantasy.
—"CULTURAL STRANGULATION: BLACK LITERATURE AND THE WHITE AESTHETIC," ADDISON GAYLE JR.

IN THIS STUDY, I build a case for redefining black aesthetics to account for nearly a century of efforts by African American poets and critics, beginning just after World War I with the New Negro Renaissance, to name and tackle issues of racial identity and self-determination on the field of poetics. Delineating the contours and consequences of African American poetic innovation in an assortment of historical and cultural moments, I aim to highlight and resituate innovative poetry that has been dismissed, marginalized, and misread: first, in relation to the African American poetic tradition, because its experiments were not "recognizably black"; and, second, in relation to constructions of the avant-garde tradition, because they were.[1]

We might begin with an inquiry: what do we mean when we designate as "black" certain behaviors, values, or forms of expression? More particularly, what did the young poets and theorists who created, developed, and associated themselves with the Black Arts Movement (BAM, also called here the Movement) beginning in the mid-1960s mean when they spoke of a black aesthetic? We think we know, even though there is hardly a "we" we could delimit, regardless of race, whose members would have a common understanding or usage of the term. We defend or disparage or dismiss it, as if we agreed upon what *it* is—as if even the originators and first promoters of the concept of a black aesthetic had come to an agreement about its parameters, its value, its reach.[2] The central theorists of the BAM also revised their own thinking over time, as the example of poet and scholar Larry Neal reveals, for instance. Renewed attention to his work demonstrates that his thinking on black aesthetics evolved significantly between the years of his early BAM writings, which focused on narrower definitions, and his untimely death in 1981. Carter Mathes, who in 2006 co-organized a two-day conference devoted to re-evaluating Neal's creative and critical work on black aesthetics, argues that if we examine his whole oeuvre, we find that "Neal went to great lengths to caution against a parochial view of the black aesthetic as a singular arbiter defining the creative and the everyday realms of African-American cultural life."[3]

Despite the complex debates about and transformations of the concept of black aesthetics during and immediately following the Movement, at a certain level of generality, a picture—a caricature, in many respects—of a BAM-era black aesthetic has taken shape in which, as frequently happens with caricatures, several of its features are exaggerated and other qualities some of us know to be present are rendered invisible. I refer herein to this caricatured version—this sloppy, slippery, well-circulated notion—as the Black Aesthetic. The capital letters signify the subsequent reification of a particularly rigid construction of black aesthetics that had its fullest, most passionate articulation during the BAM, but that does not at all exhaust the range of ideas BAM theorists raised in their ongoing dialogues concerning the politics of African American art—nor does it wholly encompass the range of work produced by the poets and other artists in that moment. The Black Aesthetic suggests, among other things, a set of characteristics of black art—poetry, in this case—that are said to be derived organically from African and African diasporic cultures and yet, paradoxically, must often be imposed upon African American poets, who would appear to be dangerously close to assimilation into European American culture.[4] These characteristics, such as an emphasis on and celebration of black music, black speech, black heroes, and black history, should and do determine both the form and content of black poetry—according to this reductive view of BAM theory that I am calling the Black Aesthetic,[5] commonly associated with militant, revolutionary politics and angry, incisive criticism of white supremacy and racial oppression.[6] How ridiculous, or offensive, or limiting it is, we dissenters say, to argue that all African American poets write from—or have a responsibility to write from—this sharply circumscribed location! How all-important, or necessary, or inevitable it is, we defenders say, to understand that African American poets can, do, and should write primarily from this rich and varied cultural heritage, this moral and politically empowering social stance!

What goes missing in the arguments on both poles of the spectrum is the kind of nuance that comes with recalling the historical context in which the concept of a black aesthetic, per se, was first expressed. As Neal makes clear immediately in his 1968 essay on the subject, the BAM emerged out of a charged political context in which radicalized young black people insisted on the interconnectedness of culture and politics. His essay begins:

> The Black Arts Movement is radically opposed to any concept of the artist that alienates him from his community. Black Art is the aesthetic and spiritual sister of the Black Power concept. As such, it envisions an art that speaks directly to the needs and aspirations of Black America. In order to perform this task, the Black Arts Movement proposes a radical reordering of the western cultural aesthetic. It proposes a separate symbolism, mythology, critique, and iconology. The Black Arts and the Black Power concept both relate broadly to the Afro-American's desire for self-determination and nationhood. Both concepts are nationalistic. One is concerned with the relationship between art and politics; the other with the art of politics. ("Black" 62)

I offer this extended quotation because it provides a relatively concise snapshot of some of the Movement's key motivations and methodologies. Its call for black nationhood reminds us that, a century after the emancipation of the enslaved and the end of the U.S. Civil War, African Americans still were not fully enfranchised participants in the nation of which they were citizens. Impatient with the pace and degree of the reforms achieved via the Civil Rights Movement, Black Power advocates sought a dramatic and, if possible, immediate restructuring of American society that would result in African Americans obtaining the political and economic power necessary to become a self-determining people. The emphasis on the artist's role in the political change that Black Power activists sought derives from an analysis of American culture that understands its denigration, demonization, and outright exclusion of black people and their ways of seeing and being in the world as an effective tool for perpetuating African American disenfranchisement. Rather than seek validation in the art forms of a culture in many ways founded upon the notion that black people are less than human or, at best, decidedly inferior to white people, Black Arts proposed to establish a new set of cultural reference points and standards that centered on "the needs and aspirations" of African Americans.

Neal's analysis assumes what Addison Gayle, in a later essay, asserts explicitly: that aesthetics are not universal, but culturally specific, and as long as black art was being written out of one set of cultural materials and values, but being evaluated in accordance with the touchstones of another culture—especially where the latter culture takes the former to be inferior by definition—black art would be found wanting.[7] To conceive of "a Black aesthetic," then, was not to indulge in a "separatist . . . Black fantasy," as Gayle suggested BAM's detractors would argue (see the third epigraph to this Introduction), but to recognize and insist upon the validity of an African American culture that encompasses not only the retentions of the African cultures from which the enslaved population was drawn, but also the unique culture that the enslaved developed out of the conditions and imperatives of their lives in the U.S. ("Cultural" 207). Black Arts, by portraying black people and their political situation more accurately, would teach them what they needed to know in order to struggle effectively for collective power. The degree to which this idea of cultural specificity is now widely accepted is one measure of the impact (and analytical efficacy) of the Movement. The democratization of American poetry, the greater formal and thematic diversity of the poetry of the latter half of the twentieth century as compared to the former, is also attributable in part to the dynamic, poetic avant-garde the BAM nurtured, along with other groups of envelope-pushing writers during that era, such as the Beats or the Black Mountain poets, of whom one more regularly reads in accounts of American literary avant-gardes. The final third of Eugene Redmond's *Drumvoices: The Mission of Afro-American Poetry: A Critical History*, written and published in the waning of the Movement, and James Smethurst's retrospective literary history, *The Black Arts Movement: Literary Nationalism in the 1960s and 1970s*, provide complementary, indispensable accounts of the scope and impact of the work achieved by BAM poet-activists.

But the Movement's problems cannot be overlooked. Most obviously, there is the problem of the constricting, racially essentialist limitations some BAM theories placed upon what a black aesthetic could encompass. These constrictions, by some accounts, would have African American poets address themselves *only* to black audiences, eschew traditional European forms, and draw solely upon African and African American speech, music, folklore, and history for subject matter. To speak of these boundaries as limitations is not to imply that the "approved" territory is small or impoverished, which is certainly not the case; rather, the impracticability and inherent contradictions of such boundaries for a people whose experience has been bound up in the U.S. and the Western cultural tradition for hundreds of years overwhelms the logic of drawing them in the first place. Thus, these limitations helped open the door to the more or less dismissive treatment of the idea of black aesthetics by the African American scholars who might otherwise have been sympathetic interlocutors, when in subsequent years—and due in part to the work of the Black Power and Black Arts activists—they entered the academy and began to develop and shape the emerging field of African American literature. Further, two additional and closely related problems engendered by the Movement's politics concern the sexism and heterosexism attendant to its (black) nationalist ideology. To the extent that the nationalist agenda typically relies upon gender norms and hierarchies in organizing the ("domestic") nation as a "home" and its people as a "family," it should not be surprising that black nationalism figured the black man as the focal point of racist oppression and the frontline warrior in the fight against racism. But such nationalist imperatives placed black women in the position of having to choose between race and gender as the source of their oppression—as if the two were mutually exclusive.[8] This false dichotomy operated upon the realm of black aesthetics not only in terms of content—for example, the appropriate portrayal of men and women in poems or the voices women poets could properly adopt—but also in relation to the formal tropes that were designated "black" and made central to the canon, which consistently privileged heterosexual masculinity.[9]

The dust from the Movement's vigorous, nationwide activity had barely settled before retrospective constructions of its scope and aims and assessments of its efficacy and legacy began to be offered. Houston Baker Jr. and Henry Louis Gates Jr., in 1976 and 1979, respectively, published essays that established their critical trajectories in relation to BAM-era black aesthetics and cleared the ground for their widely influential theoretical studies: Baker's *Blues, Ideology, and Afro-American Literature: A Vernacular Theory* (1984) and Gates's *The Signifying Monkey: A Theory of Afro-American Literary Criticism* (1988). In his essay "On the Criticism of Black American Literature: One View of the Black Aesthetic," Baker applauds the BAM critics for beginning the work of theorizing African American literature—that is, for seeking to define the "Black aesthetic" or articulate "a theoretical perspective that treats Black American literature as a distinctive body of writings" (113, 114). Gates, by contrast, in "Preface to Blackness: Text and Pretext," finds little of value in the Movement's theoretical production (and less in its artistic production), offering as merciless a critique of Jones/Baraka, the poet and theorist, and his poetic and theoretical comrades as Jones had earlier offered of the Harlem Renaissance and mid-century critics and writers. (Gates and Jones equally overstate their cases, it must be said, each to the detriment of his argument.) Gates agrees with Baker, however, that a theory of African American literature is required, one that will privilege the evidence of the text over the political ideology of the moment. Where Baker insists upon the importance of cultural context to the meaning and operation of literary language, a proposition that underwrites his theory of the "blues matrix" (*Blues* 9), Gates calls for a theory in which literary structure and form are foregrounded even as they evidence cultural specificity, which approach frames his conception of the "signifyin(g)" function of the African American "speakerly text" (*Signifying* xxv).

These two theorists, whose work has played a material role in shaping the canon of African American literature that we know today, situated their critiques of BAM-era black aesthetics, as well as, ironically, their own subsequent theories of the centuries-long African American literary tradition, in relation to efforts to define the elusive concept of blackness. Both Baker and Gates, as critics influenced by poststructuralism and postmodernism, reject the racial essentialism that openly shapes (or lurks just beneath the surface of) many BAM-era theories of black aesthetics. Yet their extremely sophisticated and elegant articulations of culturally based, rather than racially based, notions of the characteristics around which African American literature coheres still purport to identify that which is black about these textual structures and, therefore, the texts that employ them. Moreover, for all that they criticize about the construction of race in BAM-era black aesthetics, neither Gates nor Baker moves significantly beyond the problematic masculinization of blackness that those aesthetics incorporate. Thus, their critical approaches necessarily exclude texts by African American writers that are not most productively read through the lens of the blues tradition or the practice of signifying, such that black music and black speech become, once again, the defining rubrics for understanding black literature—not unlike the very BAM theories that Baker and Gates criticize. Further, insofar as Baker's version of the blues tradition writes out the women blues singers in favor of the "bluesman" and his guitar, and Gates chooses to ground his theory in signifying, typically a men's linguistic practice, these approaches also incorporate a masculine bias not unlike that found in BAM theories and no less potent for being implicit rather than overt.

Harryette Mullen identified the problem of these exclusionary constructions of the tradition about ten years ago, with particular reference to the canon-making *Norton Anthology of African American Literature*, of which Gates was a primary editor. The problem with a canon shaped fundamentally by theories grounded in oral traditions of black music and black speech, from Mullen's perspective, is that what she calls "writerly texts"—those that get their primary traction out of their written, visual elements—are marginalized, if not excluded altogether.[10] Mullen's objection arises out of her concern that a significant portion of the most innovative writing by African Americans falls under that banner of the "writerly text" and that, on this basis, a number of excellent, important writers and challenging, innovative works are inadequately written about or taught. Her generative essay "African Signs and Spirit Writing" not only identifies this problem, but in tracing an alternative to the slave narratives, most of which are authored by men, as a genre in which to ground the African American tradition, she points us toward the line of spiritual conversion narratives, for which the most well-known authors were women.[11] Thus, although gender is not an explicit focus of her argument, we are reminded that even seemingly gender-neutral rubrics like "orature" and "writerly texts" may have distinctly gendered implications for our criticism.

Renegade Poetics is my attempt to address these concerns about ways that African American critical traditions have excluded exciting, significant, and innovative writing, specifically with regard to African American poetry. Eschewing racial essentialism, but maintaining a healthy respect for "the integrity of . . . black cultures," I suggest that the term "black aesthetics," from which many contemporary critics have distanced themselves, need not be inevitably linked to static understandings of how blackness is inscribed in literary texts.[12] Instead, what is called for is a redefinition of the term, one that makes it descriptive, rather than prescriptive. While Gates and Baker took important steps in this direction, ultimately their theories return to outlining qualities that "black" texts can be expected to have. Certainly, their theories contain no political imperative that African American writers *should* deploy these qualities in their texts, as BAM theories often did; however, one might argue that these influential conceptions of the tradition suggest—in their effect, if not in their intent—a kind of conditional prescriptive: one's work should have these qualities of "blackness" if one wants the work to be ripe for canonization. That the implications of this prescription seem to weigh more heavily upon women writers is not only important to recognize, but a factor that, as we will see, raises the stakes of this project of redefinition and helps bring them into clearer visibility.

BAM-era black aesthetics—which were in the first instance powerful and empowering expressions of artistic and political agency—and both of its rearticulations (reductively, as the Black Aesthetic, and implicitly, as the unspoken grounding for culturally based theories of black textual forms like Gates's and Baker's) have deeply influenced African American poets and their poetic production. Moreover, they have had similar impact upon the dissemination and reception of African American poetry, insofar as they shape the criteria and values applied to this work by scholars, critics, editors, judges, and publishers, both academic and popular. That is, the core concept of black aesthetics that came out of the Movement has had a much longer and wider scope of influence on African American poetry than we might expect given the close identification of the term with the discrete span of the BAM and later scholars' renunciation of the Black Aesthetic for its essentialism. Thus, poets writing during and since the Movement, up to the present moment, have been directly or indirectly influenced by the explosive aesthetics of such figures as Baraka, Sonia Sanchez, Nikki Giovanni, Haki Madhubuti, Askia Touré, Mari Evans, and others whose work epitomized the defiant, unapologetically political, unabashedly Afrocentric, BAM ethos. Additionally, scholars and critics of African American literature—from the time the field was first gaining recognition within the discipline of English literature through at least the turn of the twenty-first century—have been influenced by BAM-era ideas about black aesthetics. Those ideas inform their conceptions of the canon and the larger tradition, shape editorial decisions, and, along with prevailing directions in the contemporary poetry of these decades, construct readers' expectations for African American poetry.[13] Moreover, even the way we understand African American works written prior to the Movement has been shaped by the BAM legacy—or by our reactions to it. BAM poets' and critics' assertions of the newness of "the New Black Poetry," for example, have encouraged us to see BAM poetry as a more radical break with previous work in the African American tradition than it often was, hindering our ability to see the "newness" of New Negro Renaissance poetry (and other points of commonality between these movements). The Movement has had far-ranging implications for the constitution of not just African American poetry, but multiple poetic traditions in their scholarly and general manifestations.

I propose that we think of not "a black aesthetic" or the Black Aesthetic, but of "black aesthetics," plural: a multifarious, contingent, non-delimited complex of strategies that African American writers may use to negotiate gaps or conflicts between their artistic goals and the operation of race in the production, dissemination, and reception of their writing. These strategies might be "recognizably black," as with Langston Hughes's successful experiment in bringing the blues lyric into poetry, or might not seem particularly concerned with issues of race (and, specifically, "blackness") as in the fragmented voice, disjunctive logic, and paratactic lines of Erica Hunt's poems. In any case, the "black" in the conception of "black aesthetics" I am positing is not meant to describe the characteristics or qualities of the texts, nor does it refer specifically to the (socially constructed) race of the writer. Rather, it describes the subjectivity of the African American writer—that is, the subjectivity produced by the experience of identifying or being interpolated as "black" in the U.S.—actively working out a poetics in the context of a racist society. Black aesthetics are a function of the writing process, are contingent, and must be historicized and contextualized with regard to period and place, and with regard to the various other factors that shape the writer's identity, particularly including gender, sexuality, and class as well.[14]

Insofar as I understand black aesthetics to refer to types of engagement rather than specific styles, it is conceptually akin to Nathaniel Mackey's generative notion of "othering" (as opposed to "otherness"): "The privileging of the verb, the movement from noun to verb, linguistically accentuates action among a people whose ability to act is curtailed by racist constraints" (268).[15] Rather than expecting black aesthetics to inhere in any *particular* strategies, tropes, devices, or themes, critics and readers might bring to a text this inquiry: do we find herein the "residual form" of aesthetic choices that have been motivated by the writer's desire to write with, against, around, about, and/or in spite of ideas or issues of race, particularly concerning black identity and cultures?[16] Or, put differently, what evidence is there in the text, if any, of the African American writer's wrangling with competing expectations or desires for whether and how race will function in her work?

Renegade Poetics is interested in those instances when such race-related wrangling has led the poet beyond what experience has shown will do the job and into a space of formal risk-taking and experimentation.

I am compelled by the impulse of some African American poets to coax from the available tools of language something that is felt to have been excluded, repressed, or rendered impossible in previous poetry by constructions of blackness imposed on African Americans, inter- or intra-racially. This impulse, across a number of poets' works, accounts for a staggering range of formally innovative poetic practices, encompassing those that operate by engaging blackness to such a degree that their experimentation is not perceived as falling within the field of twentieth-century poetic innovation and, at the other end of this spectrum, those that operate by engaging avant-garde poetics to such a degree that their interventions are not perceived as interrogating issues of race. Accordingly, this study addresses not only the exclusions of the African American poetry canon, but also the ways in which African American poets and their poetic engagements with black cultures can be marginalized or find their complexity diminished within the discourse around American avant-garde poetry and poetic innovation.

Admittedly, "innovative poetry" can be as difficult a term to nail down as "black aesthetics," if for different reasons. "Innovative" is one of a string of terms—including "experimental," "avant-garde," and "modernist/post-modern"—that are used somewhat interchangeably and with across-the-board dissatisfaction by poets and critics to identify work less interested in mastery and beauty (two of the literary establishment's most highly valued criteria for American poetry) than in social critique, aesthetic revolution, unbounded exploration of language, and other forms of notable unconventionality. We choose among these terms in order to make a variety of distinctions, and I have found that what matters most in discussions in this vein is not which term one employs, but that one offers a working definition and explains how the term should be distinguished from others one could have chosen. In that spirit, I will adopt the definition of "innovation" offered by Mullen in her remarks at "Expanding the Repertoire: Continuity and Change in African-American Writing," a gathering convened by Renee Gladman and giovanni singleton in April 2000, under the auspices of Small Press Traffic. On a panel concerning "The Role of Innovation in Contemporary Writing," she noted: "I would define innovation as explorative and interrogative, an open-ended investigation into the possibilities of language, the aesthetic and expressive, intellectual and *transformative* possibilities of language. Poetry for me is the arena in which this kind of investigation can happen with the fewest obstacles and boundaries" (Untitled 11).[17] With that understanding as a base, I would add that I distinguish "innovative" work from "avant-garde" work on the grounds that the latter term most usefully signifies people working in the context of a movement or a visible collectivity seeking not simply to push their own work individually, but to shift the whole discussion around poetics away from current norms. Thus, all avant-garde poetry is innovative (or aspires to be!), but not all innovative work is created within the context of an avant-garde. I prefer "innovative" to "experimental" in order to respect the fact that poets working within a wide range of aesthetics undertake experimentation in their efforts to achieve their desired effects.[18] And, finally, I use "innovative" rather than "modernist" or "postmodern" in this study for a largely practical reason: because I am treating poets who collectively span the twentieth century, it seemed useful to work with a term that I could apply similarly to all of them, instead of terms that raise complicated temporal issues outside the scope of this project.[19]

Regardless of the term used, the discourse around innovative and avant-garde poetry in the U.S. has historically constructed these categories as implicitly "white." African American poets, even when they were involved in, perhaps central to, now-canonical avant-garde movements, have been marginalized or erased from the literary histories. A case in point would be the "occlusions" of Bob Kaufman's importance to the Beats: as Aldon Nielsen, Maria Damon, and others have recently noted, for decades a "public bleaching out of the artistic movement" obscured Kaufman's intellectual and artistic influence upon his contemporaries, not to mention such contributions as his cofounding of the Beat journal *Beatitude* (Nielsen, *Integral* 149–52; Damon 105–07).

A related phenomenon concerns the recognition of avant-garde movements themselves. The typical laundry list of U.S. avant-gardes does not automatically include the BAM, in the way that the Imagists, the Objectivists, the Beats, the New York School, the Black Mountain poets, and the Language poets, for example, are ticked off like beads on a rosary. The additional omission from this list of the Society of Umbra—an early to mid-1960s group of New York–based African American poets whose "work was formally, as well as politically, radical"—licenses the omission of the BAM, and vice versa (Nielsen, *Black* 114). That is, just as attention to the earlier group makes visible some of the roots of BAM aesthetic adventurousness, recognizing the BAM as an avant-garde, in turn, underscores the influence, direct and indirect, of the innovative Umbra poets (including Lorenzo Thomas, David Henderson, Ishmael Reed, Tom Dent, Oliver Pitcher, and Rolland Snellings/Askia Touré) on the Movement.[20] In more recent years, poets and critics focused on avant-garde and innovative poetry have increasingly acknowledged, written about, and taught African American poets. From the singularity of Jones/Baraka (whom we find cited as the sole African American among the Beats or the Black Mountain poets), we arrive in the dawning of the twenty-first century at a moment when such poets as Hunt, Mullen, Mackey, Gladman, Jayne Cortez, Ed Roberson, Tyrone Williams, and Will Alexander make regular appearances on the lists, as well as on the reading circuits, that feature innovative writers. These poets experiment with language in ways that jibe with the kinds of radical formal experimentation that have long served to identify (white) avant-garde work. But as poets among this group have pointed out, when their work is taken up by contemporary critics and readers of innovative poetry, it is too often discussed as if they are neither influenced by nor in conversation with a wide swathe of African American and African diasporic poetry, past and present. The sources and materials of aesthetic innovation in African American literature and other arenas of black cultural production and performativity may not be accounted for, or may be treated in superficial, unidimensional ways. Divorced from one or more important cultural traditions informing the work, the fact that, or extent to which, black aesthetics underwrites or shapes the innovation in these writers' texts can go unnoted and unanalyzed.

Renegade Poetics brings the poetry of African American writers like these, whose formal innovation may be presumed to have little to do with black aesthetics, into conversation with the poetry of other African American writers whose work may arise regularly in discussions of black writing, but without immediately registering as innovative. In this, my project differs from (even as it is indebted to) the models offered by Nielsen's *Black Chant* and *Integral Music* and Mackey's *Discrepant Engagement*. Where Mackey's vital scholarship illuminates the cross-cultural linkages among the poetics of African American, Caribbean, and white American (specifically, Black Mountain) innovators, mine is interested in how innovative African American poets' cross-cultural influences shape and are shaped by the context of the African American poetic tradition. And where Nielsen's indispensable work uncovers the submerged tradition of African American poetic postmodernism by recalling poets who have been marginalized or erased from the canon, I seek to juxtapose the submerged innovations of poets who are not most well-known or valued for poetic experimentation (Anne Spencer, Gwendolyn Brooks, and Sonia Sanchez) with the work of poets who function more obviously within the lineage Nielsen traces (Ed Roberson, Will Alexander, and Harryette Mullen).[21]

My project might be said to take up and interrogate the idea behind a comment Lorenzo Thomas made at the "Expanding the Repertoire" conference. Thomas notes that "[t]here was a desperate period in the 1980s when—frustrated by our inability to grasp society's real prizes (however defined)—we thought that simply being Black was avant-garde" ("Kindred" 60). Citing the widespread impact and commodification of African American culture in American society, he adds: "This was not an entirely bogus position" (60). His remarks were recalled by John Keene in response to one of the questions that Terrance Hayes and I posed, as editors of *jubilat*'s recent "African American Experimental Poetry Forum," namely: "*Does it take something more or different for Black poets to be understood as experimental poets?*" (119). In the ensuing discussion, the idea of black *people* being "intrinsically experimental" (or even becoming so as a result of a common historical experience) was rejected on essentialist grounds (127). But that notion was distinguished from a different possibility also available in Thomas's formulation. As Fred Moten, in a conversation among several poets in the forum, put it: "To say that Blackness is intrinsically experimental is not the same thing as to say that Black folks are intrinsically experimental" (130). For Moten, the effort to write about "the experience of Blackness"—an arbitrary and imposed identity that some of us so-named have decided to embrace—has led him to a "mode" of writing, "taken up . . . under constraint," that "is experimental" (128, 129).[22] The expanded, descriptive conception of black aesthetics with which I am working in *Renegade Poetics* might be understood, accordingly, as referring to a mode of writing adopted by African American poets in their efforts to work within, around, or against the constraint of being read and heard as "black."

Keene's response to the forum question quoted above began with an apt question of his own: "[W]ho is it that's 'understanding' Black poets as 'experimental'?" (120). For Keene, what is at stake here is "self-determination," one of the key political goals of Black Power and a concept central to BAM conceptions of black aesthetics (120). Another productive way of thinking about this question is suggested by Timothy Yu's compelling study, *Race and the Avant-Garde: Experimental and Asian American Poetry Since 1965*. Pointing to theories of the avant-garde that emphasize such movements' impulse to propose possibilities for social change by generating "revolutionary aesthetics," Yu argues that "the communities formed by contemporary American writers of color can . . . best be understood in the terms we have developed for the analysis of the avant-garde" (2). His argument strikes me as an insightful extension of Erica Hunt's powerful discussion of "oppositional poetics" in the essay that emerged from her talk at the New School in 1988. Hunt asserts:

> There are oppositional projects that engage language as social artifact, as art material, as powerfully transformative, which view themselves as distinct from projects that have as their explicit goal the use of language as a vehicle for the consciousness and liberation of oppressed communities. In general, the various communities, speculative and liberatory, do not think of themselves as having much in common, or having much to show each other. In practice, each of their language use is radically different—not in the clichéd sense of one being more open-ended than the other, but in the levels of rhetoric they employ. More interesting is the limitations they share—limitations of the society as a whole which they reproduce, even as they resist. ("Notes" 203)

Hunt and Yu, like Nielsen, Mackey, and Mullen, are seeking to dismantle the false dichotomy that has been constructed between writing communities that identify themselves primarily in terms of shared aesthetic values and those that ground their common aesthetic concerns in a shared racial or gender identity.

This study works toward the same end, by illuminating the common relationship between black aesthetics and formal innovation among texts by African American poets whose perceived differences are ultimately the result of racialized frameworks. *Renegade Poetics* draws its title from a line in Harryette Mullen's prose poem "Denigration," a piece that reminds us of the sonic power of language through wordplay around the morphemes "nig" and "neg." It begins:

> Did we surprise our teachers who had niggling doubts about the picayune brains of small black children who reminded them of clean pickaninnies on a box of laundry soap? How muddy is the Mississippi compared to the third-longest river of the darkest continent? In the land of the Ibo, the Hausa, and the Yoruba, what is the price per barrel of nigrescence? Though slaves, who were wealth, survived on niggardly provisions, should inheritors of wealth fault the poor enigma for lacking a dictionary? (*Sleeping* 19)

By shifting between actual and false cognates—such as, "niggling," "Niger," "nigrescence," and "enigma"—in the poem's explicit and implicit lexicon, Mullen draws our attention to the seemingly inescapable racist baggage our language carries, a factor much discussed in recent debates about the ability of African Americans to recover or redeem "the n-word" by using it not to denigrate, but to affirm or express identification with one another.

The poem ends with the line that serves as this introduction's first epigraph: "Though Maroons, who were unruly Africans, not loose horses or lazy sailors, were called renegades in Spanish, will I turn any blacker if I renege on this deal?" (*Sleeping* 19). The morpheme "neg" in "renegades" has no etymological connection to the word "negro" (which is Spanish for "black"), but as the Spanish equivalent of Maroons—the name given by English speakers to black people who ran away from slavery to live in isolated, hidden communities in the hills of Jamaica or the South Carolina swamps, for example—it cannot escape the racial connotation. I use the word "renegade" in my title to signify the rebellious, nonconformist approaches the poets in this study have taken in their aesthetics. Indeed, the work examined herein might be said to have run away from (or with) the confining expectations many nonblack and black audiences hold for the styles and subjects of poetry by African Americans. But *Renegade Poetics* demonstrates that the poets writing such work leave only their confinement—not their racial subjectivity—behind. One such renegade poet, the Martinican founder of négritude, Aimé Césaire, illustrates this gorgeously in his invitation to the Haitian poet René Depestre "to break ranks and join him in an artistic secession": "marronerons-nous Depestre marronerons-nous?" ("Shall we turn maroon, Depestre, shall we turn maroon?").[23] Making a verb of the noun Maroons (as if anticipating Mackey's discussion of "othering"), Césaire appeals to Depestre to break free from the aesthetic constraints his Communist political allegiances placed upon his art, reminding him (and us) that black poets can find freedom *and* make community as "renegades"—a designation that does and does not mean "black."

THE SIX MAIN CHAPTERS of *Renegade Poetics* study some of the innovative ways that African American poets writing during the long twentieth century have negotiated tensions among influential conceptions of black aesthetics, competing imperatives of mainstream and avant-garde American aesthetics, and their own individual artistic impulses. These chapters treat through close, but thoroughly contextualized, readings the rich forms of innovation—including uncommon or unconventional ways of negotiating or engaging black history, cultures, and politics—that have often gone unnoticed or unexamined within analytical frameworks that are structured or deeply influenced by dominant Black Aesthetic approaches. The chapters are grouped in two parts, each of which coheres around an arena of poetry that has traditionally been understood to exclude poets like those whose work I take up. I purposefully locate my explorations of black aesthetics in areas of poetics that raise explicit issues of gender and are not closely associated with the African American poetry tradition to more clearly illuminate the rewards of working with the more process-oriented, descriptive conception of black aesthetics that I have proposed.

Part I, called "Voice Held Me Hostage: Black Aesthetics and Polyvocality in African American Women's Epic Poems," examines long poems by three African American women poets—Brooks's "The Anniad" (1949), Sanchez's *Does Your House Have Lions?* (1997), and Mullen's *Muse & Drudge* (1995)—all of which I argue should be understood as epics. The epic genre, historically constructed as a highly masculine form and one not regularly undertaken by African American poets of either gender, presents as a result certain formal challenges for Brooks, Sanchez, and Mullen, each of whom sought to achieve something with the epic that it was not created to do. I first became attuned to the usefulness of reading their poems together when I realized that these poets were (and are to date) the only African American women to employ lyric stanzas in building poems of epic length, scope, or structure. Confronted similarly with the genre's exclusionary norms—the singular warrior hero, the battlefield setting, the mandate to tell "the tale of the tribe" (Ezra Pound's phrase) in an elevated diction—each of these poets found ways to combine the lyric and epic modes to engender polyvocality in their poems.

The title of this part comes from a stanza of Mullen's playfully fragmented *Muse & Drudge*, which I read as suggesting the capacity of voice to bind some bodies to one another, even as they are violently silenced:

> chained thus together
> voice held me hostage
> divided our separate ways
> with a knife against my throat (13)

Taking Mullen's cue, part I of this study examines the ways that African American women poets have sought to escape the fetters or transgress the boundaries of voice in their poetry. As noted, the three works I consider, in creating epic long poems from recurring lyric stanzas, form a constellation of rarities. Combing my bookshelves and my memory, and sifting through studies and discussions in print and online, I have identified just over fifty long poems in the African American tradition—a sizeable number, but a very low proportion of the number of poems, or even books, published by African American poets. Fewer than half of these long poems appear to be at all interested in the conventions of epic poetry.[24]

But the numbers really shrink when we add the second condition of a formally regular stanzaic structure. Very few African American men have created long poems in regular stanzas, and, to my knowledge, Brooks, Sanchez, and Mullen are the only women poets in the African American tradition to have published such poems, to date.[25] What draws me to these poems, then, is the opportunity they present to consider issues of race, gender, and voice in poems that are both thematically ambitious and formally innovative.

That is to say that Brooks's, Sanchez's, and Mullen's long poems all tap into the possibilities opened by the insistent and intimate combination of the epic poem's lofty expansiveness and the stanzaic form's intricate constraints. Together, these formal structures create spaces in which the three poets can circumnavigate or productively engage with the limitations the concept of voice proposes for them, associated as it is with the (gendered) "orality"—black vernacular speech—that defines the African American literary tradition for many. There may seem to be some irony in the idea that such structures as the epic (and the long poem generally) and rhyme royal (and other received stanzaic forms) might lend themselves to African American women's liberatory poetic projects, given their construction as male and European forms. But the existence of African traditions of epic poetry, as well as a growing awareness of women's adoption of epic and other long form structures, arguably mitigates the surprise we might otherwise feel.[26] And, surprising or not, in the hands of such supremely skilled craftswomen, these potentially inhospitable poetic structures become tools that cooperatively facilitate *polyvocality*.

When I refer to the "polyvocality" of a poem, I mean the extent to which its language, tone, diction, form, and other stylistic choices generate the effect of multiplicity in a single speaker's voice or create space for a number of different speakers—an effect that runs counter to (or around) the predominant expectation for lyric poems to function as internally consistent, first-person utterances. While I of course recognize the importance of Mikhail Bakhtin's work on this subject, my thinking about polyvocality is more directly indebted to (though distinct from) Mae Gwendolyn Henderson's theory of black women writers as "speaking in tongues," which recognizes an acquired ability to "speak in a plurality of voices as well as in a multiplicity of discourses" (352).[27] To survive and thrive, she submits, black women have had to learn to speak dialogically in ways that can be heard by our "others," both through similarity and across difference. Responding creatively to the environments in which they write, particularly with respect to the ways they understand their audiences, Brooks, Sanchez, and Mullen exercise this skill by innovatively manipulating the formal elements of their poetry, so that the works might be heard differently by different listeners.

Chapter 1, "Changing the Subject: Gwendolyn Brooks's "The Anniad,'" examines the long poem that stands as the centerpiece of Brooks's Pulitzer Prize–winning volume *Annie Allen*. "The Anniad" is frequently characterized as a "mock-epic" because the poem's subject matter is seen as incommensurate with Brooks's use of highly elevated diction, dazzling and unique formal intricacy, and conventions of the Greek epic. The poem's criticism, largely produced subsequent to the BAM, reads the Movement's black aesthetics retroactively onto Brooks's earlier, post–World War II work, producing a reading of the poem that insists upon an equivalence between "blackness" and vernacular speech. This reading renders Brooks's attempt to *change the subject* of the epic (in both senses)—that is, to elevate her poor, young, working-class, female protagonist to the role of epic hero—incomprehensible, except as an exercise in ridicule. I read Brooks's innovative formal choices—including the decision to develop a unique, extremely torqued version of the rhyme royal stanza as a vehicle for her epic—instead as manifestations of black aesthetics grounded, in part, in a perceived need for a political and aesthetic revaluation of young black women like Annie.

Whereas chapter 1 expands the chronology of black aesthetics back into the 1940s, chapter 2, "Expanding the Subject: Sonia Sanchez's *Does Your House Have Lions?*," brings it forward into the 1990s. *Does Your House Have Lions?* is Sanchez's seventy-page elegy for her brother, who died of AIDS in 1980. This breathtaking poem, I argue, *expands the subject* of the traditional epic by refiguring the singular hero's quest as a collective, familial struggle. She enlarges the epic's subject not just numerically, but also temporally, casting its reach back into the era of slavery by including in her representation of the family two ancestral figures who lost their lives during the Middle Passage. Relatedly, Sanchez expands the *black* subject, insofar as she calls forth a more encompassing black subjectivity, one which can incorporate the previously proscribed identities of gays and people who are HIV-positive and/or living with AIDS. Taking Brooks as her starting point, Sanchez brings elements of the traditional Western epic, the lyric, and the contemporary narrative of slavery together in dense, highly figurative rhyme royal stanzas. Her skillfully crafted amalgamation of forms emerges as a variety of black aesthetics that both draws upon and reinterprets the aesthetics that dominated the BAM of which she was a part, enabling her to navigate cultural taboos in order to memorialize her brother and contribute to HIV/AIDS awareness and prevention in the African American community.

In her fourth book, *Muse & Drudge*, Mullen fundamentally achieved her goal of creating a text that would engage both the greater numbers of black readers (and other readers of color) who had responded to the culturally specific invitation of her first volume of poetry *and* the predominantly white community of readers who had appreciated the postmodernist techniques she employed in her second and third books. Writing in lyric quatrains composed of disjointed, fragmented lines, Mullen samples blues lyrics and black vernacular speech; references a range of diasporic figures, events, and practices; and ultimately collages these myriad sources into an epic, collective portrait of black female subjectivity. Chapter 3 of my study, "Complicating the Subject: Harryette Mullen's *Muse & Drudge* as African American Blues Epic," counters the dominant readings of the poem, whose reliance on notions of cultural "hybridity" often resolves into a binary of "black" (blues) *content* and "white" (traditional and avant-garde) poetic *forms*. I argue that Mullen's intensely polyvocal, thematically wide-ranging quatrains (which reference everything from Mexican maquiladoras to Dahomey symbols of royalty) insist upon the manifold and diasporic nature of black women's experiences. The result is a new form—an African American blues epic—that takes its language, structural cues, and expansive, non-autobiographical first-person subjects primarily from the blues and African American literary traditions, even as it foregrounds the extent to which American poetic traditions, and other aspects of American culture, have always themselves comprised complex, polymorphous mixtures. The black aesthetics underwriting *Muse & Drudge* thus rejects the BAM's racial essentialism, even as it rearticulates the Movement's emphasis on the richness and plenitude of black cultural traditions—including traditions of artistic innovation.

As part I will make clear, the differences in the way polyvocality operates in each work emerge from differences in the black aesthetics motivating each of the three poets. But all of them respond to and revise the genre of epic poetry—a contribution that the scholarship on this genre has not adequately taken into account. Lynn Keller's excellent study,

Forms of Expansion: Recent Long Poems by Women, stands out as one of the few exceptions to the general rule that works by African Americans (female and male) are ignored or relegated to the footnotes of scholarship on the long poem (whether epic or other forms). The rule has been true even of studies I have found otherwise useful, such as Michael André Bernstein's *The Tale of the Tribe: Ezra Pound and the Modern Verse Epic*, Susan Stanford Friedman's "When a 'Long' Poem Is a 'Big' Poem: Self-Authorizing Strategies in Women's Twentieth-Century 'Long Poems'"; Smaro Kamboureli's *On the Edge of Genre: The Contemporary Canadian Long Poem*; and Brian McHale's *The Obligation toward the Difficult Whole*. Keller devotes a chapter of her book to poems by Brenda Marie Osbey and Rita Dove, which she characterizes as "testifying" long poems. But where Keller contextualizes Osbey's and Dove's works as deeply invested in "African American spiritual traditions" of "tell[ing] the truth through story" (103), I focus on the ways Brooks, Sanchez, and Mullen tell African American stories and truths by wresting the epic from its traditional contexts—in part by channeling it through rhyme royal or ballad stanzas—to make it serve their unconventional purposes of societal critique.

Where part I takes off from a formal tradition, the epic genre, part II gathers together poets whose work foregrounds a subject that has not traditionally been associated with poetry by African Americans: nature. The three poets considered in this part—Spencer, Roberson, and Alexander—are drawn to what our society constructs as "nature" (in opposition to "culture" and politics), and return repeatedly to images and ideas from contexts and discourses focused on nonhuman aspects of the world. This preoccupation has contributed to the invisibility or marginality of their poetry, insofar as, for most of the twentieth century, neither the traditionally "white" genre of "nature poetry" (including the newer rubric of "ecopoetry") nor the African American poetry tradition (especially as understood from our post-BAM vantage point) has contemplated African American poets who make the garden, the wilderness, or the near and far reaches of the universe a primary concern of their writing. Simultaneously, because of this focus on nature, rather than more "recognizably black" topics and settings (such as urban neighborhoods, street culture, or overt political protest), the ways their poetry engages black culture and/or matters of politics often goes unnoticed or undiscussed.

Though it may be a less obvious point of departure for either black aesthetics or formal innovation than the generic rubric of the epic, the category of nature poetry or "ecopoetry" is likewise a productive site for analyzing the innovative strategies African American poets have used to write their way out of racially constricted spaces. Just as with the formal structures of the epic and the rhyme royal and ballad stanzas, nature poetry is a construction that comes to American poets from a European tradition (notably, Romantic poetry) whose construction has been understood to exclude African American poets, for more than one reason. The long tradition of nature poetry features the outdoors, particularly rural and scenic areas, as the site of relaxation, recreation, and contemplation; the nature poem is not about labor, except in its most romanticized sense, and, even then, the laborer is not the poet himself. For a people whose collective identity is, in a sense, defined by (but not reducible to) their status as enslaved workers or the descendents thereof, the traditional nature poem functions as the literary erasure or prettification of an unutterably significant aspect of their experience or history. The challenge this erasure presents to the would-be African American nature poet is magnified by the fact that black people have historically been constructed *as* nature: metaphorically, as savages who operate based on instinct and emotion (rather than intellect and reason); legally, as chattel slaves who were treated as being on a par with livestock; fundamentally, non- or sub-human. Add to this mix the inclination of African Americans themselves to identify blackness with the city, a strategy that can be traced as far back as the New Negro Renaissance era, when Harlem's metonymic relationship with the African American community was intended to signal the arrival of Afro-modernism. The BAM leaned heavily on the association of African Americans with urban life—that and the sheer numbers of black urban dwellers after two enormous waves of rural-to-urban/industrial migration by African American people support what has become almost an equation between "black" and "inner city" in American social discourse. In light of the foregoing, it is not surprising that the African American poets I bring together here for their interest in writing about nature beyond the human and human ecosystems employ aesthetics that are consciously (if not "recognizably") "black" and productively (one wants to say necessarily) innovative.

I have indicated that the "natural world" and "nature" are contested terms, because one of the things we learn from these poets is to be skeptical of the nature/culture dichotomy that pretends that humans and the environments we build are fundamentally distinct from everything else. Because black people (like Native Americans) have been constructed as part of "nature," African American poets are well situated to question what Lance Newman has called "[t]he first premise of most nature writing—that human and nonhuman places belong to sharply separate categories of being" (19). The title for this part of the book—"The Blackening Sun, That Standard of Clarity: The Nature of Black Aesthetics"— plays upon language from Ed Roberson's work to suggest that poets whose nature writing is informed by a black subjectivity may be able to shed some new light on environmental matters. Newman argues that "how nature writers see and understand nature has everything to do with how they see and understand the society whose relations with it they hope to change" (19). If he is correct, then African American poets' critique of this society's racism (among other concerns) must inevitably shape their conception of humanity's position within nature.

It is thus regrettable that African American poetry has been all but invisible within "the green tradition" until only very recently. Lawrence Buell begins the preface of his 2005 book, *The Future of Environmental Criticism*, by proposing that where W. E. B. Du Bois had identified racism as the "great public issue of the twentieth century," the twenty-first will be consumed with the environmental crisis. Buell justly notes that this question of whether and how the earth will continue to be a viable environment for its current inhabitants is "ultimately . . . more pressing" than the ongoing problem of race; it is hard to imagine what does not take a back seat to a problem of such all-encompassing concern (vi). Still, I think he might agree that had we done a better job over the last hundred years of understanding and eradicating racism, we might be facing a less severe environmental crisis today. For instance, how much sooner would the powerful and wealthy people of this nation have begun to insist on alternatives to toxic industrial processes and environmentally indefensible waste management practices if they had not been able to shift the burden for their choices onto the poor communities where people of color are disproportionately represented—or onto developing nations that are also, not coincidentally, home to people of color? Along with the scholarly interventions of critics like Christine Gerhardt, I have been deeply gratified to see the publication of the anthology *Black Nature: Four Centuries of African American Nature Poetry*, which provides those of us interested in African American writers' constructions of and responses to nature with nearly a couple hundred primary texts.

One of the poets anthologized in *Black Nature* is the focus of chapter 4 of *Renegade Poetics*. In "Protest/Poetry: Anne Spencer's Garden of 'Raceless' Verse," I take up the poetry of an initially well-received but now understudied poet of the New Negro Renaissance who lived and worked in segregated Lynchburg, Virginia. Her marginalization in late-twentieth-century assessments of the New Negro Renaissance can be attributed in large part to the fact that she more often drew her subjects and imagery from her beloved garden than from the cultural particularity and unjust treatment of the "New Negro." Commonly, Spencer criticism understands her garden as a space of beauty and refuge from the oppressive society in which she lived, noting her long-term commitment to civil rights work and the role of social heretic only as a counterpoint to the relative lack of racial protest in her poetry. I argue, however, that Spencer used both her poetry and her garden as spaces where she could *think* about and *experiment* with ways of conceptualizing and articulating the power dynamics among the people of her society in light of those she observed among nonhuman creatures. Given her location in the Jim Crow South, we should not be surprised to find that her "cryptic" (J. Johnson, *Book* 45), "original" (Kerlin 158), highly compressed lines not only constitute innovative poetics within the context of the Renaissance, but also participate in, rather than simply offer refuge from, the struggle for racial and gender equality she carried out in her nonliterary life.

Chapter 5, "Black and Green: On the Nature of Ed Roberson's Poetics," looks at Roberson's use of unconventional formal strategies and subject matter related to activities in realms of nature socially coded as "white" (such as, studying the Alaskan wilderness, participating in an "Explorers' Club," or working as a diver in an aquarium). These elements of his poetics remind us how the false dichotomies between nature and culture and between black and white are mapped onto one another—and, thus, can be simultaneously challenged. I argue that Roberson uses his distinctively fragmented yet hypotactic poetics to illustrate not merely the interrelation but the identity of the natural and the cultural (or political) realms, insisting through the example of his form upon the unitary character of nature. His entire thirty-year oeuvre, up through the recently published *To See the Earth before the End of the World*, treats racism and classism within human social settings as problems facing our ecosystems—reconceptualizing them as environmental issues, so to speak, and thus providing a new lens through which to see the dispersed impact of misuse of our natural (cultural) resources.

The natural realm foregrounded in the two surrealist long poems that comprise Will Alexander's *Exobiology as Goddess* challenges the geocentric conception of nature that even most ecopoetry maintains, casting its net out into the universe in a search for extraterrestrial life. Alexander's work thus takes us farther afield spatially than either Spencer's or

Roberson's, and also aesthetically, in that the key influence of Martinican poet Aimé Césaire upon Alexander's surrealist poetics moves us beyond a narrowly African American black aesthetics. Chapter 6, "Will Alexander's Surrealist Nature: Toward a Diasporic Black Aesthetics," reads his poetry in light of both his critique of the Black Aesthetic of the didactic BAM era and his enthusiastic embrace of the liberated politics of Césairian surrealism. Césaire's poetic emphasis on African mythologies and the natural environment of Martinique prove to be points of reference for Alexander's black aesthetic strategies, which turn on an embrace of ancient Egyptian cosmology. Significantly, however, although Alexander represents himself as a "psychic maroon" ("Hauling" 402) from the African American poetry canon as currently constructed, his early influences—which led him to Césaire in the first place—comprised a quasi-localized African American avant-garde of surrealist writers and musicians. An exploration of the various sources of his diasporic black aesthetics ultimately reminds us that African American black aesthetics have long influenced and been influenced by black aesthetics beyond our national boundaries.

PART I

VOICE HELD ME HOSTAGE
Black Aesthetics and Polyvocality in African American Women's Epic Poems

ONE

CHANGING THE SUBJECT
Gwendolyn Brooks's "The Anniad"

AT THE CLOSE of their interview in 1990, critic D. H. Melhem asked Gwendolyn Brooks if there were any literary genres she had yet to try in which she would like to write. Brooks replied briefly and directly: "Yes. An epic. An honest-to-goodness epic" (Brooks, "Gwendolyn" 154). Surprisingly, Melhem did not follow up on this stunning declaration, which flies in the face of the assessments of critics who had already begun to describe not one, but two of Brooks's poems as being examples of, or deeply engaged with, the epic: "The Anniad," published in her 1949 Pulitzer Prize–winning volume *Annie Allen*, and "In the Mecca," the title poem of a collection published in 1968.[1] Indeed, the title of the former poem, which visually or sonically evokes two of the best-known epic poems of Western culture (*The Iliad* and *The Aeneid*),[2] its relative length within Brooks's oeuvre, and certain technical devices she uses therein (about which more later) together invite us to read "The Anniad" within the matrix of the epic tradition. Given this context, I am compelled to ask: what work is the qualifier "honest-to-goodness" doing in Brooks's interview response?

Brooks's qualifier, as I read it, speaks to the issue of legitimacy, or authority. An "honest-to-goodness epic" would be one that indisputably employs the conventions of that genre in ways recognizable to any reader familiar with it. Was "The Anniad" an epic in this sense? Apparently, in 1990, Brooks did not think so. But her retrospective view does not preclude us from reading it as precisely that: a *legitimate* epic. This chapter argues that "The Anniad" can and should be read as a poem whose scope and form staked its claim to the status of legitimate epic, a poem which therefore held the potential to legitimize her as a poet in the eyes of the literary establishment, as she intended it to.[3] The kind of artistic authority the establishment could—and, in fact, did—bestow upon her would have been attractive and helpful to many eager young poets. But this would be especially so for a poet like Brooks, who, though exacting and ambitious, might easily have been dismissed by potential readers in mid-twentieth-century America, because of assumptions based on her race, gender, or class.[4] But even as "The Anniad" reaches for this kind of legitimacy, it does so without sacrificing—or, more precisely, it does so in the service of—the cultural and sociopolitical values Brooks holds dear. This point is important, as I will discuss later in more detail, because it registers the type of black aesthetics she was working with in the late 1940s. (Another kind of "legitimacy"—black cultural legitimacy, or "authenticity"—replaced the former sort as Brooks's ambition between the time she wrote the poem and the time she spoke with Melhem about it, reflecting her engagement with some of the more exacting cultural nationalist iterations of BAM-era black aesthetics.) In writing this poem, Brooks successfully maps her interest in literary legitimacy onto her interests in representing the life of a young, African American, working-class woman and offering a critique of the racial and gender constraints limiting that young woman's development. Importantly, she manages to do this despite the divergence of her heroine and her poem's critical perspective from the warrior protagonists and celebratory stances of traditional epic works. In other words, as I will demonstrate, Brooks's black aesthetics lead her to *change the subject* of the epic in some fundamental ways.

Her subject matter and politics make her foray into the territory of the epic genre quite logical, if not predictable. The broad scope of the epic offered the room she needed to develop an unconventional protagonist who would nonetheless be compelling to the poem's readers, while the genre's traditional function of representing a people's culture and mythology supported her concern with featuring particularly African American experiences.[5] Brooks generates ingeniously innovative approaches to form (including a reconstruction of the epic subject and a tour de force reworking of the rhyme royal stanza) in order to reconcile her potentially competing interests in literary legitimacy and the honest treatment of black experiences in World War II–era Chicago. Attention to her strategies reveals the operation of a black aesthetic in her work that, while different from—indeed, invisible to—the black aesthetic that began influencing her work in the late 1960s, is nonetheless critical to both the poem's apparent aims and its formal innovations. By analyzing the initial reception of "The Anniad" and the collection *Annie Allen,* the later scholarship on this work, and the existing evidence concerning the author's own shifting relationship to her achievement, we can elucidate the distinctly gender-conscious black aesthetics that motivate and shape Brooks's "honest-to-goodness" epic poem. Of particular import are the strategies which together create polyvocality in the poem. I argue that, to manage the delicate balancing act necessary to achieve the legitimacy she wants for her poem, Brooks creates a speaker who can be heard as addressing at least three different audiences simultaneously—the effects of which were not entirely predictable or manageable. Polyvocality, then, is a key source of both the work's brilliance and its deeply mixed reception, as well as its long critical history of partial misreadings and grudging admiration.

AN IMPRESSIVE LONG POEM of 43 stanzas and 301 lines (though certainly shorter than many modernist long poems), "The Anniad" is the centerpiece of *Annie Allen*.[6] The volume as a whole gives us the life of its eponymous heroine from her birth through the first several years of her adulthood. Her story is divided into three sections; the second section, "The Anniad," constitutes the bridge between "Notes from the Childhood and the Girlhood" and "The Womanhood." While agreeing with scholars like Jenny Goodman that the book is a unified sequence of poems about one woman's experience, I am interested here specifically in how diverse readings of "The Anniad"—a long poem within a long poem, we might say—are shaped by its juxtaposition with the epic tradition.[7] I understand Annie's explicitly gendered journey from youth to maturity, which transpires over the course of "The Anniad," as taking the form of an epic quest—though not a triumphant one. Considered as a quest to realize the illusory dreams that have made her girlhood feel less constricting (or less "pinchy," to take a word from "birth in a narrow room," an early poem in the book), it could even be called disastrous, as critics have noted.[8] But if we consider it a quest to survive and resist the poisonous effects of racism and sexism on her life as a working-class black woman in mid-twentieth-century Chicago, we can recognize Annie's achievements, even as we suffer with her the disappointments and losses of her journey. The poem follows Annie from her youthful fantasies about the "paladin" who will come and rescue her from the economic limitations of her situation, through her courtship by a "tan man" who is much more mundane than divine, their impoverished (in both senses) and disillusioning marriage, and her desperate search for an identity independent of this relationship. We see her emerge, in the end, subdued, but not destroyed: a young woman who has learned the hard way that, although she cannot change her reality with romantic fantasies, she has the necessary resources within herself to meet the challenges her life entails. This self-knowledge, however, is gained through a painful stripping away of certain illusions this society encourages young women to harbor. The poem's beauty lies not only in the emotional arc of its narrative, but in its formal intricacy, from its organization in seven-line stanzas of varying three-rhyme patterns (strongly reminiscent of rhyme royal) to its soaringly Latinate, sometimes archaic, and strikingly unusual vocabulary.

As already noted, *Annie Allen* was deemed worthy by the literary establishment of one of the nation's highest honors, garnering for the thirty-two-year-old Brooks the belated honor of being the first African American to win a Pulitzer Prize. This must have been as surprising to her as it was to others, because the collection had received very mixed reviews from critics upon its publication. While reviews of her previous book, *A Street in Bronzeville* (1945), had uniformly praised her poetic technique, many critics—even those who wrote the most encouraging responses to *Annie Allen*—were put off by the very self-conscious display of formal expertise, elevated diction, and linguistic whimsy that Brooks lavished upon the new volume. More than one reviewer deemed it "uneven" and "awkward"; Stanley Kunitz, for example, mixed his praise of the collection's strengths with a pointed reference to "an uncertainty of taste and direction" he perceived in the work (Kunitz 11, 12; Humphries 8; McGinley 177).[9] Not surprisingly, perhaps, in a number of reviews the focal point for both positive and negative criticism of the volume was "The Anniad."[10] Another noteworthy aspect of these contemporary commentaries is the fact that the reviewers frequently make implicit gestures toward the metaphor of voice in their negative critiques; assertions that, for example, her word choice is "out of key" or "her ear [. . . has gone] all to pieces" call attention to the poem as a "heard" object and to the poet as an embodied speaker (Kunitz 11; Humphries 8).[11]

Ultimately, the initial reception of "The Anniad," and *Annie Allen* generally, comprised responses so varied as to raise the question of whether all the reviewers were reading (hearing) the same work. The subsequent scholarship is similarly divergent. The handful of scholarly analyses that began to appear in the late 1970s, like the circa 1950 book reviews noted above, tend to differ widely from one another in their characterizations of the volume and its significance.[12] These later assessments encompass a good deal of variety in terms of values and emphases, much of which is channeled through a debate about the role and degree of satire in the poem that has continued to shape the scholarship into the twenty-first century. "The Anniad" has engendered such diverse, even conflicting, interpretations and responses in large part because the poetics Brooks employs in "The Anniad," particularly its formal idiosyncrasies, produced a poem that could be "heard" differently by audiences with differing ideologies, tastes, interests, and perceptions about the operation of race, gender, and class in U.S. society. The combination of her voice (the poetic projection of a working-class black woman) and her subject (the coming-of-age of Annie Allen, also an ordinary working-class black woman) could have rendered her text effectively inaudible. Brooks was well aware that the largest audience for American poetry—including not just readers, but also the literary critics who would evaluate a poet's work and contribute to the amplification or muting of her voice—was then (more than now) composed predominantly of middle-class and wealthy white people.[13] The majority of her African American readership would have attained some postsecondary education. She would have been cognizant of the various expectations readers would have for her work and the different biases (including gender biases) they would likely bring to bear on it. Some readers would be interested in a window opening onto a view of "authentic" black life; others would hope to see the struggles of black people depicted in heroic (read: masculine) terms, in the service of racial protest.[14] Some readers would be sympathetic to a recounting of a girl's development into a woman; others would find the narrative of her romantic and domestic life trivial or, at best, diverting. Some readers would value the masterful use of poetic technique almost regardless of subject matter; others would see little value in modernist poetry that emphasized style to the detriment of clear meaning. The challenge, then, was for her to present Annie's life in poems that would engage as many of her potential audiences as possible, despite the fact that this placed competing, if not conflicting, demands upon her work. This task called for a black aesthetic highly attuned to the interplay between race, gender, and class.

Brooks's strategy was to inscribe her putatively mundane story about an unremarkable young woman within a highly formal structure that combined epic conventions with an intricate, rhyme royal–like stanza. Her deployment of the traditional significance of these forms calls attention to the generosity, creativity, and strength of will—the nobility, we might say—with which Annie struggled against the constraints of race, gender, and class upon her life, highlighting these qualities for audiences that might otherwise have not registered them. At the same time, however, this particular combination of content and form resulted in a poetic voice that critics have heard in quite different ways than those I am suggesting, as we have seen. These disparate responses suggest both the possibilities and the limitations of the production of polyvocality in "The Anniad."

The epic genre, which facilitates Brooks's polyvocality in significant part, was not a likely formal challenge for her to tackle. To cast a poor, urban, African American woman's struggle, fought largely on the *home* front, as an epic was a remarkably gutsy move on Brooks's part in 1949, years prior to the time when the second wave of the women's movement would force American society to rethink its assumptions about where history is made and who makes it. For the epic tradition is about history—most often, the history of a particular people, joined by cultural and national bonds—and the history-makers, as represented in the epics that European and (African) American literature celebrates, have almost always, until very recently, been men. Bernstein follows Ezra Pound in referring to the epic poem as "the tale of the tribe" (7). In exploring the origins of Pound's articulation in a talk given by Rudyard Kipling, Bernstein suggests that the epic has traditionally been concerned with "articulating the common aspirations, ethical beliefs and unifying myths of a people." The epic poet, then, records "the deeds of warriors, priests, and men of action . . . , providing a storehouse of heroic examples and precepts by which later generations would measure their own conduct and order the social fabric of their lives" (8). As both Lynn Keller and Susan Stanford Friedman have remarked in their respective and welcome studies of women's long poems, this masculinist bias can seem almost inextricably embedded in the epic genre. Friedman helpfully points to the few women who wrote poems that might be characterized as epic prior to the last century: for example, Elizabeth Barrett Browning (*Aurora Leigh*, 1857), George Eliot (*Spanish Gypsy*, 1868), and, significantly, for our purposes, Frances Ellen Watkins Harper (*Moses: A Story of the Nile*, 1869), an African American writer best known for her novel, *Iola Leroy* (16–17). Brooks was one of only a few women—including Gertrude Stein, H. D., and Mina Loy—to publish a long poem, epic or otherwise, before the 1960s (Friedman 17). Her decision in the late 1940s to write a long poem, and to invoke the epic tradition with its very title, at that, was not a matter of course.

That it was unusual, however, does not signify that it was unthinkable. Yet it marks her as a poet of great ambition (a point to which I will return). Indeed, this unusual decision required her to determine how to re-envision the epic and, moreover, how to persuade her audiences to take this revolutionary form of epic journey with her heroine. The poem begins:

> Think of sweet and chocolate,
> Left to folly or to fate,

Whom the higher gods forgot,
Whom the lower gods berate;
Physical and underfed
Fancying on the featherbed
What was never and is not.[15]

The first line recalls the epic poem's tradition of commencing with an invocation of the muse, by way of a substitution. Instead of calling upon a goddess to help her bring the narrative to life, Brooks urges the audience to participate actively with her in imagining her heroine. Requests in this format recur twice more within the first five stanzas—"Think of ripe and rompabout," "Think of thaumaturgic lass"—and four more times subsequently, until their tone becomes unstable, sometimes sounding more like a demand, while at times taking on the quality of a plea (99, 100, 104, 105, 109, 109). Brooks repeatedly wraps her descriptions of Annie into these appeals to her readers, as though anticipating that they would need to be pressed and cajoled into investing their imaginations in seeing a working-class, dark-skinned African American woman as the central figure of an epic.[16] The poet's acknowledgment of the liberties she is taking with the epic comes in lines 3 and 4. She calls upon her audience, rather than a muse, because such "higher gods" have forgotten about Annie. Or, interestingly, if we doubt that Brooks's and Annie's world includes such divinities as Calliope and Mnemosyne, this allusion to "higher gods" might actually refer to people like the more powerful and privileged members of the poem's audience, who need to be reminded repeatedly of the existence of young women like Annie. In that case, the "lower gods" who "berate" her would logically include her mother, Maxie Allen, whose tone in "the ballad of late Annie," for example, is distinctly scolding.[17] Brooks's challenge to the reader is intensified by the stanza's last three lines, in which she juxtaposes the "physical" reality of the "underfed" Annie's meager means (and otherwise constrained circumstances—she is hungry not only for literal food) with the young woman's ability to "Fancy . . . / What was never and is not." If Annie's imagination is strong enough to hold such contradictions in place, then surely the reader will be able to conjure up a poor, black epic heroine, the text implies.

Friedman has said of contemporary "long poems" (a term she contests for its tendency to obscure the masculinist bias of the category) that their "departures from epic convention gain their particular power from being read within the epic grid. . . . As re-scriptions of epic conventions, modern long poems depend for their ultimate effect on our awareness of the epic norms they undo and redo" (16). My reading of the first stanza demonstrates the applicability of Friedman's insight to "The Anniad." By working through Brooks's engagements with epic conventions, we learn from this stanza not only the basic outline of Annie's looks and temperament, but also how Annie fits within the society into which she was born. And, beyond that, we get a sense of what is at stake for the poet: her ability to enable her audience to imagine Annie in a context that might seem as farfetched to Brooks's readers as Annie's romantic fantasies would seem to her mother.

Readers have indeed had difficulty accepting Annie as an epic heroine, as the scholarship on this poem demonstrates. The majority of critics who have considered the genre of "The Anniad" in relation to the title's allusion to Homer have deemed the poem a mock-epic, fiercely or compassionately critical of Annie's response to the passive gender role her society assigns to women.[18] This interpretation relies upon a conception of Brooks's aesthetics that I find unsupported by the text and insupportable in the larger context of her oeuvre and her asserted poetics. In an essay on the ramifications of the use of the mock-epic by women writers, Adeline Johns-Putra defines it as a genre that "exploits the discrepancy between the elevation of its style and the triviality of its subject" (para. 1). She explains that this "technique of mockery through deflation . . . has been a popular means with which to carry out socio-political satire, for it is a way . . . of 'putting down the mighty'" and that its motivation may be either "good-naturedly tolerant or seriously condemnatory" (para. 1). Should we understand Annie as one of "the mighty" who require a mocking "deflation"? I argue against such an interpretation; Brooks represents herself—directly and in her oeuvre—as an artist who would be much more sympathetic to Annie than even a "good-naturedly tolerant" mock-epic framework implies.

To begin with, when asked whether its title was intended to be "a classical reference," Brooks explained: "Well, the girl's name was Annie, and it was my little pompous pleasure to raise her to a height that she probably did not have, and I thought of the *Iliad* and said, I'll call this 'The Anniad'" (Brooks, "An Interview" 46). This explanation points toward two reasons for not locating the poem in the mock-epic tradition. First, Brooks acknowledges that Annie's social status would not place the young woman among the obvious candidates for the role of African American hero.[19] She tells us she felt "pleasure" in elevating Annie's stature and that she consciously chose to invoke a literary work that is revered, written in a genre, the epic, that is reserved for the doers of the "notable deed"

(Bernstein 8). Johns-Putra's definition of the mock-epic tells us that satire is typically aimed at the powerful and notorious; though it can target folly as well as hypocrisy or villainy, I am not persuaded that Brooks would raise Annie up for the express purpose of deflating her. Brooks's oeuvre has been dedicated to complicating and enriching the literary depiction of ordinary African Americans. Rather than making a satirical target out of one of the least powerful members of mid-twentieth-century American society, it would be more in keeping with her poetics for Brooks to produce work which demonstrates, in Hortense Spillers's words, "that common life is not as common as we sometimes suspect" (129).

Brooks's comment subtly points toward a second reason to resist reading "The Anniad" as a mock-epic: the fact that Brooks's autobiography is so heavily implicated in *Annie Allen*.[20] Like Annie, Brooks is from an urban, working-class home; although Brooks's father supported the family on a janitor's income (a low wage that dipped even lower during the Depression), he and her mother took pains to provide the kind of orderly conventional home-life that is suggested by the poem "the parents: people like our marriage: Maxie and Andrew," which appears in the first section of *Annie Allen* (Kent, chapter 1). Again like Annie, Brooks is dark-skinned ("chocolate" is her word for Annie) and has felt that she was neglected and rejected by black people—particularly potential suitors—on that account (Brooks, *Report* 57, 86); indeed, intraracial colorism is a theme much of her work emphasizes (Davis, "Black and Tan" 91). Particularly interesting for our purposes is this report from her biographer, George Kent:

> As she moved over the threshold of adolescence, she would also fantasize about boys, who behaved differently in these dreams than in her day-to-day life. At night in bed, she would dream of their embraces and of marriage, of being the mother of one child and loved to distraction by this boy/man. More often, she would be the center of attention and the object of the heart-longings of more than one boy. Like the knights of the fairy tales she read, they would fight for her favor and possession. (18)

What reader of "The Anniad" is not reminded of the "fairy-sweet" fantasies "littering the little head" of the poem's heroine, which include an impossible lover who will somehow be "Ruralist and rather bad, / Cosmopolitan and kind" (99), all at once? As these passages indicate, the young Brooks shares with Annie the central characteristic some cite as the subject of the poem's ridicule and the source of its humor: both base their fantasies around the cultural myth that women's happiness lies in being swept away by a valiant hero—unlikely enough to occur in the most privileged women's lives and all the more improbable for an African American woman whose suitors would typically be in the working class.[21] Thus, while Brooks had achieved sufficient distance from her subject at the time she was writing that we can observe irony at work in the poem and humor at play, it is nonetheless improbable that "The Anniad" is a send-up of Annie. Consider Brooks's telling response to the question whether, in her poem "The Chicago Picasso," she was "satirizing those people who do stay home and drink beer" rather than go to art galleries: "No. No, I'm not satirizing them, *because I'm too close to them to do that. I 'stay at home' (mostly) and drink Pepsi-Cola. I can't poke fun at them*" (Brooks, "An Interview" 37; emphasis added). I am basically arguing, to return to Brooks's explanation of the poem's title, that the reason her "pleasure" in placing Annie at the center of an epic poem is "pompous" (which is defined as "revealing self-importance") is because, by doing so, she implicitly makes a heroine of herself. Indeed, one has the sense, reading her exchange with the interviewer about "The Anniad," that Brooks was a trifle embarrassed to acknowledge this indulgence (or defiance), even indirectly. It would only be later—significantly, during the four-year period in which she was separated from her husband—that Brooks would begin, first in her 1972 autobiography, *Report from Part One*, and subsequently in interviews, to reveal enough about her life to allow us to draw such conclusions.

Report from Part One makes no bones about the fact that her one published novel, *Maud Martha* (1953), was autobiographical—"much in the story was taken out of my life"—though she adds to her admission the caution that she "twisted, highlighted or dulled, dressed up or down" the material, "to spare others and one's self" (Brooks, *Report* 190–91). Scholars of *Maud Martha* regularly note this relationship between writer and text and its implications for understanding the novel.[22] Yet, to my knowledge, no one has remarked upon, let alone studied, the deep similarities between *Annie Allen* and *Maud Martha*, which further underscore the autobiographical grounding of the former. From their alliterative titles to their deeply domestic heroines, from the "tan" and "low yellow" husbands to their infidelities with light-skinned women, and beyond, Brooks's texts, published only four years apart, seem to be doppelgängers for one another. Though they are by no means identical, each shadows the other uncannily, *Annie Allen* treating the story in narrative poetry and *Maud Martha* relating it in lyrical prose. This comparison underlines my argument that Brooks is not satirizing Annie in "The Anniad." Though Maud Martha also has highly romantic dreams about what marriage and her future will bring, she is not deemed ridiculous in the novel's scholarship. That Annie has been understood so differently from her literary "sister" is attributable to the challenges Brooks faced as a young poet in terms of audience and the strategies she employed in order to meet those challenges. Not only is "The Anniad" *not* a mock-epic, but its status as an epic is crucial to our understanding of how Brooks negotiated problems of voice writing for a post–World War II audience that would include racist, sexist, and class-based resistance to the subject and concerns about which she wished to write. Recognizing the poem as an epic is a necessary step toward an account of her specific black aesthetics.

By taking on the mantle of epic poet, Brooks lays claim to a genre imbued with the authority she wants her voice to project and the importance she wants her subject to possess, but she simultaneously creates certain problems for herself. The first is a problem of content. Her subject is not a triumphant male warrior, but a young woman whose quest appears to be for an ideal(ized) marriage, whose battlefield is no larger than a room or two, and whose fate is only victorious insofar as the defeat of her illusions by her realities evidences her achievement of a clear-eyed, if disappointed, maturity. The epic tradition that Pound references with regard to the *Cantos*, according to Bernstein, comprises tales in which valiant men provide "a storehouse of heroic examples and precepts by which later generations would measure their own conduct and order the social fabric of their lives" (8). Brooks must persuade her audience of the gravity of the challenges Annie faces, as well as of Annie's viability as a "heroic example" for the "tribe" she represents. While a decidedly masculine experience can, for many readers, easily represent the experience of a nation or people, they are often less willing to accept a woman's differently gendered engagements as a model for everyone in a mixed-gender group. Mary Helen Washington discussed this phenomenon in connection with the reception of *Maud Martha*, which is, again, strikingly similar to *Annie Allen* in terms of the identity and struggles of the two protagonists. Criticizing the reviews of *both* books as "condescending and dismissive," Washington interrogates reviewers' "resistance" to locating the novel within either an African American or "mainstream American" literary tradition (*Invented Lives* xv–xvi). She asks whether such resistance could be attributed to the fact that "few critics could picture the questing figure, the powerful articulate voice in the tradition as a plain, dark-skinned housewife living in a kitchenette apartment on the south side of Chicago" (xvii; emphasis added). This is precisely the issue that arises for Brooks when she asserts her authority as an epic poet.[23]

The second problem posed is a problem of language, which is so closely related to the problem of content that teasing them apart is no small task. Ralph Ellison has addressed these issues of content and language, in the context of the novel, as a singular concern, calling the question of how to deal with "social change" and "social ideals" in "a work of art"—as opposed to "a disguised piece of sociology"—a "problem of rhetoric" (91). He asks (in terms that ironically both foreground *and* erase gender):

> How does one . . . persuade the American reader to identify that which is basic in man beyond all differences of class, race, wealth, or formal education? How does one not only make the illiterate and inarticulate eloquent enough so that the educated and more favorably situated will recognize wisdom and honor and charity, heroism and capacity for love when found in humble speech and dress? (91)

Ellison's questions indicate the significance of this problem for the novelist, but the requirements of the epic layer it with genre-specific complications of particular relevance to the African American poet.

Ironically, those complications are connected to the construction of the epic narrator as particularly authoritative—which, I have argued, is precisely part of its appeal to Brooks. Walters reminds us that the ceremonial nature of the epic is traditionally evidenced in a "style which is deliberately distanced from ordinary speech and proportioned to the grandeur and formality of the heroic subject" (354). At the same time, as Keller's discussion of the epic points out, "the dominant narrative voice" of the epic poem should function "as the voice of the community's heritage, representing values significant for communal stability and social well-being" (24). While these two expectations for the epic are not inherently in conflict, they might be seen as incompatible—as creating a problem of language, in other words—for an African American poet, if "the voice of [her] community's heritage" is understood to be, by definition, a black vernacular voice. One wonders to what extent a discomfort with her "less identifiably Negro" voice stood behind criticism that predominantly white contemporary reviewers of *Annie Allen* leveled at Brooks's "experimentation in language" and attraction to "the big word" (*Annie Allen review, Booklist* 79; *Annie Allen review, New Yorker* 130; Humphries 8). In any case, there is clearer evidence that African American critics and scholars writing later—during or in the wake of the Black Arts Movement—have been influenced to some degree, in their criticism of *Annie Allen,* by the high value BAM art and aesthetic theory placed on black vernacular expression. In 1972, Don L. Lee (Haki Madhubuti), a close friend of Brooks's and a vocal proponent of a rigidly prescriptive Black Aesthetic, wrote that although the book demonstrates Brooks's "ability to use their [whites'] language while using their ground rules," as a result "she suffers by not communicating with the masses of black people" (19). While not following Lee in dismissing the poem's value for African American audiences, subsequent critics who interpret "The Anniad" as a mock-epic appear nonetheless to have been influenced (directly or indirectly) by his perspective on Brooks's language. This influence is made manifest in readings of the poem as a mock-epic that explicitly or implicitly turn on the claim that Brooks's language is *too* "deliberately distanced from [the] ordinary speech" of most African Americans to be anything but satirical as a vehicle for an "ordinary" young African American woman's story.[24]

But is it ridiculous to term Annie's husband's mistress "a maple banshee," a "sleek slit-eyed gypsy moan," or a "mad bacchanalian lass" (104), given the havoc she helps to wreak in Annie's life? Brooks, when she wove her soaring, sparkling lexicon into "The Anniad," was not writing within the BAM or post-BAM context and, by extension, was not flouting a consensus or even a widely circulating opinion that the African American poet should write her work specifically *to*—and, thus, in the common discourse of—the vast majority of African American people. Those poets preceding her who are most known for writing in "Negro dialect" or vernacular, such as Paul Laurence Dunbar, Langston Hughes, and Sterling Brown, did not argue that black poets *should* write like most African Americans talk, but rather that they should *be able* to do so and still have their work recognized as art.[25] These poets all also wrote significant bodies of poetry in "standard" (American) English and, especially in the case of Dunbar and Brown, in traditional Anglo-European meters.[26] Brooks, too, had written poetry in a black vernacular diction (for example, the "Hattie Scott" sequence in *A Street in Bronzeville*); indeed, part of what seems to have struck reviewers so mightily is that she was able and inclined to cast her voice so far away from the simplest (or least erudite) registers of her first book's poems.[27] Ultimately, it requires an ahistorical imposition of BAM ideology upon a 1940s context to argue that Brooks's decision to employ a high, Latinate diction in "The Anniad" can only have been intended to mock the life and longings of her dreamy and disempowered young black heroine. That late-twentieth-century African American women critics—employing black feminist perspectives—have read the poem as a mock-epic on this ground illustrates the continuing influence of the Black Aesthetic upon the construction of the African American poetry canon, as much as a decade or two after the Movement that launched it was said to be over.

The impulse to read Brooks through a critical lens tinted by this itera-tion of the Black Aesthetic is understandable insofar as Brooks, begin-ning around 1967, so deeply identified herself, her poetry, and her politics with BAM concerns and priorities—or those of black cultural nation-alism more generally. But in 1949, Brooks's black aesthetics would have been more likely shaped by New Negro Renaissance–era thinking, which connected antiracist politics with art in different ways than BAM artists would later do.[28] For example, as Maureen Honey notes in her introduc-tion to *Shadowed Dreams: Women's Poetry of the Harlem Renaissance*:

> The Renaissance generation . . . conceived of itself as carrying on the struggle [for equality and opportunity] through attaining the highest possible level of literary accomplishment and surpassing the boundaries that a racist society tried to impose. Writers saw no contradiction be-tween social activism and the production of nonracial literature because the two were fused in their minds: artistic achievement moved the race upward. (xxxvii)

Though I would quibble with Honey about the designation "nonracial," she provides a useful description of the context for Renaissance-era po-ets' decisions to engage traditional Anglo-European forms, whether writ-ing explicitly about racism or not.[29] Within that context, there is no basis for assuming that Brooks herself would understand the epic genre, and the "grandeur and formality" it calls for, to have an automatically anti-thetical relationship to content critical of a working-class black woman's particular experience of oppression—even if she was well aware that some members of her audience might.[30] Along with New Negro Renais-sance poets, Phillis Wheatley also constitutes a potential influence upon Brooks's aesthetics; her biographer tells us that, around 1959 to 1960, Brooks was planning to write a "verse biography" of Wheatley, which demonstrates that she was familiar with at least some of her predecessor's work (Kent 134, 149–51). In the mid-twentieth century, well before Amiri Baraka's dismissive assessment of what he would deem the enslaved poet's poetic and political shortcomings ("Revolutionary" 139), Brooks may have found Wheatley a model for the potential of elevated language to confer distinction upon the "lowly."

Indeed, far from seeing it as necessary on racial grounds to retreat

from the epic's traditionally ceremonial register, Brooks raised the aesthetic stakes by choosing to write her epic poem in a metrically regular
stanzaic form—a variation upon the rhyme royal stanza, no less. Brooks
grew up reading the Romantic poets, such as William Wordsworth, Sam-
uel T. Coleridge, and John Keats, as well as earlier English poets, like John
Donne (Brooks, Newquist interview 30; Brooks, Howe and Fox interview 143); she not only learned many of the fixed forms that were part of
the English poetry tradition, she rigorously taught them to her students
(Brooks, *Report* 80).[31] It proves difficult to determine absolutely whether
she was consciously innovating upon rhyme royal when she devised her
stanza; however, the similarities between that form and hers call for the
comparison. Just as reading her "The Anniad" against the more typical
epic illuminates her poem's structure, we can better appreciate the brilliance of her stanza by juxtaposing it with the similar rhyme royal stanza.
Both are seven-line stanzas built around three rhymes. Rhyme royal lines
follow the pattern *ababbcc*, conventionally in iambic pentameter—a
challenging, exacting form in which to work. If anything, Brooks's stanza
is even more technically demanding. First, her lines are consistently in
trochaic tetrameter with a catalectic final foot—arguably a more difficult
meter to sustain than iambic pentameter, which is commonly held up
as the meter nearest to the "natural rhythms" of English speech. And,
second, rather than repeating the rhyme scheme exactly throughout the
poem, Brooks shuffles the organization and combinations of her stanza's
three rhymes to produce thirty-one different schemes, only reusing patterns in twelve stanzas. The rhymes are woven together intricately and
unpredictably—to read the poem aloud is to give voice to the melody
that accompanies the dance of words on the page. Indeed, the degree
to which the aural and writerly qualities of the poem reinforce one another underscores the importance of recent critiques of the tendency of
scholars to overstate the oral tradition's significance for African American
literature.[32]

Writing her epic in this stanzaic form, Brooks only emphasizes the
poem's ambition and magnitude. The rhyme royal stanza, which Brooks
revises (or at least evokes), brings with it a powerful pedigree. It was originated by Chaucer in his long poems, such as *Troilus and Criseyde*, and
gets its name, purportedly, from its association with King James I, who
used it in his own verse. When asked, twenty years after publishing "The
Anniad," Brooks said she "can't remember exactly" why she chose a seven-line stanza; but if she did intend to invoke rhyme royal, as is likely, this
stanza's history would certainly lend itself to the project of "rais[ing]"

Annie "to a height she probably did not have" (Brooks, "An Interview" 46). Consider the verbal pyrotechnics produced within this combination of epic genre and stanzaic form, as illustrated by these stanzas describing the self-satisfied response of Annie's "tan man" to her dream-fueled adoration of him:

> Narrow master master-calls;
> And the godhead glitters now
> Cavalierly on his brow.
> What a hot theopathy
> Roisters through her, gnaws the walls,
> And consumes her where she falls
> In her gilt humility.
>
> How he postures at his height;
> Unfamiliar, to be sure,
> With celestial furniture.
> Contemplating by cloud-light
> His bejeweled diadem;
> As for jewels, counting them,
> Trying if the pomp be pure. (100–01)

The stanza's reverberating rhymes and compressed lines encourage and showcase Brooks's predilection, already apparent in her first book, for alliteration ("godhead glitters"), assonance ("hot theopathy"), and consonance (the *l*s in "celestial," "contemplating," and "cloud-light"). Further, the foreshortened meter (in comparison to traditional rhyme royal) foregrounds Brooks's increasing tendency to torque her syntax. For instance, notice how she implies, rather than announces, subjects and objects of her sentences (as in the final sentence of the second stanza above), and how she builds energy by layering clauses one upon the other (as in the final sentence of the first stanza). Add to these elements Brooks's fondness for the spectacularly exact image, which only heightens the serviceability of her elegant vocabulary, and we have the mix of qualities that comprise the dense décor of "The Anniad."[33]

Speaking about her work on this poem, Brooks has emphasized how much time she put into perfecting it, how lovingly she revised it, how deeply she "wanted every phrase to be beautiful," and how "enjoyable" the writing process was for her (Brooks, "An Interview" 46–47). She also recalls being "very much impressed with the *effectiveness* of technique" at the time she was writing *Annie Allen*, which indicates she was quite conscious of the instrumentality of formal prosody in shaping the experience of readers (Brooks, "A Conversation" 6–7; emphasis added). Her descriptions of the self-conscious care that went into this poem belie the comments of those contemporary reviewers who suggested that her use of "the big word or the spectacular rhyme" and her "moments of extravagance" display an "uncertainty of taste" or a failure to be in command of her craft (Humphries 8; Rev., *Booklist* 21; Kunitz 12). Among the few reviewers who appreciated the explosive poetics of "The Anniad" was Thomas Hornsby Ferril, writing for the *San Francisco Chronicle*; he appeared to understand that Brooks's stylistics were deliberate:

> This brilliant Negro girl does things which can't and mustn't be done: she'll bring in big and impossible poster-words; she loves garish alliteration; but her particular magic makes everything work perfectly. The explanation is obvious: She has the keenest sort of mind, and a severe lyrical concreteness is always in control, no matter what extravagant areas of imagination she wanders into. (18)

This focus among contemporary reviewers upon the "extravagance" of Brooks's writing suggests the applicability of Karen Jackson Ford's argument that certain women poets and poets of color have adopted a "poetics of excess," which "carr[ies] the poem forward against the resistances of her readers and of language itself" (42). Ford understands these resistances as arising largely from gendered expectations for the poetry of women to remain controlled, demure, sedate—*feminine* (see 26–27). Whereas women have used "poetic excess" as a strategy for countering their gendered boundaries, Ford explains, BAM poets "reinvented" it for racially disenfranchised people to use "when the dominant culture encouraged their silence" (167). Both of these axes of oppression—gender and race—apply to Brooks, of course.

"The Anniad" is deeply invested in the "poetics of excess." Brooks admits, with no little chagrin, that one of her "motives" for "being technically passionate" in writing "The Anniad" was that she "wanted to *prove* that [she] could write well," which recalls the point about her ambition I made earlier in this chapter (Brooks, "Update" 96; emphasis in original).[34] In order to overwhelm the critical establishment with her poetic prowess, we might say, she "honed [the poetry in *Annie Allen*] to the last degree it could be" (Brooks, "A Conversation" 6–7). This strategy is both facilitated and necessitated by the structural forms Brooks chose to work with: the epic and rhyme royal call for elevated diction, grand rhetorical gestures, and technical intricacy. Brooks not only embraces these formal requirements, but "makes them new" in ways that transgress the boundaries which different kinds of readers apparently would have liked her to respect. The result is a polyvocality that the diversity of critical opinion starkly evidences. Though she might not have predicted some of the specific ways her readers would hear "The Anniad," Brooks's provocative poetics constitute a defiant refusal to allow the poem to be ignored. Her formal choices challenge the racist and sexist inclinations some might have to look upon Annie as a curiosity or a nobody. Casting Annie as the central character of an epic, Brooks pushes readers who might not see the young woman as capable of representing the "tribe" (whether constituted as black women, women, black people, or working-class people) to reconsider the extent to which her quest speaks to the "community's heritage" and "values" (Keller 24). And by taking a stanza that innovatively signifies upon the venerable rhyme royal stanza and *wizarding* it across 301 lines of poetry, Brooks (also potentially a curiosity in some eyes) demands that her audiences see *her* as a poet powerful enough to project a "narrative voice" capable of supporting the necessary "cultural, historical, or mythic heritage" (Keller 24).[35] Equally important are the closely related choices she makes about her subject matter. Brooks's poem depicts the material disadvantages and psychic damages suffered by many, many Americans because of race, gender, and class oppression, and it mounts a strong, if implicit, critique of the powerful, systematic structures that wreak such havoc in so many lives. It does this precisely by depicting the quest of a single person—one who must deal with the full intersectional force of racism, sexism, and classism—for an empowering subjectivity and a social environment in which that subjectivity can be realized. The "ordinary," "mundane" hurdles Annie faces, in the context of epic poetry, are revealed for the trials of strength, intelligence, and character that they are, and her determination in pursuing her quest, despite all setbacks, is rightly portrayed as heroism.[36]

WITH THE FOREGOING in mind, we can elaborate the reading of the poem that our more nuanced take on Brooks's black aesthetics makes available. The underlying structure of "The Anniad" comprises four portions of about equal length. The first eleven stanzas depict Annie, her romantic fantasies about the wonderful "paladin" in her future, and the unfolding of her actual courtship and marriage. In these stanzas we come to understand Annie's quest, which is set up in large part by poems in the first section of *Annie Allen*, "Notes from the Childhood and the Girlhood." The opening poem of that section ("the birth in a narrow room") tells us that she has been born into a "pinchy . . . room," connoting the tight, domestic constraints of her poverty and her gender role that surround her from birth (83). She is not aware of these constraints at first, but after some years, she begins to internalize what her society has taught her about herself: "I am not anything and I have got / Not anything, or anything to do!" (83). Her way of dealing with this disturbing knowledge is to retreat into fantasy, to prance "nevertheless with gods and fairies," where she can imagine a different fate than the one her society assigns to her (83).

The conflict between fantasy and reality that emerges in "The Anniad" is also foreshadowed in "Maxie Allen" and "the ballad of late Annie," in which her mother's pragmatic realism comes head-to-head with Annie's fanciful hopes. We see Annie attempting "to teach her mother / There was somewhat of something other" than the basic gratitude for life and health that Maxie tries to instill in her (84). Maxie listens to her "stipendiary little daughter" (the first adjective underscoring how uncomfortably connected the familial and the financial are for the working poor) as the girl chatters about "fleet love stopping at her foot / And giving her its never-root / To put into her pocket-book"—that is, Annie's view of romance as a way out of an immobilizing poverty (84). What Maxie thinks, but does not say, is that she, too, is a woman; and she has learned from hard experience that marriage does not work the way it is depicted in the fairy tales:

And you don't have to go to bed, I remark,
With two dill pickles in the dark,
Nor prop what hardly calls you honey
And gives you only a little money. (85)

Annie soon will learn that, not only does romance often vanish—as suggested by Maxie's substitution of eating comfort food for having sex—but she is just as likely to have to "prop" her husband up as to be supported by him, financially or otherwise. Though Maxie Allen is often painted as a two-dimensional character, utterly conventional and symbolic of the societal forces that constrain Annie, she might more sympathetically be understood as a victim of the same limitations that confine Annie—and as a mother who sees no better way to protect her daughter from seemingly inevitable disappointments than to nip Annie's dreams in the bud.

But we soon learn that Maxie's efforts have been in vain. Had Maxie's own experience suggested to her that the "something other" than a

gender-constrained domesticity—the sense of purpose in life—that Annie longed for could have been sought outside the realm of romantic love,
she might have been able to save her daughter from some heartaches. But,
in "the ballad of late Annie," we see that she offers Annie only a choice
between the known domesticity of her parents' home and the unknown
of her husband's: "Get a broom to whish the doors / Or get a man to
marry" (90). Faced with these options, who can blame the young girl for
choosing *wishing* over "whish[ing]"? Thus, as "The Anniad" opens, Annie
is "[w]aiting for the paladin / prosperous and ocean-eyed" to come and
rescue her from her "pretty tatters" (99).

While Annie is identified racially as African American ("chocolate"),
her ability to serve as an epic "Everywoman" across racial lines is signaled in the stanza that tells us how impossible her fantasies are.[37] She is
"[w]atching for the paladin / Which *no woman* ever had," regardless of
race and class, the speaker insists (99; emphasis added). The gender roles
of American society are written with middle-class women in mind, but
financially speaking, middle-class men are only slightly less improbable
as "paladins" than men of the working class. What distinguishes Annie
from many women in her situation is her ability to persist in achieving
some relief from the dismal aspects of her reality by keeping her imagination alive. In the stanzas quoted earlier as examples of her poetics of
excess, Brooks deftly allows the reader to see how ill-fitting the mantle
of "paladin" is on the shoulders of the tan man, even as she illustrates
Annie's ongoing devotion to this fabricated image of him. When instead
of removing her from poverty, the new husband "[l]eads her to a lowly
room," Annie does not give in to despair or the kind of bitterness that
marks her mother, Maxie (101). Rather, "she makes a chapel of" the kitchenette apartment that "his pocket chooses" (101). She will not concede
defeat or disillusionment:

> And her set excess believes
> Incorruptibly that no
> Silver has to gape or go,
> Deviate to underglow,
> Sicken off to hit-or-miss. (101)

Only the coming of war—perhaps the gold standard for excess—manages
to tear down her defenses.

Though "The Anniad" is Annie's story, the second portion of the poem
comprises eleven stanzas sketching the wartime adventures of tan man,

who is drafted into World War II. This portion strengthens Brooks's implied claim, as epic poet, to speak for the "tribe" of African Americans, across gender (in addition to that of women, across racial boundaries), by giving attention to the way racism infiltrates and shapes a black man's experience of war, manhood, and marriage. In doing so, it provides a wider context for our understanding of the raced and gendered American power structure in which Annie must operate. This part of the poem, too, is fleshed out by poems outside "The Anniad." The "Appendix to the Anniad" gives us three poems, including Brooks's famous "sonnet-ballad," that depict her sorrow over her husband's departure—or should we say his defection? For he is headed into the traditional realm of the epic poem, into war, with the opportunity to see other parts of the world and to achieve honor and glory of the sort that is denied to women. And he will never return, the poem suggests—not fully, not as he was when he left.[38] Upon his return from "[t]he hunched hells across the sea," he finds it impossible to squeeze himself back into the (racially) constricted life he had previously lived (102). Although war implies the paltriness of any life ("Life was little as a sand"), it also means "drama," excitement, and "power"; war takes with one hand and gives with the other ("[s]uffocation, with a green / Moist sweet breath for mezzanine") (102, 103).

But, regardless of the allowances made for soldiers during World War II, black men, much like women, were not allowed to wield power and privilege, as a matter of course, in 1940s American society. Here, the poem's epic scope enables Brooks to draw illuminating connections between social groups whose political similarities have been inconsistently acknowledged; she casts her "voice" in such a way that black men and women of any race might simultaneously hear her speak to their constrained condition. When "tan man" is required to surrender his uniform and, thus, his power, he seeks to counter this symbolic castration with a show of sexual potency. But to demonstrate true manhood, he must "hunt"; a wife will not suffice (103). "Not that woman! (Not that room! / Not that dusted demi-gloom!)," he insists, feeling just as "pinched" in his marital kitchenette as Annie does (104). What he needs, apparently, is an undomesticated woman, "a gorgeous and gold shriek," which is a far cry from "sweet and chocolate"—and a sore point with Brooks, as I have noted (104).

Brooks thus makes a point of identifying the contribution of intra-racial colorism to Annie's hardships. This point becomes especially interesting with regard to later critics who accuse her of speaking only to white audiences in *Annie Allen*. J. Saunders Redding, one of the very few African American critics to review *Annie Allen* (and the only one I have discovered reviewing it for a major national publication—the *Saturday Review*)—takes note of Brooks's treatment of the topic. Speaking about another poem addressing colorism that appears later in the book, he writes: "Who but another Negro can get the intimate feeling, the racially-particular acceptance and rejection, and the oblique bitterness of this?" (27). His concern is that Brooks not indulge in writing "coterie stuff—the special allusions, the highly special feeling derived from an even more special experience," by which he means poems about situations so particular to black people that white audiences will not be able to identify with, or even understand, them (27). His caution makes an ironic counterpoint to an assessment like Lee's, which, as noted above, complained that *Annie Allen* did not "communicat[e] with the masses of black people" (19). Polyvocality, then, operates within time, not outside of it; what one critic alleges in 1949 can be heard *only* by black audiences, another critic proclaims is virtually inaudible to blacks in 1972.

From the news of the tan man's betrayal we move back to a focus on Annie, in the third portion of "The Anniad," which is composed of twelve stanzas following the movement of her quest beyond the traditional domestic sphere, for the most part, as she begins to look for ways to define herself outside of marriage. This portion of the poem is the least thoroughly discussed in the criticism on "The Anniad," despite its significance for understanding the scope of Annie's epic quest. For it is only here that she begins to perceive that romance is but one means of attaining a sense of self-worth and cultivating beauty in one's life. These stanzas begin by recalling Annie to the foreground through a return to the invocation of reader-as-substitute-muse: "Think of sweet and chocolate / Minus passing-magistrate, / Minus passing-lofty light," the narrative voice asks of us, continuing to list all the things that Annie is now "minus," or lacking (104). Importantly, Annie is "[m]inus symbol, cinema / Mirages, all things suave and bright"—she has been forced to let go of the cultural myths that Hollywood has fed her about the meaning of romance and marriage for women's lives (104). Though cast in terms of lack, this letting-go represents progress on her journey. Annie now goes out-of-doors, literally, and spends the next year of her life in a series of seasonally characterized, socially isolated forays into self-definition. She "[s]eeks for solaces in snow," only to find that it "[c]hills her nicely, as it must" (105); she then "[s]eeks for solaces in green" springtime, but in that season dwell the untrustworthy creatures of her former fantasy life: "Hyacinthine devils," "unseen / Pucks and cupids" can offer her nothing more substantive than "a fine fume" (105). In summer she finds herself

tempted by the sensuality of the palate, but quickly learns that the pleasures of "gourmet fare" are not amenable to "solitaire" (105). Annie at last
discovers her feelings of loss accurately reflected in the autumn landscape,
"her true town"; the "November leaves / All gone papery and brown" are
like herself, she realizes, "falling falling down" (105).

Recognizing that she is withering in her loneliness, Annie gives up her
retreat into nature to look for rejuvenation in the social arena. She offers
herself to "friends"—not real friends, but those members of the "popu-
lace" whom she can only tempt to her side with "philanthropist" prom-
ises of "rubies" and other "flirting bijouterie" (106). She learns soon that
"Glass begets glass," and moves on to seek her society among the philoso-
phers of the past: "Plato, Aeschylus," and a list of other wise men of the
ancient world (106). While this company may have wisdom to offer, she
comes to see that she will not "find kisses pressed in books" (106). Too
young and too passionate yet to resign herself to an asexual existence, her
final adventure in the sphere of the social world is to play her husband's
game and take a lover.[39] Having "lost her twill / . . . her fur," those sturdy
and warm fabrics representing the relative security of marriage, Annie
"[t]ests forbidden taffeta" and "shivers in her thin hurrah" (106). Though
there is "pleasant" enough music in this endeavor for a time, ultimately
"the culprit magics fade," and because her motive for pursuing the relationship is more "compulsion" than attraction, she has to admit finally
that "no music plays at all" below the relationship's ornamental surface
(106–07). "Shorn and taciturn," Annie "[f]rees her lover" and retreats
back into domesticity, where the role of "mother" remains to her. But her
"children-dear" cannot protect her from the "desert" of her loneliness,
whose "[h]owls . . . and countercharms" she still has neither conquered
nor come to terms with (107).

It is into this vacuum that tan man creeps, as we move into the final
portion of the poem. He has a disease contracted during his wartime
travels and, sped along by "[w]ench" and "whiskey," it is killing him (107).
The narrative voice addresses him directly, advising him to:

> Pack compunction and go home.
> Skeleton, settle, down in bed.
> Slide a bone beneath Her head,
> Kiss Her eyes so rash and red. (108)

Here we see a reversal of the roles they played at the beginning of their
relationship. Then, he wore the "godhead . . . / Cavalierly on his brow"
(100); now, the capitalization of the pronoun referring to Annie signals

"Her" divinity. This is ambiguous and fleeting triumph, at best; he is dying, after all, and she is being idolized for taking on a very traditional and constricting gender role: woman as caregiver and nurse. He is soon dead, leaving behind the children he has largely neglected and who will "forget him" before long, and the "mistress" who will similarly "dismiss / Memories of his kick and kiss," as she prepares to "[s]lit her eyes and find her fool" for the next season (108). Only "his devotee," Annie, will remember him, every time she "pass[es] by his chair / And his tavern," every time the telephone rings (109). Outwardly, she is going through the motions—"washes coffee-cups and hair, / Sweeps, determines what to wear"—but inside she is battered, stung, and reeling (109). Two lines that are frequently misinterpreted as referring to tan man's funeral are in fact a metaphor for Annie's internal state in the moment when she succumbs to utter disillusionment and a kind of death of the self: "Harried sods dilate, divide, / Suck her sorrowfully inside" (109).

If the poem ended here, it would be more a tragedy than an epic. The "sweet and chocolate," "ripe and rompabout," "thaumaturgic lass" we meet at the beginning of the poem has shown herself to possess a vibrant imagination and an even livelier sense of determination. She has faced down the collapse of her fantasy world and walked bravely into the natural and social worlds in search of a new sense of purpose. She has embraced her role as mother and her capacity to serve as a caregiver, but without accepting the gendered prescription that her personal fulfillment as a woman necessarily lies therein. For this Annie to find in her husband's death the total negation of her own being would be such a tragedy that it would threaten to overwhelm the powerful sociopolitical critique the poem makes. Instead, Brooks makes the emotionally satisfying and technically sound choice to include but not to end "The Anniad" with this dark moment of despair. The epic requires a "heroic example . . . by which later generations [can] measure their own conduct and order the social fabric of their lives" (Bernstein 8). If Annie is to be, fundamentally, more than just a model of what not to do, her strength of will, creativity, and persistence must be underscored and rewarded with a final, arguably successful heroic act. Recalling the audience to its function as muse once more in the closing stanzas, Brooks essentially resurrects Annie from the death of the soul she has suffered, and depicts her as beginning life anew—not with a clean slate, but having succeeded in recognizing that she must search first *within herself* for the nurturance and the resources she needs to create a satisfying life in the face of the challenges she faces as an African American woman:

Think of tweaked and twenty-four.
Fuschias gone or gripped or gray,
All hay-colored that was green.
Soft aesthetic looted, lean.
Crouching low, behind a screen,
Pock-marked eye-light, and the sore
Eaglets of old pride and prey.

Think of almost thoroughly
Derelict and dim and done.
Stroking swallows from the sweat.
Fingering faint violet.
Hugging old and Sunday sun.
Kissing in her kitchenette
The minuets of memory. (109)

Brooks carefully balances the pain of the past with hope for Annie's future. She is "tweaked," yes, but at "twenty-four" she is still young—almost shockingly young to have already experienced marriage, war, betrayal, motherhood, and widowhood. Her life is still ahead of her. The color has drained or been leached out of her world and her "eye-light" is scarred, but "behind a screen" of this bleached existence, Annie is nurturing a new self (109). Brooks's metaphor, "the sore / Eaglets of old pride and prey," suggests rebirth, as the young eagles are born almost phoenixlike from the ashes of Annie's past (109). They are "sore," but in this adjective of ache we hear the homonym of flight.

In the final stanza, we are asked to "think" of what Annie has "*almost*" become—and the doors that are opened by this qualifier cannot be overemphasized (italics mine). "Stroking swallows from the sweat" is an impossible line to interpret literally; however, noting that it offers a recurrence of bird (and thus potentially flight) imagery is one way of connecting it to the line of interpretation I am unfolding (109). Considering the swallow's significance in English poetry as a mythological reference, it might also stand as a symbol of the metamorphosis of a wronged wife (Procne) into a creature with a new life (Hamilton 270–71). The line is also significant as evidence of Annie's redirected agency and renewed creative powers, whether her fingers are coaxing music from her throat or transforming waste fluid into potable water. The signs of rejuvenation grow even stronger, though they are still weighted with reference to the past, as the stanza and the poem come to a close. Color ("violet") has returned, if "faint[ly]" (109). Annie is "[h]ugging . . . sun," which again suggests color: perhaps it is still a faint color, insofar as the sun is "old"— but equally arguable would be a very bright sun, whether based on the audible pun in "Sunday" suggestive of another familiar myth of resurrection or simply on the echoing, doubled glow of "*Sunday sun*" (109; emphasis added).

In these final lines, Annie is alone and still in the kitchenette that represents her cramped and impoverished circumstances; nonetheless, she has learned how to gather the tender and imaginative energy that she used to direct outwardly and to activate it in ways that ease her confrontation with the constraints upon her life without blinding her to them. The verbs of this stanza—"stroking," "fingering," "hugging," and "kissing"— portray her as lavishing upon herself the romantic caresses that she once bestowed upon the largely undeserving tan man (109). The "music" that did not "play . . . at all" during her last attempt to define herself through a romantic relationship has returned to her life as "minuets of memory," which are not fantasized, but real (107, 109).

The outlets for this reborn Annie's active, creative agency are not many, but in the aftermath of World War II there are somewhat expanded opportunities for women in the labor force and in other nontraditional public sector roles. Racism continues to further limit her possibilities, as it did Brooks's own,[40] but, as historian Stephanie Shaw's research teaches us, it would be a mistake to think of black women in this period as entirely excluded from the public and professional realms. With self-confidence and the support of family and community, black women could aspire to personal achievements in these realms that would enrich the women's families and communities in return.[41] The poems that follow "The Anniad" do not specify how Annie supports her family as a widowed, single mother, but it is clear that she does. By the close of *Annie Allen*, our heroine can state with authority that "There are no magics or elves / Or timely godmothers to guide us. We . . . must / Wizard a track through our own screaming weed" (140).

The third section of the volume, "The Womanhood," allows us to see, obliquely, the development of Annie's hard-won authority. The poems depict her reentering life as a mature woman, thoughtfully mothering her children, interacting with her community, and critically analyzing the American society that places such an oppressive foot on her neck. Brooks displays Annie's heroic stature by having her articulate the clear-eyed, witty insights of poems like "I love those little booths at Benvenuti's" and "Beverly Hills, Chicago," in which she astutely assesses the racial and class dynamics at the intersections of white and black Chicago. More than one of her white contemporary reviewers, as well as her editor at Harper, took her to task for her "reportorial" poems on "problems of caste and prejudice," but she apparently saw this "poetically 'reportorial'" writing unambivalently as her task, because her writing thereafter grew increasingly "indignant" (Kent 78; Kunitz 10). [42]

Brooks's poetic politics, upon her identification with Black Arts Movement aesthetics, became even less palatable to critics from the literary establishment, as she grew more and more explicit and Afrocentric in her engagement of race in her poems. But her poetry never became more explosively *excessive* than it was in *Annie Allen*. The excesses of "The Anniad" were fostered by Brooks's ingenious decision to tell a black story—a poor, black, woman's story—by using two highly traditional, highly ceremonial (masculinist) formal structures: the epic genre and a rhyme royal–like stanza. She freely and distinctively modified both forms until, transformed, they served her story's needs. This "experimentation," which was initially widely recognized, even when it was not uniformly celebrated, was not undertaken simply for its own sake (though I do not mean to disparage such a motive); Brooks innovated, we might say, because her black aesthetics called for it. Shaped by the legacy of the New Negro Renaissance, her aesthetics motivated her to "*prove*" her ability to write as well as or better than any American poet at that time—and her Pulitzer Prize suggests that she achieved this goal. But she proved it without moving one step away from the subject matter that had fueled her first book and would furnish all her books to come: the lives of the people she knew, the people of Bronzeville—writ small and writ large—including herself.

The failure of most modernist critics to see beyond Brooks's traditional forms to her formal innovations mirrors the failure of many BAM and BAM-influenced critics to see beyond her elevated diction to her very socially grounded subjects. The combined result of these blindnesses has been the relative obscurity of one of her masterpieces, despite the fact that both her early and later works have been canonized within the broadly accepted American and African American traditions (in different but overlapping ways). In particular, the significance of Brooks's work in "The Anniad" for the modernist project has been vastly underestimated, a critical oversight that becomes especially visible when we compare the disproportionately sizable critical response to Robert Frost's brand of modernism, which is not significantly less engaged with traditional meters and forms than Brooks's. [43] The most innovative contributions of Brooks's modernism, unlike those of Frost's, have gone largely unremarked and undervalued because they require a contextualization in which the meaning of race and gender for both production and reception is fully examined and appreciated. I have provided a measure of such contextualization here.

This chapter takes a step toward (re)situating *Annie Allen* in the critical landscape of the American and African American poetic traditions, and, notably, the "avant-garde" tradition as well. By tracing the poet's awareness of her various audiences and their potentially conflicting expectations as manifested in the inventive approaches she uses to bring her subjects and forms together, this chapter also begins an exploration of the aesthetic value of polyvocality produced in stanzaically regular long poems by African American women poets. Analyzing the relationship of these explorations in polyvocality to these women poets' apparent need to develop modes of black aesthetics that diverge from the masculinist norms of the African American literary tradition is a project I continue in the next chapter, which examines a poem directly inspired by "The Anniad."

Sonia Sanchez, having begun to publish during the Movement that so deeply influenced Brooks's later work, turns in her later years to the mix of lyric and epic modes that the young Brooks had developed for historically distinct black aesthetic purposes. In the 1990s, for very different but equally complicated reasons, Sanchez also needs to write a poem that can "speak in tongues." Her poem must interpellate readers with deeply held black nationalist (masculinist) beliefs in the primacy of the heterosexual family, as well as readers who, like Sanchez herself, are mourning the impact of HIV/AIDS on the African American community (and black populations, generally) from more inclusive, less (or non-)homophobic standpoints. As I discuss in chapter 2, she will need to innovate upon both the epic and the rhyme royal stanza once again, taking them in a different direction than Brooks did, in response to a black aesthetic that is drawn from her BAM-era commitments, even as it revises them.

EXPANDING THE SUBJECT
Sonia Sanchez's *Does Your House Have Lions?*

SONIA SANCHEZ, whose forty-year writing career took off in the late 1960s within the flowering of the Black Arts Movement, engaged from the start with some of the most prescriptive forms of black aesthetics (those that make up what I have been identifying herein as the Black Aesthetic, that now overshadow alternative versions). During these same decades, however, she has also employed black aesthetics in ways far more fluid—and far more complicated—than most retrospective constructions of the Movement would lead one to expect. Committed to creating art that supports and nurtures her readers—particularly, though not exclusively, her African American readers—Sanchez confronted a signal challenge, aesthetically and otherwise, in the writing of *Does Your House Have Lions?*, her searing, soaring, seventy-page elegy for her brother, Wilson Driver Jr., who died of AIDS-related complications in 1980.[1] Driver's death occurred just a year or so before the condition that became known as Acquired Immune Deficiency Syndrome was deemed an epidemic ("The Global HIV/AIDS Timeline"). Yet, seventeen years later, when *Lions* was published, it was among the very first handful of HIV/AIDS–related literary works produced by African American writers who were themselves neither gay nor HIV-positive—and, of these, it was the only one written in verse. This literary silence, against which out gay, insistently black artists like Essex Hemphill, Marlon Riggs, and Melvin Dixon cast their works, suggests why this poem presented such a challenge to Sanchez. Her two goals for the poem—to honor her brother's memory and to raise awareness about HIV/AIDS in the African American community—were thornily in conflict with one another. The productive tension they generated prompted her to write what is arguably the most innovative poem of her oeuvre—no small feat for a poet whose improvisatory spirit, openness to cross-cultural influences, and unconventional approaches had already inspired Kalamu ya Salaam to pronounce her work "a model of Black postmodernism" (77).[2]

In this chapter, I argue that *Lions*, like "The Anniad," again revises the traditional Western epic by bringing a distinctive configuration of black aesthetics to bear on its norms. If Brooks, as we saw in chapter 1, *changes the subject* of the traditional epic by instating a young, black, working-class woman in place of the strong and powerful male warrior as the hero(ine) of her text, Sanchez *expands the subject* of the epic by refiguring the singular hero's quest as a collective, familial struggle. While the epic hero has always conventionally symbolized his whole "tribe," by presenting a black family (symbolic of the Black Family, writ large) as the collective hero of her poem, Sanchez removes the focus from the individual on both sides of the symbolic equation. Moreover, as she enlarges the epic's subject numerically, she also opens it up temporally: she demonstrates the reach of this epic struggle back to the era of slavery, by representing the family so as to include ancestral figures who died hundreds of years ago during the forced transatlantic journey from Africa to North America. In so doing, she brings together the conventions of the epic with those of the contemporary narrative of slavery (or the "neo-slave narrative"), a genre deeply rooted in African American history and culture. Add to this mix the formal elements of both lyric elegy and dense, highly figurative rhyme royal stanzas, and we begin to appreciate the stores of creativity, African American cultural knowledge, and technical virtuosity Sanchez called upon to produce this carefully crafted amalgamation of forms. The resulting poem speaks not simply to those members of the black community already dealing with the taboo subjects of homosexuality and HIV/AIDS, but also to those who actively avoid the realities of queer sexualities and AIDS-related deaths among black people.

In this sense, as well as in the sense of her poem's multiple speakers, Sanchez invests *Lions* with a polyvocality that emerges formally from the hard-earned balance between epic scale and lyric compression inspired in part by Brooks's "The Anniad." Mae Henderson's discussion of polyvocality, upon which I draw, points out the "simultaneity" of "familial, or testimonial and public, or competitive discourses" to be found in black women's writing—"discourses that both affirm and challenge the values and expectations of the reader" (351), precisely as I am suggesting Sanchez's writing does in *Lions*. Sanchez's inscription of polyvocality into the fundamental structure of the poem foregrounds her commitment to an ethical and evolving black aesthetics—an aesthetics that employs (and re-forms) the conventional rhyme royal stanza, even as it expands the subject of the traditional Western epic. Attending to her nuanced black aesthetics enables us to see clearly the range and sophistication of her formal strategies and to assess what is gained and what is lost in the negotiation with audience that those strategies represent. Attempting to coax her resistant audience far enough into the poem for her message of aware acceptance to take hold, she ultimately risks reaffirming the very prejudices she sought to challenge. We will be required, then, to consider the extent to which she also expands the *black* subject—that is, the degree to which Sanchez succeeds in calling forth a more encompassing black subjectivity, one which can incorporate the previously proscribed identities of the homosexual and the person who is HIV-positive or diagnosed with AIDS.[3]

BEFORE TAKING UP the poem itself, I need to outline two important reasons for the resolute literary silence around HIV/AIDS and homosexuality among African Americans and the taboos that silence evidences.[4] One of them arises from the history of white racist constructions of black people's sexuality, as it intersects with the emergence of AIDS awareness in the U.S. Preliminary information about HIV/AIDS led the medical community to associate its origins and transmission with populations that were already stigmatized, to varying degrees, within dominant U.S. discourses—especially Africans, Haitians, and homosexual men. These social stigmas (as racist, discriminatory, and unwarranted as they were) tended to magnify the stigma of being diagnosed with an incurable, fatal, contagious virus, and vice versa. As the 1980s progressed, it became increasingly clear that being gay, like being from Haiti, was in no way a prerequisite for contracting HIV/AIDS. Nonetheless, the initial association of the virus with gay men (and the perception of AIDS as a modern-day "plague" sent by the Christian God to wipe out "sinners," à la Sodom and Gomorrah) remained powerfully operative in popular understandings of AIDS for years.[5]

Since the black women's club movement emerged in the 1890s to defend black womanhood from charges of hypersexuality and licentiousness, African American communities have embraced the ideology of respectability as a means of countering enduring racist stereotypes and racial discrimination.[6] Candice Jenkins, in her brilliant study *Private Lives, Proper Relations: Regulating Black Intimacy*, writes: "One not-so-surprising reaction to . . . narratives of black sexual and domestic deviance is the attempt by blacks, particularly black women, to regulate black behavior in the service of creating an inviolable respectability," efforts which involved "the embrace of the very same Victorian values that had been used to exclude black people from the ideals of kinship and sexuality" (12). Jenkins calls this "desire" of black women to achieve respectability as a defense against "narratives of sexual and familial pathology" the "salvific wish" (13–14). In more recent decades, the persistence of this ideology appears in the way some African Americans have distanced themselves from homosexuality by, among other things, denying or ignoring the existence of HIV-positive people and AIDS-related deaths among them. It was not until 1991, when the famous, highly respected (and avowedly heterosexual) African American basketball player, Earvin "Magic" Johnson, announced publicly that he was HIV-positive, that the cloud of silence around HIV/AIDS in African American communities began to lift ("Global"; Román 204).[7]

The second factor contributing to African American responses to queer sexuality and HIV/AIDS, including the literary silence on these subjects, concerns the Black Arts Movement context in which Sanchez emerged as a poet, publishing her first book, *Home Coming*, with the independent, black-owned Broadside Press in 1969. As Phillip Brian Harper's compelling account details, in *Are We Not Men?*, BAM's demonization of homosexuality in the service of black nationalism worked to discursively exclude homosexuality from the "authentic" African American community by equating effeminacy and same-sex desire with a highly class-inflected notion of white male impotence and degeneracy.[8] Thus, homosexuality in black men was deemed detrimental to the struggle for liberation and self-determination, from black nationalist perspectives, because it symbolized male weakness and ineffectuality in a context "in which the masculine body and mind indexed the race's political standing" (Murray 10). The literature of the Movement participated in the construction of homosexuality as a "white thing"—and a "blacks-who-want-to-be-white thing"—both by castigating black gay men for their purported emasculation and by treating so-called "assimilationist" behavior (conflated with middle-class aspirations or status) as evidence of homosexuality in black men.[9] In other words, to the extent that BAM writers understood black liberation as resulting from (and equal to) black manhood—where "manhood" and gay sexuality are irreconcilable—homophobia constituted an entrenched element of their black aesthetics.

To put this in context, today, the issues of gay marriage and out gays in the military are still hot-button, election-deciding controversies, and the continuing perpetration of hate crimes against gays, lesbians, bisexuals, and transgendered people make it clear that vast numbers of Americans, irrespective of race, remain unwilling to relinquish heterosexual privilege and proscribe homophobic behavior.[10] That African Americans make up some of these numbers should neither be surprising nor a singular indictment of blacks; as poet and activist Cheryl Clarke has put it, "homophobia among black people in America is largely reflective of the homophobic culture in which we live" (197). Contrary to popular wisdom, African Americans are not any "more homophobic than the heterosexist culture" of America as a whole—despite their being more vulnerable to, and having more to lose from, being stigmatized as "sexually deviant" within dominant American discourse (Clarke 205; Jenkins 16–21).[11] Nonetheless, Sanchez's creative expression of the emotional and material impact of HIV/AIDS on black families and communities over a decade ago placed her within the vanguard of black writers on the subject.[12] Sanchez was undoubtedly aware, as she drafted *Lions*, that breaking the cultural silence about AIDS by writing about her brother's sexuality and death would require both herself and her audience to confront the existence within the African American community of practices and conditions that have typically been repressed.[13] Editor Kadija Sesay was not exaggerating when she called Sanchez's decision to do so a "brave step" (Sanchez, "Sonia Sanchez: The Joy" 150).

Her self-imposed task was made all the more challenging insofar as Sanchez was a highly visible artist and activist within the Black Arts Movement and remains one of its most iconic figures. Some of her visibility and longevity, I propose, arises from her relative success at not allowing the Movement's gender norms to overdetermine her poetics. The early books that established her reputation demonstrate her willingness and ability to wield the same ("masculine") tools as the men poets—including profanity and calls for literal revolution—without relinquishing the celebration of black love and voicing of women's perspectives that marked her poetry as "feminine," all in the service of African American liberation.[14] For example, she makes both gestures in these lines from "Indianapolis/Summer/1969/Poem":

> if mothas programmed
>   sistuhs for
> good feelings bout they blk/men
> and i
>   mean if blk/fathas proved
> they man/hood by
>   fighten the enemy
> instead of fucken every available sistuh.
> and i mean
>   if we programmed/
>   loved/each

other in com/mun/al ways
                    so that no
blk/person starved
                    or killed
                          each other on
a sat/ur/day nite corner.
then may
            be   it wud all
come down to some
                    thing else
like RE VO LU TION.
                          i mean if. (*I've Been* 22)

Here, she skillfully blends concern for black interpersonal (heterosexual) relationships with a critique of the masculinist politics of black nationalism, tracing the relationship of both to the Movement's political goals and, equally important, establishing herself as an artist whose commitment to black people is evidenced—rather than weakened—by her ability to identify their shortcomings. Her continued insistence, over the course of a long and fairly prolific career, upon the viability of an often overtly political and racialized poetics (including her championship of rap and politically conscious rap artists) has kept her, like Amiri Baraka, in view of successive generations of African American poetry consumers.[15] The magnitude of respect Sanchez commands as a cultural figure is suggested by the establishment in 1996 of *BMa: The Sonia Sanchez Literary Review*, a journal created "to provide an interdisciplinary forum for the critical discussion of Sonia Sanchez and other Black Arts Movement artists."[16] My point here is that Sanchez's stature and popularity, particularly vis-à-vis the African American community, is rooted in her connection to BAM and her commitment to black people and cultures. A large part of her most devoted audience, then, is likely to bring expectations to her work that accord with the black aesthetics typically associated with the Movement, which included, as we have seen, a deeply homophobic— and heteronormative—thread.

To be sure, Sanchez was rarely as strident as many BAM writers in her treatment of homosexuality. Elisabeth Frost notes, however, that Sanchez's early work, "at times, engages in the same homophobic rhetoric that [LeRoi] Jones and others exploited" (77). Traces of this appear in the poem excerpted above, which illustrates the economic impact of racism on African American communities by pointing to the prostitution of "young brothas" to white men; as critical of the *sale* as of the orientation of the sex, she writes that these young men get

> picked up
> > cruised around
> > > till they
> asses open in tune
> > to holy rec/tum/
> > > dom. (*I've Been* 21)

Still, poems in her first three books more commonly deal instead in *implicit* heterosexism. The focus in her early books on the "revolutionary" potential of black "(hetero)sexual love" constitutes a less offensive poetics, to be sure, though it is grounded in the same problematic understanding of normative sexuality that was thought to justify the ridicule and castigation of gays in works by other BAM writers (Frost 79). Sanchez has since dropped the objectionable language altogether and increasingly writes poems that are explicitly critical of homophobia and inclusive of gays and lesbians, a shift that seems to have taken place between her award-winning *Homegirls and Handgrenades* (1984) and *Wounded in the House of a Friend* (1995), the book whose writing interrupted the writing of *Lions*.[17] But the fact that her audience has always included a significant segment of people whose views on gender and sexuality are influenced by heterosexist black nationalism would necessarily inform her approach to composing a poem honoring a black gay man and challenging homophobia. Indeed, it is chiefly to that segment of her audience that *Lions* is addressed.

Sanchez explained in a recent interview why she felt *Lions* is an "important" book:

> [B]ecause it will speak to some of the issues in our community. How we jump up and talk about and laugh at gay people. You even have people who think they can go out and beat up on gays. They're following other people's examples, you know. But we can't do that because we've seen that already in our neighborhoods. We've got to understand that we are not to treat people the way we've been treated in the world. ("Interview" 60)

Drawing a powerful connection between racism and homophobia, Sanchez asserts that her poem will encourage members of the African American community to stop ostracizing and abusing others because of their sexuality. Significantly, however, this unequivocal rejection of the homophobia—and, by extension, the homophobic constructions of "blackness" woven through BAM-era writing—that she appears once to have accepted *does not* evidence a wholesale break with black aesthetics. As I noted in the Introduction, even for key players in the Movement, black aesthetics is, and has always been, an elastic and contested concept, contrary to the subsequent constructions of the Black Aesthetic as a set of agreed-upon rules circumscribing "black art." Just as Sanchez challenged the sexist gender norms that permeated BAM-era aesthetics while she was participating in and promoting the Movement's cultural nationalism (Frost 68), she does not allow her inclusion of gay sexuality to preclude her from embracing other powerful aspects of black aesthetics that BAM engendered.

In fact, it is Sanchez's ongoing commitment to another well-known element of black aesthetics that underwrites her decision to create a poem that works against the black nationalist condemnation of homosexuality: the principle that "black art" must empower black people. Carolyn Fowler wrote for *Black World*, at the height of cultural nationalism, that the "notion of survival, since it has been so important in our historical evolution as a people, may remain part of the Black Aesthetic" going forward (qtd. in Spady 47). One tenet of the black aesthetics being worked out by Movement theorists and artists posited that art created in accordance with a black aesthetic was importantly connected to political action—might even be a form of political action—to the extent that it "further[ed] the psychological liberation of [black] people" (Neal, "And Shine" 656). There exist forces that could and would destroy the black community; thus, poet and theorist Larry Neal argued, black artists "must address ourselves to this reality in the sharpest terms possible" (654). The insistence on art that spoke "to black people," rather than *about* them to whites, if embraced, would save the work from the status of "protest" literature. As Neal put it: "You don't have to protest to a hungry man about his hunger. You either have to feed him, or help him to eliminate the root causes of that hunger" (654). In other words, the artist could address the very real threats to African American survival through direct action or through the creation of art that would enable African Americans to better understand and resist those threats.

The rate at which HIV/AIDS has spread through the African American community—not to mention Africa—certainly qualifies it as a threat to black people's survival.[18] Another BAM poet, Haki Madhubuti (Don L. Lee), has also set aside previous expressions of homophobia to recognize this crisis. In the Foreword to an anthology published by his own Third World Press, *Fingernails across the Chalkboard: Poetry and Prose on HIV/AIDS from the Black Diaspora*, Madhubuti writes: "AIDS . . . has the potential of devastating the Afrikan population unlike any weapon we've known since the Afrikan holocaust, the enslavement of Afrikan people by Europeans" (x).[19] Similarly, as we will see, Sanchez invites an analogy between AIDS and slavery in *Lions*, a move facilitated by the elaborate formal framework she creates stanza by stanza and section by section. Having seen firsthand what AIDS can do to the human body as she cared for her brother during his illness, Sanchez crafts a poetic resistance to the threat represented by the mounting numbers of AIDS-related deaths. Her poem exemplifies her recognition that helping to reduce the deadly impact of AIDS on the African American population necessarily involves an intervention in the homophobia located in the black community.[20]

LIONS IS DIVIDED into four sections—"sister's voice," "brother's voice," "father's voice," and "family voices/ancestors' voices"—a structure which immediately foregrounds the importance of polyvocality to the work. Despite the clear autobiographical impetus behind the poem, the characters remain unnamed, indicating that they ultimately function more symbolically than specifically. The narrative unfolds in a temporally fascinating way, moving back and forth in time, not unlike a pendulum, but in increasingly wider arcs. In the first seven stanzas, the "sister's voice" introduces us to the speaker's half-brother at the age of seventeen. He has come north to take emotional revenge upon his father (and, to a lesser extent, his sister) for leaving him and his mother behind in the South while he was still a very young boy. In the "brother's voice" section, nine stanzas long, he addresses his father, sister, and mother in turn, taking the reader back to his childhood and adolescence as he describes his relationships with his family. He then picks up where the "sister's voice" left off in relating his experiences as a young man in the North, moving us forward through his young adulthood.

The "father's voice" speaks next, giving his children (and the reader) the history of his marriages—initially to the sister's mother, his one true love who died all too soon in childbirth, and later to the brother's mother, who refused to parent her predecessor's child, forcing the father to choose between his children and precipitating the move north that separated him and his daughter from his son. As these eleven stanzas move from the father's past to the brother's adult life, we become more aware of the young man's development of inexplicable health problems, which would only after his death be understood as HIV/AIDS. The book's final section, "family voices/ancestors' voices," distributes thirty-two stanzas among the three previous speakers, as well as the dying man's mother and, significantly, two long-dead ancestors, one male and one female. As the narrative circulates among the speakers, the narrative scope expands backward as far as the Middle Passage and forward, through the progression of the brother's illness and his reconciliation with his family members, both the living and the ancestors, who are prepared in the final stanza to receive him on the other side of his transition.

At 418 lines, *Lions* is not a great deal longer than "The Anniad." But with each of its 59 stanzas centered on an individual page and comprising a book, it visually projects the kind of gravitas appropriate to the epic that Brooks's poem, an unbroken stream of stanzas forming only a section of a volume of poetry, has to earn in other ways. By contrast, a search for visual markers of the black aesthetics characteristic of Sanchez's work would be disappointing. The idiosyncratic typography and orthography that Sanchez once used to suggest the sound of black vernacular speech and "score" the pacing and intensity of the lines—also a sign of the orality typically associated with the African American literary tradition—are largely absent.[21] Compared to the eye-catching appearance of her BAM-era poems, especially her pathbreaking, improvisatory jazz poetry, the book's visually consistent rhyme royal stanzas—seven-line blocks of text following the standard *ababbcc* pattern—do not immediately announce either their "blackness" or their innovativeness. There are certainly signs that the poem's embrace of received form is not wholly deferential: Sanchez's characteristic move of generally dispensing with capital letters, for one, as well as decisions to slant her rhymes at dramatically inclined angles and to discard meter altogether in favor of a fluid, conversational rhythm that showcases her ear for speech (decisions which distinguish her work from Brooks's). But while these are unconventional variations upon the rhyme royal form, alone they do not necessarily evidence an innovative black aesthetic at work.

While the poem does contain visual signs of "blackness" that I will account for presently, three other equally telling (if less visible) markers of Sanchez's black aesthetics that are woven instead into the formal fabric of *Lions* require our attention first, as they help us understand how she achieves the polyvocality her taboo subject matter requires. All of these elements participate in her radical revision of the epic—the ways she *expands the subject* of the genre. The first concerns Sanchez's response to the epic's typical narrative structure, which, as we recall from chapter 1, relies upon an authoritative, highly ceremonial voice that projects "the community's heritage" and communicates "values significant for communal stability and social well-being" (Keller 24). Where Brooks sought to claim that voice of authority for herself, in the service of her very unusual (black woman) epic hero, Sanchez works to literalize the notion of a communal voice by refusing to authorize a single speaker. Instead, she disperses the conventionally singular, privileged role of the narrator nonhierarchically among several members of a black family: men and women, parents and children, mortal and spiritual beings—all have their say. In this way, the poem's structure recalls that of dramatic works (and may have suggested itself to Sanchez because of her work as a playwright); as in a play, there is no authorial voice to frame or mediate the words of the speakers, nor is there an omniscient narrator or chorus (as in some plays) to perform those functions.[22] The poem simply begins, in the "sister's voice," with a description of the brother's reasons for moving to Harlem: "this was a migration . . . / . . . to begin / to bend a father's heart again," "to repay desertion at last" (3). The narrative, with all of its temporal shifts, must be integrated by the reader from the distinct (and occasionally inconsistent) accounts and perspectives the speakers offer. I see Sanchez's use of this strategy as an important (black) feminist act of decentering authority, insofar as it counters the masculinist assertions of authority embedded in both the epic tradition and BAM's black nationalism.

The poem itself does not proclaim the "communal values" it promotes; rather it invites the reader to identify and empathize with each member of this troubled family and, in so doing, enables the reader to practice one of those values, in the very act of reading. Sanchez's rejection of the prerogatives and additional measure of narrative control that attach to the voice of the poet-speaker in conventional epics distinguishes *Lions* from other (black aesthetic) revisions of the epic, such as Brooks's "The Anniad"—arguably a feminist work, in 1949, precisely because it does claim the epic's authoritative voice for a black woman writing about a black woman—or works like Derek Walcott's *Omeros*, which presents the speech of many different figures, but all subordinated to and contained within the voice of the narrator.

One effect of this device is to gradually move the reader from seeing the poem simply as an elegy for a beloved brother—though it is that—to understanding the poem as an epic, in which the life and death, not of an individual but of a family, are at stake.[23] Ultimately, it is that whole family, rather than just the brother, whose collective actions can fulfill the quest for survival at the heart of this epic. Moreover, the reader begins to see the unnamed members of this family as symbolic of the familial roles by which they are instead identified and comes to understand this particular (black) family as symbolic of the Black Family, the ethnic and racial collective. Sanchez foregrounds this symbolic level of the narrative by way of the second element of her formal black aesthetic innovation: her merger of the traditional Western epic genre with the contemporary narrative of slavery, a genre rooted in the African American literary tradition.

According to Arlene Keizer, the "contemporary narrative of slavery" (which includes the neo–slave narrative, but is finally a much broader category) is a genre of fiction that emerges in the mid-twentieth century and embraces narratives set during the historical period of slavery, narratives set in later periods that draw explicit connections to slavery, and narratives that incorporate scenes from both the slave past and the present (2–3). *Lions* falls into this last category, insofar as the poem's speakers include two ancestral figures who lived during the era of the Middle Passage and can speak about the experience of enslavement firsthand. For example, the female ancestor testifies, in language that hauntingly collapses the distance between the past and present: "i hear the water whistling in squads / of blue comings, the ocean has become a thief / i see our souls transported . . ." (58). By including two contemporary generations of the family and, additionally, extending the scope of the narrative back to generations probably from the eighteenth or nineteenth century, Sanchez places *Lions* in relation to not only traditional epic poetry, but also the popular prose genre of the epic saga. Alex Haley's *Roots*, a text which is also one of the most widely known contemporary narratives of slavery, is a particularly apt example of this prose epic.[24] Sanchez's black aesthetics are in operation here, in her recourse to these literary and popular genres that are likely to be more familiar and inviting to a good part of her target audience than is the traditional Western epic.

The third marker of Sanchez's black aesthetic revision of the epic genre—and one which will lead us into a close reading of the poem—is what we might call, after Henry Louis Gates's theory of African American literature, her "unmotivated Signifyin(g)" on Brooks's epic poem, "The Anniad." To call Sanchez's gesture "unmotivated Signifyin(g)" is to say that it is not motivated by a negative critique (as with other forms of "Signifyin(g)"), but rather is deeply "intent on underscoring the relation of her text to" Brooks's "antecedent" work, in an act of "homage" (*Signifying* xxvi–xxvii). With *Lions*, Sanchez becomes the first poet in the African American tradition (or the American tradition, for that matter) to follow Brooks in using rhyme royal stanzas as the building blocks of an epic poem.[25] Gesturing back to "The Anniad" fulfills a tenet of the most rigid version of the Black Aesthetic, which stresses the importance of "black art" taking its formal models from within black cultural traditions. There is some irony in this, of course, to the extent that Brooks's poem was not understood by BAM-era and BAM-influenced critics to be a particularly "black" poem, for reasons I discuss in chapter 1.[26] But, just as Sanchez's poetic homage contributes to the reinscription of "The Anniad" in the African American poetry tradition, Brooks's groundbreaking work in bringing a (feminist) black aesthetic to the epic tradition clears a space for the approaches to epic that Sanchez takes in *Lions*. We might say that in this way, fittingly, the two poems "vouch" for each other's "blackness," as well as each other's belonging in a (revised) tradition of epic poetry.

Sanchez was teaching "The Anniad" in two courses simultaneously when the first lines of *Lions* came to her—as a stanza of rhyme royal—in her sleep (Sanchez, "Form and Spirit" 32). She had been thinking, not about the epic, but about elegizing her brother, and came to appreciate how the rhyme royal stanza's formal constraints would give shape to her overwhelming grief and signal her intent to honor him ("Form and Spirit" 32; "Form and Responsibility" 197). Moreover, Brooks's highly torqued stanzas and dizzyingly compressed language provided Sanchez with a powerful example of how culturally resonant ideas, expressed in tightly wound, elliptical images, could communicate the traditional epic's ceremonial style via the kind of "elegant Black linguistic gesture" that Stephen Henderson compared to the "lightning arpeggios on difficult changes" originated by jazz musicians (*Understanding* 33).

This model was critical for Sanchez, who needed to write a poem that would proceed through indirection. Though *Lions* has been described as "difficult," "complex, . . . and challenging" (Wachman 27; Asim 27)—in tension with the Black Aesthetic principle that "black art" must be "accessible" to those members of the black working classes who have little patience for "difficult" poetry—its dense, allusive style makes it in other ways more likely to reach the readers upon whom she wants to have an impact.[27] By not staging an immediate or explicit textual confrontation with the brother's sexual orientation, the poem lures a wider range of readers into a narrative that ultimately argues for the recognition of black gays' belonging in the Black Family. Sanchez's signifying not only identifies "The Anniad" as her stylistic model for heightened compression, but also facilitates the work of encoding references to her brother's gay life.

Specifically, allusions to Brooks's poem enable Sanchez to be understated in conveying the sexual nature of the brother's exploration of his new, New York City freedom.

For instance, the "sister's voice" introduces the figure of the brother by inviting the reader to "imagine him short and black / thin mustache draping thin lips / imagine him country and exact / thin body, underfed hips" (4). These lines recall the syntax Brooks's speaker uses in introducing her poem's protagonist, Annie Allen: "Think of sweet and chocolate" (*Blacks* 99). Sanchez follows Brooks in this twist on the epic's traditional invocation of the muse that I discussed in chapter 1: both poets charge their readers, as stand-ins for the muse, with helping to bring their figures and narratives to life. Additional allusions in the "sister's voice" section create and capitalize upon a strong association between the brother and Brooks's Annie—for example, both are "underfed," physically and emotionally (*Lions* 4; *Blacks* 99). Further both are unsatisfied with their circumstances and long for something else: she, "[w]atching for the paladin" who would come to fulfill her paradoxical dreams of "what was ever and is not"; he, "watching at this corral of battleships / and bastards. watching for forget / and remember. dancing his pirouette" (*Blacks* 99; *Lions* 4). But gender makes a difference. Annie's heteronormative gender role prescribes that she wait passively for sexual fulfillment, which comes in the form of "a man of tan"—her awaited "paladin"—who consumes her virginity: "Eats the green by easy stages, / Nibbles at the root beneath / With intimidating teeth" (Brooks, *Blacks* 100). By contrast, the brother can become, like Annie's "tan man," a sexual agent, "grabbing the city by the root with clean / metallic teeth" (Sanchez, *Lions* 5). He is done with "watching": "he turned changed wore / a new waistcoat of solicitor / antidote to his southern skin / ammunition for a young paladin" (*Lions* 7). In noting that the brother can both desire and *become* the "paladin," Sanchez repeats a "signature" Brooksian word, a clear signal of her unmotivated signifying.

While the allusive language confirms that the brother is exploring his sexual agency, his gay sexuality is even less directly communicated. The reader must read between lines like these:

and the nights flickering through a slit
of narrow bars. hips. thighs.
and his thoughts labeling him misfit
as he prowled, pranced in the starlit
city ... (9)

Phrases and words like "flickering through a slit" and "prowled" con-
note sexuality, but one that could easily be heterosexual. Yet Sanchez's
inspired combination of zeugma and ellipsis in the second of these lines
nudges the reader towards an image of young men's bodies, rather than
young women's, as the objects of the brother's desire—that is, if "narrow" is read as modifying "hips" and "thighs," as well as "bars." This interpretation is supported by the immediately subsequent suggestion that
the brother feels out-of-place or abnormal—"misfit," as some gay men in
pre-Stonewall America (even in New York City) must indeed have been
made to feel—and by the verb "pranced," which is commonly associated
with a particularly flamboyant homosexuality. Sanchez pursues this strategy of indirection in the "brother's voice" section as well. The first stanza
spoken by the brother alludes to his sexuality, rather than asserting it:

> father. i despise you for abandoning me
> to aunts and mothers and ministers of tissue
> tongues, nibbling at my boyish knee.
> father. forgive me for i know not what they do (13)

Here, the brother implies that his father's absence left him to grow up in
a wholly feminine domestic environment, vulnerable to improper sexual
contact with closeted religious leaders. The passage activates a familiar
heterosexist (and sexist) narrative in which gayness emerges as the unfortunate, preventable result of forces (such as black "matriarchal" homes
and "predatory" gay preachers) that preclude black (heterosexual) men
from providing sufficient role models of (heteronormative) manhood.[28]
The currency within African American culture of this construction of
homosexuality's so-called causes may actually engender sympathy for
the brother among readers inclined to see him as a victim of domestic
circumstances. At the same time, Sanchez's subtlety avoids terminology
that might trigger audience resistance. If these and other clues Sanchez
incorporates seem like fairly transparent indications of the brother's sexual orientation to some readers, they are nonetheless *clues*, and would remain more or less opaque to others. Compared to quite straightforward
descriptions of his other activities during this period—even disreputable
behaviors (such as, "enslaved his body to cocaine" [6])—these images
remain ambiguous, or at least indirect, in their implications for his sexuality. Nowhere is he (or any other speaker) more explicit than in the passages I have quoted here in referencing his sexual orientation.

It is important to note that Sanchez balances the strategy of compression and indirection with other techniques designed to assure a broad African American audience that, despite the elaborate and possibly unfamiliar form, the poem is speaking to them. In particular, she relies upon her expertise with vernacular to infuse the language with black rhythms and cultural references. This stanza from the "brother's voice" section, describing a moment that was the catalyst for a new direction in his life, serves well as an example:

> came the summer of nineteen sixty
> harlem luxuriating in Malcolm's voice
> became Big Red beautiful became a city
> of magnificent Black Birds steel eyes moist
> as he insinuated words of sweet choice
> while politicians complained about this racist
> this alchemist. this strategist. this purist. (18)

Sanchez does not shy away from Latinate terms, but neither do they dominate the stanza. What gives her language its complexity is less about diction than it is about compression, enjambment, and unpredictable imagery. Though she requires the reader to work out where highly figurative phrases begin and end, largely without punctuation cues, Sanchez also offers the African American reader words that Stephen Henderson termed "mascons"—that is, allusive words that hold a "massive concentration of Black experiential energy," such as "harlem" and "Malcolm" ("Saturation" 108). Such words, like the subject of this stanza—the powerful impact of Malcolm X on African Americans and others—carry readers who might be put off by rhyme royal through the poem, as does Sanchez's syntactic wizardry. As this stanza concludes, for example, repetition (anaphora), rhythm, and rhyme come together in a moment that blends rhyme royal with contemporary rap.[29] Throughout the poem, Sanchez strikes this balance between forms of compression and linguistic elegance that are quite "recognizably black" and those that are less so. We must recognize that the stanzaic form she has chosen, following Brooks's model, facilitates her employment of devices that will be particularly resonant with African Americans, as well as strategies for avoiding the explicit treatment of issues that are likely to be discordant for those same readers. Importantly, Sanchez's black aesthetics principles underwrite both her choice of the traditional, European rhyme royal stanza and her inclusion of black vernacular diction and cultural references.

With an understanding of Sanchez's black aesthetics as a flexible, dialectical interchange between cultural imperatives and cultural resources and of how her black aesthetics shape the formally innovative structure of the poem, we can appreciate the deft, compelling ways she moves *Lions* toward a conclusion that underscores for her audience the importance of familial reconciliation and unity for the survival of the Black Family in the age of HIV/AIDS. That the poem assigns a significant—indeed, heroic—role to family in countering the devastating impact of HIV/AIDS on the black community is indicated from the outset, even before the table of contents identifies the speakers as members of a family, in the poem's title. The question it asks—*Does Your House Have Lions?*—is attributed in the front matter of the book to musician Rahsaan Roland Kirk. Sanchez explains that, as the statues of lions outside of important public buildings and homes symbolize that those spaces are protected, each of us needs "a reconciliation with our children, our parents, our families, and our larger families," for we are one another's lions and "need to protect each other" (Asim 27). The title, then, reflects her understanding that only when gays are not ostracized, only when people living with HIV/AIDS meet with compassion, will members of the African American community feel safe to obtain the information and protection necessary to prevent the spread of HIV. Sanchez creates a poem that argues for forgiveness and love to be extended to all members of an inclusively defined Black Family—a way, as I have argued, of expanding the black subject.

But the very notion of the African American population constituting a "family" owes its currency to the BAM-era black nationalist ideology that has long excluded black gays and lesbians from belonging. Indeed, one of the grounds for that exclusion has been the importance of the survival of the race. As Stefanie Dunning notes in her illuminating study of the connection forged in black discourse between gay sexuality and interracial desire:

> The solution to the threat of extinction, then, is to exist and continue to exist. The call for the reproduction of the nation through heterosexual and monoracial sex is one that is fundamental to black nationalist politics. Like Eurocentric nationalist discourses, black nationalism perceives threat through the trope of reproduction. Therefore, sexual acts that make impossible the birth of "black" children are denounced by black nationalism ... (46)

There is, ultimately, no small irony that *Lions* proposes to reduce the threat to African American survival posed by HIV—a virus associated with gay sex and stigmatized for precisely this reason—through recourse to a construction of a racial family that has, so to speak, no roles for gays *as such* to play. Analyzing how Sanchez navigates the terrain marked out by her project can teach us much about the elasticity—and the limits—of her black aesthetics.

One critical way in which Sanchez sets the stage for reconciliation and inclusion is by suggesting that the brother's and the father's lives, for all their superficial differences, have followed quite a similar pattern. The poem opens with the "sister's voice" describing the brother's reasons for moving from the South to Harlem:

> this was a migration unlike
> the 1900s of black men and women
> coming north for jobs. freedom. life.
> this was a migration to begin
> to bend a father's heart again
> to birth seduction from the past
> to repay desertion at last. (3)

This stanza places the brother's quest for emotional revenge against his father in a larger historical context, evoking the Great Migration that had taken place early in the twentieth century even as it distinguishes the brother's journey from those others. Though the reader will only learn this later in the poem, this journey toward freedom (which, as Sanchez has noted, recalls the northward escape route of the authors of the so-called "slave narratives") is the journey the father had made when the brother was just a child ("i was a southern Negro man," he says, "prisoner since my birth to fear" [26]). The brother describes the father as "always a guest / never a permanent resident of my veins / always a traveler to other terrains," lines which invite us to think about migration as inherited (14). The brother, following in his father's footsteps, literally and figuratively, in heading for Harlem, also finds freedom, work, and a new life (as later stanzas reveal). His migration thus parallels his father's and, insofar as this familial legacy reproduces the African American historical pattern of recurring waves of migration out of the South, underscores this family's symbolic significance.

A further, more telling parallel concerns the extent to which the brother, in defining himself as a young man in relation to the loss of (or abandonment by) his father, is once again following in the older man's footsteps. The father's adulthood was fundamentally shaped by his love for his first wife—"a high yellow woman who loved my unheard / face, who slept with me in nordic / beauty"—and his utter despair over her loss (26). Her compassionate love—and her "nordic beauty"—seem to have been sufficient compensation for the harsh constraints placed upon him by the Southern system of segregation; however, her death in childbirth left him, like his son, utterly changed and seeking both consolation and an outlet for pain and rage in the course of promiscuous sexuality. He explains that he "became romeo bound" (just as the brother becomes a "paladin" on the "prowl") and, with other routes to personal fulfillment dramatically limited or foreclosed by Jim Crow laws and customs, "placed [his] swollen / shank to the world, became man distilled / early twentieth-century black man fossilled / fulfilled by women things" (28). Both father and son, however, understand their many sexual conquests to be a poor substitute for the kind of manhood to which they aspire. The brother begins to wonder "how to erect respect in a country of men" when he must "return from" an "exile" characterized by "swollen / tongues crisscrossing [his] frail domain" (a line that echoes the earlier, similarly coded reference to "ministers of tissue / tongues" and also recalls the father's "swollen shank") (21, 13). Meanwhile, the father, after a lifetime of womanizing in the South and in Harlem, finds himself at 78 years old "sing[ing] a dirge of lost black southern manhood" (31).

The initial impetus for the brother's shift away from the lifestyle he adopted upon his arrival in New York is the example set by Malcolm X. This heroic figure, "with speeches spilling exact and compact," politicizes black people, generally, and inspires the brother, in particular, to reinvent himself (19). What precisely defines this new identity is not specified, but we know the shift is dramatic and renunciatory: "then i made my former life an accessory" (20). There are suggestions, though not conclusive ones, that the brother counts his gay sexuality among the vices of his "former life" (which included the use of profanity and drugs), which are to be excluded from his racially redefined future, following the example of Detroit Red's ascension to Malcolm X's heroic black manhood. Sanchez relies again upon the ambiguity facilitated by her rhyme royal stanzas, as here:

> then i began an awakening a flowering outside
> the living dead became a wanderer of air
> barking at the stars became a bride
> bridegroom of change timeless black with hair
> moist with kinks and morning dare (20)

I quote several lines to demonstrate how heavily enjambed they are and how many possibilities she creates for when and how to punctuate them. The images provide the reader with a clear impression of newness and revival in the brother's life, yet remain nonetheless difficult to interpret, even in the performative sense. How does one negotiate that third line break? Is the brother-speaker embracing the gender transgressivity of gay identity, claiming the ability to be both "bride" and "bridegroom," maybe even simultaneously? Or is he correcting himself after misspeaking, leaving the "bride" behind him in the third line, and claiming the masculine term instead as defining his relationship to "change"?

The poem includes other language in the "brother's voice" that makes available, but inconclusively, a reading of his character as having internalized his society's homophobia. Sanchez seems to court this ambiguity, as in the line "how to learn to love me amid all the pain?"—a question the brother asks himself immediately after wondering how to earn respect "in a country of men" from which he has been in "exile" (21). Though it remains possible to interpret his desire "to love me" as a desire to embrace his whole self, including his sexuality, in the face of societal homophobia, the former reading would tend to sustain the brother's status as a sympathetic figure for the homophobic reader. In at least one other moment, the brother's language suggests that he may have embraced heteronormativity; well into his illness at that point, he asks his sister to "tell me about this marriage crown / you wear, tell me how to claim it all without fanfare / . . . / i want a rocking chair child for my heir" (48). Today, in the midst of debates about and fluctuating access to gay marriage and gay adoption, his interest in marital commitment and reproduction may read simply like a hedge against mortality. But given the status of those issues in the 1990s, when Sanchez was writing *Lions*, and in the 1970s, when her brother was in the throes of his illness, a less progressive reading of these lines seems indicated.

The sister is also attributed lines that, like the lines above of the brother's, may have the effect of keeping the resistant reader engaged. In describing the brother's early years in New York as debauched, she makes no distinction between his drug addiction, for example, and his pursuit of gay sex, as if both were equally "profane" (6). It is the sister who suggests that the brother saw himself as a "misfit," presumably because of his sexuality, and who associates his "prowl[ing]" and "pranc[ing]" with "unreconciled rites" (9). To the extent that Sanchez is understood to be (the model for) the sister in the poem, she portrays herself as homophobic, a move that has the benefit of giving homophobic readers a character with whom to identify early in the poem—and, later, with whom to move towards an acceptance and embrace of the HIV-positive brother.

Significantly, however, while certain lines in the sister's and brother's voices raise the possibility that his gay sexuality might be an obstacle to his "return" to his family's embrace, neither the father nor the ancestors—and, ultimately, not even the sister—condition their welcome, their love for him, or their caring for him in his illness upon a renunciation of his sexual orientation. The father does not once upbraid his son for being gay. To the contrary, it is the "father's voice" section of the poem that reveals the parallels between his life and his son's life, noted above, and that invites the reader to see both men as in need of reconciliation—and facing the same challenge to achieving it: the need to repair the damage to familial relationships caused by years of sexual promiscuity. Intentionally or not, both men deeply disrupt their families with their efforts to compensate for anger and pain by having sex indiscriminately, and with the consequences of that behavior. The father's multiple, loveless marriages and infidelities ("[i] wrapped my heart in gauze") end up forcing him to leave one child behind in order to care for another, and the brother, as a result, grows up surrounded by his mother's "tears" and righteous anger at the "husband who left [her] shipwrecked with child" (14, 16). The brother, in his resentment, uses "the bars. the glitter. the light" to "discharg[e] pain from his bygone anguish," which leads to his becoming HIV-positive and brings him and his sister to blows, as he tries to turn her against their father and she defends him, as a step toward forging a peace between the two men (8). Sanchez's decision to focus part of the "father's voice" section on his own young adulthood proves crucial in providing a context in which the reader can rethink the issue of the brother's sexuality as a problem of wantonness, rather than orientation. The sympathy the reader might extend to the father for using promiscuous sex as a balm to soothe the wound he incurred upon his first wife's death might also be extended to the brother, the poem suggests. Thus, when the brother asks for forgiveness ("O forgive me mother / O forgive me father / O forgive me sister"), it need not be for a different reason than the one his father has for "begging pardon" (62, 31).

The "ancestors' voices," which appear for the first time in the final section of the poem, underscore this reading of the section in the "father's voice." The male and female ancestors both metaphorically, but clearly, criticize the brother for having indiscriminate sex, but in terms that offer no indication that his sexual orientation is at issue. The male ancestor asks the brother, "did you take your weapon, huh? / rattle it on any mattress, hey? / til you became powerless?," while on the facing page, the female ancestor follows this same line of questioning: "did you take your coastal / blood to any playground ayyyyyy? / to every resident clown?" (42, 43). They accuse him of being too free with his body, but make no reference to the matter of the gender of his sexual partners. It is in this section where the brilliance of Sanchez's formal innovations—particularly her employment of a polyvocal structure and merging of the epic genre with the contemporary narrative of slavery—are most in evidence, in relation to the role of the ancestors in the poem. To begin with, I would recall my argument that the polyvocal structure of *Lions* leaves the reader without a voice of ultimate textual authority to legitimate or delegitimize any of the perspectives articulated in the text. As a consequence, the poem can, on one hand, offer language in the "brother's voice" that *could* be interpreted as heterosexist—thus giving expression through him to ideology that might make her resistant audience at once more sympathetic to the brother as a figure and more comfortable with the poem itself. On the other hand, the poem refuses to place heterosexist language in the mouths of the ancestral figures. Because of the traditional cultural significance of the ancestors, their silence on the issue of sexual orientation may in fact speak louder than suggestions of homophobic or heteronormative views embedded in the brother's (and sister's) stanzas.

That is, the powerful role the ancestors play in African American culture makes their intervention—what they say, as well as what they do not say—critical to the way black readers understand the poem.[30] West African religious systems, prior to colonial contact, were ancestor-based, rather than deity-based. Since the majority of the Africans who were brought in slavery to (now) U.S. territory came from West Africa, the impulse among African Americans to honor and remember ancestors may well be a surviving trace of West African cultures, nurtured in part by the interest in and study of African cultures that blossomed during the BAM. In any case, the word *ancestors* is a "mascon" (in Henderson's terms), which is to say a clear invitation to many African American readers to consider *Lions* a book for and about them, and Sanchez acknowledges that she was counting on her inclusion of the ancestors "to [help] make her book accessible and relevant to readers" (Asim 27). To the extent that some readers might still be put off by the formality and density of Sanchez's rhyme royal stanza, for example, the "ancestors' voices" offer the example of their own fearless engagement with the form. Indeed, they bring their own language to the stanza—which is to say that Sanchez may be the first poet to write lines of rhyme royal in Wolof, a West African language.

The last stanza in the "father's voice" section foreshadows both the entrance of the "ancestors' voices" and the brother's approaching transition by beginning with three full lines in Wolof. Although it might not occur immediately to the reader who does not speak Wolof, one soon realizes that despite the difference in how these words look on the page (they appear in italics, which heightens their "foreignness," so to speak), the lines in Wolof nonetheless follow the traditional *ababbcc* rhyme scheme.

But when the ancestors themselves speak, they begin immediately to make themselves even more at home in the rhyme royal stanza. They introduce ritualistic chanting, relying upon identical rhymes made upon the sounds used for emphasis, as in this stanza in the "ancestor's voice (male)":

do you remember me,	huh?
when our teeth were iron,	huh?
did you drum about me,	hey?
and not babylon,	hey?
did you take your weapon,	huh?
rattle it on any mattress,	hey?
til you became powerless?	hey, huh, heyyyyyyyy? (42)

Such chanting is a trademark of Sanchez's poetry, and when she reads this stanza aloud, she gives it the kind of percussive emphasis she is famous for—and with which the rhyme royal stanza is not typically associated, to put it mildly. Here, even as these lines start to push at the boundaries of the stanzas—in terms of the internal spacing and the pattern of the chanted words—the ragged, internal line endings (if such a paradox can be admitted) continue to acknowledge the traditional pattern. But increasingly, the ancestral energy, we might say, tends to overwhelm the rhyme royal form.

In the last few stanzas, in addition to incorporating Wolof phrases consistently, the ancestors begin to disregard the seven-line structure of the form in favor of longer or shorter stanzas that correspond to the requirements of their rituals. An important example of this is when the female and male ancestors engage in call and response, a form of interaction that is known to anyone familiar with African American culture, whether music, religion, or literature. The female ancestor calls, in Wolof, *"jamma ga fanan"* ("good morning") and the male ancestor responds, in English, with a rhetorical question about the brother's apparently indeterminate phenotype, a series that requires—and receives—an eight-line stanza. In the book's final stanza, when the ancestors' voices are joined by the brother's, the rhyme royal stanza is ruptured altogether. The reader is instructed that the stanza is "TO BE SUNG," and what follows are the exchanges signifying the brother's arrival and the ancestors' welcome, in the form of eleven basically unrhymed lines in three columns, the left identifying the speakers, the center offering phrases in Wolof, and the right providing English translations. On one level, I see this progression as evidence that Sanchez's black aesthetics call for engagement with traditional European forms, but on traditional African (American) terms. On another level, I suggest we might read the ancestors' explosion of the rhyme royal stanza as a formal model for breaking out of conventional modes, whether they be poetic conventions or social conventions, such as those grounded in heterosexism.

For all of these reasons, the fact that the ancestors are not concerned with the gender of the brother's sexual partners, but with the number of them, puts significant weight behind the poem's vision of an inclusive Black Family—quietly, but importantly, and perhaps more persuasively to homophobic readers than the explicitly anti-heterosexist invitations ("Come celebrate the poor / the women / the gays / the lesbians") Sanchez makes in other recent poems (*Shake* 155). *Lions* leaves the reader little doubt that had the ancestors intended to condemn the brother's sexual orientation, they would have—because they are unambivalent and insistent in their critique of the behavior to which they object: namely, failing to honor and remember one's ancestors. In the stanza quoted in full just above, we see the male ancestor interrogating the brother on how he has spent his time: remembering those who died in the Middle Passage or dissipating his energy in indiscriminate sex (42). Similarly, the female ancestor asks whether he dreamed about her or the "betrayal" represented by taking his "coastal / blood to any playground . . . / to every resident clown" (43). They connect his earlier behavior to his failure to pay the proper respect to his ancestors, but in terms that oppose his individualist, escapist pursuits to the unifying and empowering work of remembering his ancestors' suffering. The ancestors' voices communicate that it is the responsibility of the living to "state our history" and memorialize the dead, thus keeping the ancestors (and, more broadly, the past) alive in the contemporary moment (45).

In this, Sanchez's poem joins the work of myriad African American artists and intellectuals in insisting upon the importance of remembering the history of capture, the Middle Passage, enslavement, and the long, ongoing quest for a substantive freedom. Sara Clarke Kaplan has argued that this "conjoined refusal and inability of racialized subjects to simply let go of past [collective] griefs" can be understood as "*diasporic melancholia*": a "militant refusal" "to declare the past resolved" that "can . . . produce meaning out of lost histories and histories of loss" (514; emphasis in original). This act of remembering is not simply a gesture toward the past, but an essential element of future survival. The role of the ancestors, we learn, is to guide the dying through their transition from this life to the next. But if the living do not remember the ancestors during their lives, the ancestors will not remember us during our deaths. Thus, the female ancestor's questions—"have you prepared a place of honor for me? / have you recalled us from death?"—indicate the critical importance of a kind of spiritual reconciliation for the brother, who is now near the end of his life, though he does not yet know it (45).

In the late 1970s, his symptoms and illnesses mystified the medical community: "the doctor says my temperature is like a trickster" (50). The attention Sanchez gives to the brother's physical condition and the way his sister and father helped him through his physical crises remind us of the importance of his reconciliation with his living family, as well. Some of Sanchez's most moving innovations upon the rhyme royal stanza are those that manipulate the form to reveal the effects of the brother's AIDS-related illnesses upon his body. One such stanza turns the rhyme scheme into onomatopoeia: "sister tell me about this cough i cough / all of my skin cradled in this cough / my body ancient as this white cough, i cough / all day and night" (49). Another dissolves the rhyme scheme into repetition, thus depicting an inescapable pain so exquisite that it hurts to be touched, even by helping hands:

> hold me with air
> breathe me with air
> sponge me with air
> whisper me with air
> comb me with air
> brush me with air
> rinse me with air. (65)

These stanzas highlight the vulnerability of the body and the need experienced by those dealing with the later stages of AIDS-related illness for loved ones to provide physical and emotional care.

In Sanchez's masterful work, the issue of the brother's reconciliation with his family is, first, juxtaposed against and, finally, merged with the issue of reconciliation between present-day African Americans and their ancestors. Casting the poem not simply as an elegy, but also as a contemporary narrative of slavery, enables Sanchez to foreground the parallel between HIV/AIDS and the transatlantic slave trade, in terms of the potential of the former to devastate the African American community. The ancestors both explicitly draw a comparison between the two threats. The male ancestor, after stressing to the brother (and, by extension, Sanchez's African American readers) that "it is necessary to remember the sea / holding your ancestors in a nightmare / of waves," asks: "is there no anguish no balm of Gilead for the dead? / is there no amulet for this coming dread?" (51). By the same token, the female ancestor instructs him to "drink this tea / (bitter-heyyyyyy?) as bitter / as my bones hugging the sea" (53). Sanchez thus recharacterizes the AIDS epidemic as "a black thing"—not exclusively, of course, but in the sense of the significance of its threat to the Black Family. In so doing, she rejects the assumption held by a sizeable (but now decreasing) segment of her African American audience that HIV/AIDS is an issue that black people can ignore. That ancestral figures give voice to this view conveys it powerfully to her readers, by integrating a concern with HIV/AIDS awareness and prevention with African (American) cultural values and the collective inherited wisdom that the ancestors represent.

If Sanchez is successful in making the case for removing the taboo around HIV/AIDS within the African American community, framing it as a matter of the community's survival, is her attempt to challenge the community's homophobia equally realized? A stanza from the final section in the voice of the sister concludes with the beautiful (and unrhymed) couplet: "O i will purchase my brother's whisper. / O i will reward my brother's tongue" (44). Does the final line, ending with the image of the tongue (which signified gay sexuality in earlier passages of the poem), suggest the sister's intent to praise her brother's sexuality? Or, given the proximity of "tongue" to "whisper," here, is it instead the brother's speech—particularly his talk of renunciation of his past, his interest in marriage and fatherhood, his requests for forgiveness—that the sister finds worthy of "reward" (20, 48, 62)? In the closing stanza, the ancestors call the brother, "*kai fi African* come here African," indicating their readiness to accept him among them, and he responds, "*mangi nyo* i am coming" (70). But does answering to this name require him to reject others by which he might be called?

This kind of ambiguity keeps *Lions* from being as visionary a poem as one might hope. But that same ambiguity, I argue, serves an important purpose that other, more direct challenges to homophobia might not.[31] Sanchez's strategy of restraint generated stunning, black aesthetic innovations that make the poem accessible and inviting to readers of varying tastes, varying familiarity with the literary tradition, and varying levels of comfort with the subjects of gay sexuality and AIDS. Admittedly, this strategy, by accommodating her readers' prejudices to some degree, also risks reinforcing them. But there is something to be said for the canniness of her approach: using polyvocality (expanding the epic subject), she gives voice to popular heteronormative notions in order to move readers away from them. Acknowledging—indeed, representing— alternative perspectives, she makes a compelling case for expanding the black subject to include people who do not fit the heteronormative box within which so many have sought refuge from the storm of American racism.[32] Ultimately, I am persuaded that the ambiguities Sanchez mobilizes in *Does Your House Have Lions?* enact and enable a dialogue that is vastly more productive than the silence it interrupts.

In the next chapter, we will see Harryette Mullen's poem, *Muse & Drudge*, similarly negotiating the constraints of "blackness," in order to reach multiple audiences with seemingly incompatible expectations for "black poetry." Where Sanchez's expansion of the subject of the epic seeks to elasticize the boundaries of "blackness" so as to create a more inclusive whole, Mullen's poem explodes what we think we know about both the epic genre and the definition of "blackness." The effect of her work is not to render these categories meaningless, but to make them more, if differently, meaningful.

THREE

COMPLICATING THE SUBJECT
Harryette Mullen's *Muse & Drudge* as African American Blues Epic

Sapphire's lyre styles
plucked eyebrows
bow lips and legs
whose lives are lonely too[1]

WITH THESE LINES, Harryette Mullen opens her fourth book of poetry, *Muse & Drudge*, a long poem comprised entirely of small, irregular quatrains, printed four to a page for a total of 320 stanzas over 80 pages. The postmodernist techniques upon which this poem turns—she eschews narrative and linearity and embraces collage, the fragment, and a variety of meaningful and nonsensical types of wordplay—might seem to distinguish it categorically from the tales of heroism that Gwendolyn Brooks and Sonia Sanchez offer in their long poems. The innovations of "The Anniad" and *Does Your House Have Lions?* require us to accommodate new kinds of heroes and quests, previously unrecognizable as such because of the race, gender, class, and sexual presumptions that have attended the genre of the epic as it developed within the Anglo-American literary tradition. But however much these two works might stretch the imaginations of their readers, their gestures toward the epic genre are sufficiently engaged with its conventions to be clearly legible, once we have determined to look for them. *Muse & Drudge* presents a more difficult case—but one no less important to make. The least obviously epic of the three works, *Muse & Drudge* does the most to reshape the genre. Drawing its language, themes, and artistic strategies from among the riches of African American culture, Mullen crafts what I will call an African American blues epic—a genre that has the same broad scope and wide-reaching concerns as the tradition of epic poetry that has come down to American literature from Homer, but composes that expansiveness out of the "kinky" lyric quatrains of the blues tradition.[2] Mullen's poem thus has some important, if ostensibly improbable, correspondences with Brooks's and Sanchez's works. By reading Mullen's poem in light of the only other two long poems in stanzaic form published by African American women (a different approach to *Muse & Drudge* than those taken to date), we see more fully its relationships to and significance for both the epic and the tradition of African American (women's) poetry.[3] The broader understanding of the poem and of Mullen's aesthetics that emerges from this reading complicates and complements the currently predominant construction of *Muse & Drudge* as a "hybrid" or "mongrel" poem.

LIKE "THE ANNIAD" and *Does Your House Have Lions?*, Mullen's poem can be fruitfully understood as the proffered solution to an aesthetic problem concerning audience. In most of her interviews on the book, Mullen explains that *Muse & Drudge* was specifically intended to address a shift in the audience for her work that troubled her. Her first book, *Tree Tall Woman* (1981), had been a collection of lyric poems largely in a southern, black vernacular voice, describing the speaker's family and community, their lives, her relationships with them, and the way this (black) cultural context shaped her sense of self. Mullen has credited the Black Arts Movement's racially politicized aesthetics with empowering her to treat her family and black culture more generally as poetic subjects (Mullen, "Interview" para. 2–3). Her second and third books—*Trimmings* (1991) and *S*PeRM**K*T* (1992)—recorded her simultaneously admiring and critical response to Gertrude Stein's prose poem *Tender Buttons*, even as they parsed the gender politics underlying women's fashion and the marketing of food and groceries. She cites the influences of Stein and Language poetry upon her work in these two books; for example, she identifies Stein's syntactical "elegance" and the Language poets' attention to the "new" or "paratactic sentence" as elements she works with to achieve the playful ambiguity that facilitates her cross-cultural, motivated, and unmotivated signifyin(g) upon her poetic predecessor's work (Mullen, "Interview," *Postmodern* para. 16).[4]

Muse & Drudge emerged out of the discomfort Mullen experienced when she realized that the types of readers drawn to the latter books were apparently not the same as those who had supported her debut collection:

> [W]hen I went around reading from [*Tree Tall Woman*] there were a lot of black people in my audience. There would be white people and brown people and maybe other people of color as well. Suddenly, when I went around to do readings of *Trimmings* and "Spermkit," I would be the one black person in the room. . . . I mean I'd find myself in a room that typically had no other people of color in it—which, you know, I could do,

and . . . it was interesting. But that's not necessarily what I wanted, and I thought, "How am I going to get all these folks to sit down together in the same room?" *Muse and Drudge* was my attempt to create that audience. I wanted the different audiences for my various works to come together. (Mullen, "Conversation" n.p.)[5]

Rejecting the commonly accepted construction of "black" and "innovative" as mutually exclusive ways of characterizing poetry, Mullen made it her goal to create a work that would unmistakably "signal" to potential readers that *Muse & Drudge* is "a black book," even as she pursued her interests in the materiality, ambiguity, and disjunctive quality of language and the destabilization of how "black" signifies.[6] In addition to the visual cues she incorporated in the design of the cover, Mullen indicates to black readers of *Muse & Drudge* that "this [book] is yours" by loading the poem with enough black vernacular language and black cultural references that nearly every quatrain signifies (on) some aspect of African American experience ("An Interview" 417). The blues—both the lyrics and the culture that centers around the musical form—are, in particular, the source of significant amounts of linguistic and thematic material for the poem. But, the blues are also, to a much larger degree than the criticism suggests, the source of many of the poem's most innovative formal and structural elements.

As I will discuss in greater detail later, scholarship on *Muse & Drudge* typically recognizes the blues as having some impact on the shape the poem takes. But consistently, and often in ways that are linked to constructions of the poem as a culturally "hybrid" work, the influence of the blues (and black culture, generally) is most associated with the poem's content, while its formal innovation is attributed largely to the same avant-garde poetic influences that engaged Mullen so deeply in *Trimmings* and *S*PeRM**K*T*.[7] Indisputably, the aesthetics Mullen absorbed from Stein's work, Ron Silliman's discussion of the "new sentence," and other statements and practices of avant-garde poetics continued to inform her writing as she worked on the poem that became *Muse & Drudge*. But critics tend to leverage this observation to celebrate *Muse & Drudge* as an example of how the concerns and techniques associated with poetic avant-gardes (typically constructed as "white" in their membership and literary influences) can be brought to bear upon black cultural material. To the extent that black culture is relegated to a secondary, underacknowledged role in the conceptual genius and the formal innovations of the poem, however, these analyses—even as they celebrate the "mixing" of black and white cultures—may unintentionally reinforce certain white/black binaries that privilege "whiteness" as the source of order, theory, and concept and relegate "blackness" to the realm of raw product, the "stuff" which can be abstracted into an intellectually grounded art via the right experimental approaches.[8] When Mullen explains that she wrote *Muse & Drudge* to counter the problematic "idea that you can be black *or* innovative," it was not simply to replace the "*or*" with an "*and*," leaving the fundamental dichotomy intact. *Muse & Drudge* is a poetic exploration of the proposition that Farah Griffin makes in a public conversation with Mullen, with which Mullen expresses her agreement: "to be black *is* to be innovative" ("Conversation").[9]

The blues is critical to Mullen's challenge to the opposition of "blackness" to "innovation" in poetics, and not only in terms of the structures it suggests. As an endlessly rich source of language and of emotionally charged scenarios of (inter)personal conflict, the blues underwrites Mullen's ability in *Muse & Drudge* to interrogate the dichotomization of the "liberatory" and "speculative" modes of "oppositional poetics," to borrow Erica Hunt's terminology ("Notes" 199, 203–04). Briefly, in Hunt's account, "liberatory" poetics, such as those espoused by Black Arts Movement poets, "have as their explicit goal the use of language as a vehicle for the consciousness and liberation of oppressed communities," seeking to harness the undeniable persuasive force of words and rhetorical structures. By contrast, "speculative" poetics, such as those embraced by the Language poets, "engage language as a social artifact, as art material, as powerfully transformative," and, relatedly, as a set of seemingly neutral rules (of syntax, punctuation, plot, and the like) that in fact replicate social hierarchies and produce obedient subjects for hegemonic groups (203).

Influenced by the politically informed aesthetics of both the BAM and the Language poets, Mullen explores the extent to which their competing priorities can be rendered compatible within a single work, taking as the ground for her experiment the contested territory of the first-person speaker of lyric poetry—or, "the lyric *I*." More specifically, Mullen raises the stakes of her venture into black-poetry-*as*-innovative poetry by working the poem's black cultural material into an investigation of the particular question of black women's identity. In a late-twentieth-century (American) context in which subjectivity, so long a privileged province denied to both people of color and (white) women, is suddenly deemed by the theories underwriting "speculative" poetics to be suspect, illusory, and/or fragmented at best, Mullen's decision to write a poem that turns on the experiences and subjectivity of black women constitutes a real challenge to the aesthetics of the audience for the books that immediately preceded *Muse & Drudge*. At the same time, her approach to black women's subjectivity, which is one of questioning and complicating rather than reifying it, challenges assumptions about the essential nature of black womanhood that likely held currency with the audience for her first book, *Tree Tall Woman*. As a cultural site associated for black women (as performers, songwriters, and subjects of blues lyrics) with both authority and fluid identity, the blues offers the perfect foundation for this project.[10]

IF THE PROBLEM that *Muse & Drudge* addresses is one of audience, the means of addressing that problem, the poem proposes, is via voice—or, to be more precise, voices. This should not surprise us, after having studied the issues of production and reception concerning "The Anniad" and *Does Your House Have Lions?* Mullen's experience of a racially marked split between the audiences of her first books is in many ways analogous to the dilemma Brooks faced in pitching her poem so that it would be properly heard by different audiences. As we saw in chapter 1, Brooks's challenge was to reveal the survival of her young, black, female protagonist, under deeply oppressive yet common and normalized circumstances, as heroic, and to reveal that heroism to both the (predominantly white) literary establishment and the (overwhelmingly black) community from and about which she wrote. Sanchez confronted a similar divide in perceptions of racial meaning, but in her case the division was intraracial. Competing understandings of "blackness" held among African Americans shaped the possibilities for her book, which seeks a sympathetic hearing on the subject of HIV/AIDS–related death from readers who define the Black Family, in its authentic state, as excluding gays. Both Brooks and Sanchez deal with their issues of audience via strategies that capitalize, though in different ways, on polyvocality. Mullen, too, takes recourse to polyvocality in her poem, seeking to have it speak to the sometimes conflicting criteria of value held by a white, literary community that is different from Brooks's (if similarly exacting) *and* by a black readership that, like Sanchez's, holds more or less rigid notions of an "authentic" or essentialized "blackness." Mullen, too, achieves this multiplicity of voices at the intersection of lyric and epic modes, building her long poem of formally consistent (yet "kinky") stanzas—in her case, not rhyme royal, but quatrains.[11]

In other words, Mullen's project can be productively understood as an instance of black aesthetics. Unsatisfied with the unspoken but literally visible racial coding of her innovative poetry as "white," Mullen creates

Muse & Drudge as an aesthetic response to the imposition of an untenable, racialized circumscription of the creative possibilities of African American poets, herself included. Her work is like the work of BAM poets, in this sense, even as she uses the poem to interrogate the BAM-inspired tenet—itself a circumscription—that would insist upon the existence of a unified and "essential" black (female) identity. This might seem ironic, if it were not that Mullen has been unambiguous about acknowledging her debt to the Movement, as well as her distance from it. For example, discussing her first book in an interview with Cynthia Hogue, Mullen explains:

> Part of what people were doing with the Black Arts movement was, in a sense, to construct a positive image of black culture, because blackness had signified negation, lack, deprivation, absence of culture. . . . I wanted to write within the space that had been created [by the BAM project] without necessarily repeating exactly what those folks had done. (para. 3)

But where *Tree Tall Woman* embraced "a kind of restricted idea of what it meant to write . . . with a black voice" (para. 3)—an idea inherited from the BAM emphasis on the black vernacular as "authentic" black speech— *Muse & Drudge* pushes black vernacular to such extremes that it ceases to function as the authentication of a coherent, singular black identity. Rather than "a black voice," *Muse & Drudge* presents a parade, a crowd, a chorus of black (women's) voices. Hinging her poem thematically and formally on the blues enables Mullen to explore the efficacy of lyric, first-person assertion and epic, communal sensibility, simultaneously, in a critique of representations of black women.

The poem's ability to function as both individual and collective expression emerges from the relationship of the blues to African American history. Angela Davis follows Amiri Baraka in noting that, for a variety of reasons, emancipation opened the door for individual expression to take a more central role in African American music. In his landmark study, *Blues People: Negro Music in White America*, Baraka (then LeRoi Jones) points to the emotional limitations upon creativity attendant to having one's existence and identity circumscribed by the term "slave" (60). For the vast majority of African Americans, with emancipation came the possibility of "a normal human existence," including, importantly, leisure time, which meant that there was room for songs not created in service of labor (as were the "shouts" and work songs) and not focused on the next life (as were the spirituals), but articulating the choices one was making for one's life here and now—specifically, the blues (61). Davis concurs, describing the blues as "aesthetic evidence of new psychosocial realities within the black population" (5). She calls attention to the fact that, as a music of leisure time, the blues could be performed while the individual singer accompanied himself or herself on an instrument like the banjo or guitar (5). Yet, even as the blues offered a space for expression of individual sorrows and dilemmas, the common themes that developed among blues singers across the culture evidenced the commonalities of African Americans' experiences at that moment in history.[12] And, ultimately, as an art form that emerged from and remains deeply associated with "the social and psychic afflictions and aspirations of African Americans," the blues functioned culturally as a site where the problems facing the individual could be "restructured as problems shared by the community" collectively (Angela Davis 33).

In other words, one of the things that made the blues such a versatile and transportable art was the fact that the *I* speaking in a stanza of blues lyrics would often articulate "intensely personal" (and typically private) woes, but because those woes were widespread among African Americans and were figured in broad, metaphorical terms in the lyrics, nearly *anyone* in the community could speak that *I*.[13] Take these lyrics from a blues written and performed by Gertrude "Ma" Rainey: "I'm running away tomorrow, they don't mean me no good" (Angela Davis 239). The new mobility African Americans had gained (though not entirely unfettered, as Rainey's lyrics suggest) meant that blues lyrics were spread by travelers from locale to locale, and the best verses were taken up by new singers (Jones, *Blues* 64). The blues could thus be personal without being literally autobiographical and could be collective in both theme and compositional process.[14] This made the blues an ideal model for Mullen's long poem.

Mullen has shared that her use of the first-person pronoun in *Muse & Drudge* is almost always in the context of a line she is quoting or "recycling from tradition," be it the blues tradition, the literary tradition, or the black vernacular tradition of common idioms and overheard lines. As she puts it: "The 'I' in the poem is almost always someone other than myself, and often it's any anonymous 'I,' a generic 'I,' a traditional 'I,' the 'I' of the blues, that person who in reference to any individual experience also speaks for the tradition, speaks for the community" ("Solo" 653). While not insisting on the absolute absence of autobiographical material in the poem, Mullen stresses that those moments are nonetheless rendered "abstract" and "generic," so that she can keep the personal reference within "a blues conception of the individual, a subject that speaks but not simply as oneself" ("Solo" 665). But at the same time, all of the "generic" moments are potentially her own, because, as she says, the poem is "about black women primarily, and I am a black woman" ("An Interview" 408). In *Muse & Drudge*, she emphasizes, "[t]he individual and collective merge, as in the blues" ("An Interview" 408).

An example might help to ground this discussion, and also begin to illustrate some of the techniques Mullen folds into her quatrains. We might consider, for example, the second stanza on page 53. If that sounds like an unlikely place to commence a close reading, I should pause here to explain why we can jump in almost anywhere to examine the operation of this poem's specific language. This characteristic of the poem is actually further evidence of how much Mullen draws upon the model of the blues for many of the most innovative moves *Muse & Drudge* makes. She has explicitly noted that her decision to create quatrains that "can be free standing and shuffled in and out of the work" derived from the "compositional strategies of the blues" ("Solo" 654). "Blues verses," she continues, "are actually shuffled and rearranged by the performer, so new blues can be composed on the spot essentially by using different material in different orders" (654). Accordingly, when Mullen reads from *Muse & Drudge* in person, she might begin on any page of the book and thereafter skip ahead or backward at whim, in each case reading the four quatrains on the page she has selected. Treating the page as the unit for purposes of her readings seems to be a more or less arbitrary decision, however, in terms of how units of meaning might be understood. Sometimes a whole page, or even two pages, might be made of lines that have a common theme or thread (for instance, page 53 is filled with references to birds), but because "change is one of the rules" of *Muse & Drudge* ("Solo" 662), more often her splicing of lines and allusions builds to a single quatrain and then begins again.[15]

Thus, we may begin on page 53 to look at ways the "individual and collective merge" in a representative stanza of this blues epic:

> don't eat no crow, don't you know
> ain't studying about taking low
> if I do not care for chitterlings
> 'tain't nobody's pidgin

We see immediately that the quatrain functions in one sense as a collection of language pulled from or placed within the black vernacular.

"Eating crow" is a well-known figure of speech for humbly acknowledging a grievous error. Mullen assigns it to a presumably African American speaker, as signaled by her deployment of the characteristic double negative of the black vernacular. This move, first, increases the quatrain's assonance and rhyme, adding "no" to "don't," "know," and "low." It also contributes to our initial sense of the punning this quatrain will do. By adding to the tone of defiance the hint of a boast, echoing faintly the way a hip-hop head's freestyle lines might emphasize her claim that she is never (or never forced to admit being) wrong by underlining it with rhyme—"don't eat no crow, don't you know"—Mullen reminds us that "crow" is a verb (meaning to brag or boast), as well. The phrase "ain't studying about" is a familiar one to users of the black vernacular, signifying a refusal to pay attention to, accept, or even acknowledge the existence of something or someone. Here, the something is "taking low"—a phrase that rings no specific bell for me, but suggests, in context, the speaker's rejection of anything she considers beneath her, a refusal to accept some low status or low-budget alternative to what she deserves.

That interpretation is supported by the next line, which foregrounds the issue of class status within the African American community. Suddenly, the diction shifts from black vernacular to a hyper-"proper" locution associated culturally with middle-class aspirations and, in a negative sense, assimilationism. Mullen, whose mother was a teacher and basically a Northerner, was greeted with suspicion and accusations of inauthentic blackness by her classmates when she began school in Ft. Worth, Texas, because she was "talking proper"—a stinging condemnation, all the more bewildering (and thus alienating) for its paradoxical phrasing.[16] The negative response to such carefully correct speech—note that the speaker avoids even the grammatically acceptable contraction "don't"— arises from the way black "strivers" have used language and other class markers to distance themselves from the "masses," the majority of African Americans who lacked access to or interest in bourgeois middle-class education, income, and lifestyles. Such linguistic performances (which term should not suggest relative "inauthenticity") traditionally went hand in hand with the rejection of other actual or stereotypical markers of blackness-*as*-poverty, such as eating "chitterlings" (the small intestines of a pig, when prepared as food). This dish became part of African American cuisine during slavery, because black people were only allowed— and, later, could only afford—the unwanted parts of the animals slaughtered to feed the white people. As such, it represented for some upwardly mobile African Americans the kind of link to slavery and poverty that they were trying to leave behind.

So is the "I" in this line a strictly individual speaker, perhaps even a self-referential moment for Mullen? We need to read through to the stanza's conclusion to answer this question. In the last line of the quatrain—"'tain't nobody's pidgin"—Mullen is alluding to the popular blues song (sung by Bessie Smith, among others) "'Tain't Nobody's Business If I Do." Mullen's "quotations" are rarely verbatim; they are typically "fragmented" and "altered," and this instance is no exception (Mullen, "An Interview" 405–06). We now see that the "if I do" of line 3 doubles as the completion of the song's title and refrain (a second reason for her to have avoided the contraction "don't"). The final line brings the issue of the relation between class and language to a head. Offering "pidgin" as a playful homophonic substitution for "business," the stanza concludes with a humorous truism: for a speaker to assert in "proper" (that is, standard American) English that "I do not care for chitterlings" is, by definition, not a use of "pidgin" English. Another layer of humor emerges, as we appreciate the near rhyme formed between "chitterlings" (pronounced "chitlins") and "pidgin," insofar as it pokes fun once again at the "strivers" who, in their efforts to be hyper-"proper" English speakers, have been known to *mispronounce* the word as it looks. (This would be akin to mispronouncing "victuals," out of a wrongheaded, classist certainty that the Beverly Hillbillies' pronunciation—"vittles"—could not be correct.) The attempt to disavow the black vernacular here would not only lead to a mistake in pronunciation, but also spoil this quatrain's rhyme scheme (*aabb*). Finally, Mullen brings a third play to the line, through the pun of "pidgin" on "pigeon"—a bird that recalls the "crow" in line 1 and leaves us, in the wake of the question of eating chitterlings, with a humorously literal reading of the claim "don't eat no crow" to go with the metaphorical one we began with.

To return now to the question of the "I" of this quatrain (explicit in line 3 and implied in lines 1 and 2), I would argue that we are not invited to imagine Mullen or any identifiable individual speaker uttering the lines of this stanza as straightforward expression. My argument here reminds us that the lyric *I* does not emerge solely in putatively autobiographical poetry; persona poems and dramatic monologues, such as Robert Browning's famous "My Last Duchess" or contemporary poet Patricia Smith's powerful "Skinhead," illustrate my point. The lyric *I* (as opposed to the word "I") appears in "poems [that] characteristically project literal scenes of utterance, in the detailed context of which (context mostly implied, and having to be carefully excavated) the words uttered acquire their force" (Attridge and Staten 9). It would be hard to imagine a scenario in which these statements, taken together, could be made as actual assertions. For their logic as literal utterances, they remain tied to the distinct contexts from which the lines are metaphorically lifted for Mullen's sampling purposes. In terms of the unit of the quatrain, by contrast, the lines exist only to do the complex work outlined above.

That is, this quatrain's logical context is in this poem, where its lines must be seen and heard to be fully appreciated. Together, they function as a deeply layered cultural critique, one that performs the versatility, sophistication, and richness of black vernacular speech, rather than making an argument for it. And even as the quatrain sends up a segment of the African American population for its willingness to jettison culture to attain class mobility, it refuses to settle into an easy romanticization of the black vernacular. The performance of code switching—in this stanza and in the poem as a whole—is implicitly defended by the speaker, who suggests that it "ain't nobody's business if [she] do." Moreover, it prevents the reader from forgetting that the work is being created by a poet who has both vernacular and "standard" English fully at her command. The literary use of this code-switching technique connects Mullen quite clearly to one of the writers she has often noted as an influence: Zora Neale Hurston. Hurston's method of blending and shifting between the black vernacular she spoke in her childhood home and the standard English that took her through a degree at Barnard in her novel *Their Eyes Were Watching God* fully deserves the chapter it is given in Henry Louis Gates Jr.'s scholarship and its extensive attention in black feminist criticism generally. Mullen, much like Alice Walker, writes in the lineage of Hurston's "speakerly text" (Gates, *Signifying* xxv). I argue that a close reading of the quatrain supports the reading Mullen has suggested of her poem, generally: that the "I" we encounter is a blues singer's "I"; a generic (rather than personal or autobiographical) "I"; a lyric *I*, but one that gets at subjectivity as much through the communal, cultural sensibility of the blues as through an articulation of an individual's experience; an *I* that means potentially any African American woman and, collectively (but not uniformly), all of us.[17]

Thus, working off of a blues model facilitates Mullen's ability to explore the possibilities of the lyric *I* without projecting the kind of unitary subject that comes under suspicion amongst Language poets (Mullen, "Interview" para. 22). It also foreshortens the conceptual difference between the lyric and epic modes of poetry. Mullen touches upon a vast array of black women's experiences—particularly experiences of living with and pushing back against overdetermined, stereotypical representations of black womanhood—by purposefully collecting and juxtaposing the different voices that have articulated and described those experiences in song, in literature, in kitchens, in churches, and in all manner of other cultural spaces. Expressions of individual black female subjectivity, as well as objectifying representations of black women imposed upon them by others, are "fracture[d]," "compress[ed]," and "blend[ed]" in her work to highlight the multiplicity, the contradictions, the mysteries, and the diversity of black women's subjectivity (Mullen, "Interview" para. 21; Mullen, "Solo" 657, 662). In other words, Mullen opts for neither an autobiographical nor a coherent lyric *I*, but an unpredictable, disorderly, rambunctious "blues chorus" of lyric *Is*.[18] In the aggregate, these lyric voices evidence a temporally, geographically, and experientially vast community and compose and deliver a long blues song that is ultimately epic in its scope. Admittedly, *Muse & Drudge* looks very little like the traditional masculinist epic, with its individual hero at the forefront of a quest to save the community. But we have already seen, in chapter 2, Sonia Sanchez's effective revision of the genre that puts a collective hero—the Black Family—in the questing role.[19] I would argue that Mullen similarly presents us with a collective hero, the great "tribe" of black women who have lived in the U.S., on a quest no less identifiable for her refusal to treat it in a single, linear narrative: a quest for self-determination.

Elisabeth Frost has argued that, by "splicing together lyric fragments into a discontinuous whole, Mullen critiques the hierarchy that elevates epic over lyric," following the lead of Callimachus in the lines that Mullen uses as the epigraph of *Muse & Drudge* (156). But I am not convinced that she critiques this hierarchy only to turn it on its head. Mullen—who has repeatedly cited classicist Diane Rayor's book of archaic lyric translations, *Sappho's Lyre*, as an influence upon her work in *Muse & Drudge*[20]—was surely familiar with Rayor's introduction to the volume, which establishes that lyric poets of the archaic period frequently borrowed conventions of the epic for their poems. Rayor also distinguishes therein between two types of lyric poetry: monodic lyric and choral lyric. While monody focused on the types of personal relationships and reflections typically associated with what we call "lyric poetry" today, choral lyric had a great deal in common with the epic in terms of its stance and concerns (5–9). "[C]horal lyric," Rayor writes, "represents the voice of a community" and was sung on "formal and ceremonial occasions" by a choir of several voices; moreover, it shared with epic an orientation toward public, civic matters and the way such matters were informed by history (7, 6). Mullen's resistance to elevating the epic over the lyric mode, then, may simply indicate that she recognizes their shared history and compatible sensibilities.

Acknowledging that Mullen has used the term "serial lyric" to describe *Muse & Drudge* (Mullen, "An Interview" 413), I nonetheless read her engagement therein with the epic genre as extending beyond her critique of its dominance—its greater literary caché—relative to short form, lyric poetry.[21] Lynn Keller, citing André Bernstein's *The Tale of the Tribe: Ezra Pound and the Modern Verse Epic*, calls our attention to women poets' interest in "the communal project of the epic—its narration of the audience's cultural, historic, or mythic heritage; its attempt to address an audience of citizens using the voice of the community (rather than the voice of a single sensibility)" (8). Mullen's project evidences such an interest in several of the characteristic concerns of the epic—including "community, nation, [and] history" (9). *Muse & Drudge*, I argue, is among those women's long poems described by Keller as "enact[ing] a search for structural and metaphysical principles and for histories and historiographies that can replace those of the traditional heroic narrative" (8). Mullen's poem's search turned up the blues, which does indeed provide her both formal structures and metaphysical notions with which to construct a revisionary, black feminist account of the heroic quest. Mullen *does not* tell us a story of African American women in search of the power and freedom necessary for them to put to rest the competing stereotypes and misrepresentations, and to articulate for themselves their complex, varied, and—yes—competing black, female identities. Rather, her eighty-page collage of allusions, quotations, and language games opens up hundreds of windows on black women's experiences and the heroism entailed in our survival over the centuries of our habitation in the U.S. To look through even a third of those windows, in the course of reading *Muse & Drudge*, is to come away with a sense of the range and richness of black women's identities and of the heroics involved in shaping habitable (indeed, gratifying) subjectivities in the face of the oppressive, reductive representations typically imposed upon our bodies and lives.

ONE STANZA (AMONG MANY) that further exemplifies my argument about what Mullen is up to and demonstrates the density of her writing is this one:

> you have the girl you paid for
> now lie on her
> rocky garden
> I will build my church (22)

The first line addresses an unspecified, but probably male figure, who has "paid for" a woman. The immediate association for many readers will be prostitution and, in the context of a book about representations of black women, the particular way racists have hypersexualized black women since the earliest days of New World slavery. Black women were for many years constructed as prostitutes, almost by definition, their sexuality available to any potential purchaser for cheap, if not for free. But Mullen may also be gesturing toward feminist critiques of marriage as a form of prostitution in which the woman offers sexual (and reproductive and domestic) services in exchange for the man's financial support. This dual reading of the line resonates with a number of implications that rapidly unfold among the multiple and staggered rereadings of the language demanded by each new line. For example, "now lie on her" means one thing to the paying customer. But, in the context of a marriage contract, it echoes the old quip about accepting the consequences of one's acts: "You made your bed; now lie on it." The rhyme of "paid" with "made" reinforces the reading of the stanza's first line as a palimpsestic overlay for the first clause of the old saying. The lines now suggest that the "you" must resign himself to his chosen woman or wife.

If this sounds ominous, it well might, given that *Muse & Drudge* begins with a reference to an infamous African American wife: the notorious Sapphire, married to one of the characters on the *Amos 'n Andy* show, and portrayed as a loud-talking, nagging shrew. Though Mullen's opening stanza (quoted at the very beginning of this chapter) acts to recover Sapphire's character from the stereotype of black women as aggressive and emasculating by re-envisioning her as a Sapphic-poet-cum-blues-singer, it also inaugurates the laundry list of stereotypical representations of black women that *Muse & Drudge* evokes in order to question and criticize them.[22] The speaker here suggests, on one level, that the male addressee may find himself saddled, so to speak, with a difficult or "rocky" woman; but the "paid"/"made" rhyme boomerangs back, to imply that, in addition to having made an exchange that he must now live with, this man has, in a sense, *made* the woman's "rocky garden." That is, the stanza invites us to see (black) men as having contributed to this stereotypical construction of black women, whether by (mis)representing our efforts at self-determination and self-protection as domineering and emasculating—which is also to (tell a) "lie on her"—or by actually acting toward black women in ways that encourage the anger and indignation the men later condemn.

The "rocky garden" reference serves at least two more purposes. First, it once again recalls the folk saying identified as underwriting this stanza, insofar as the word "garden" subtly suggests the word "bed." Second, it functions as a hinge between the ideas discussed so far in the stanza and another set that take off in a different, unexpected direction. Readers familiar with the Christian New Testament Bible are prepared by the word "rocky" to see line 4 as an allusion that requires a rereading of the last two-thirds of the quatrain: "on her / rocky garden / I will build my church." These lines revise the words of Jesus to his disciple, "[t]hat thou art Peter, and upon this rock I will build my church" (Matt. 16:18). This is, perhaps, an utterly appropriate verse for an inveterate punster to gravitate toward, as Jesus himself is punning here upon the fact that Peter's name (in Greek, "Petros") means "little stone." We might note that the *I* in this distorted fragment of borrowed language, at least in the first instance, is not Mullen. The poem's lines encourage readers to rethink Jesus's words in relation to black women—not to rewrite the Bible so much as to rewrite the stereotypical narratives about black women that the Sapphire reference symbolizes. Specifically, it calls up a counter-narrative that recognizes black women as the backbone of the black church: as the majority of those attending, as more faithful tithers and givers, and as those who perform a disproportionate amount of the labor that makes the church function.[23] The traditionally male leadership of the church obscures the extent to which black women have indeed been the strong and stable "rock" upon which the black church is built. Mullen's twist upon the biblical language—changing "rock" to "rocky garden"—suggests that there is a strong relationship between the troubled and hard existence many black women have had and the strength and commitment they bring to their religious faith, their support of the church, and their many other endeavors.[24] We are now in a position to note that the lyric *I* speaker of this stanza could, secondarily, be a black woman (Mullen or any other), who asserts her faith, so to speak, in that very hard-won strength that she and her sisters have cultivated in their "rocky gardens."

As the analysis of this stanza illustrates, part of Mullen's genius in this poem is the (nonlinear) mileage she gets out of conjoining the fragment and the quatrain. The fragment supports Mullen's deliberate lexical variety, making it easy for her to introduce new voices rapidly, literally one on top of the other at times, each speaking its own version of the languages of American culture. Take this example:

dry bones in the valley
turn over with wonder
was it to die for our piece
of buy 'n' buy pie chart (37)

Here, Mullen asks us to think about the struggles of previous generations of African Americans against racism in relation to more recent constructions of black freedom as the opportunity to participate in American consumer culture. To compose this stanza, she pulls in fragments from a variety of registers. She alludes to religious songs significant to the black church ("them bones, them bones, them dry bones" and "in the sweet by and by"), echoes the folk saying that indicates ancestral displeasure ("so-and-so will turn over in her grave"), twists the exclamation of the very gendered and classed shopper ("it was to die for!") into a question, and ends with the language of advertising and corporate America ("buy 'n' buy" and "pie chart"). These rapid-fire changes and tight juxtapositions of disparate voices enable readers to infer a critique of a certain black middle-class ideology. We might also hear, in the final line, a reference to the popular Don McLean song "American Pie," a song whose nostalgia for "simpler times" calls to mind arguments some have made that the mall has replaced the church in American culture. If it is true that we as a society worship the almighty dollar, why would it be any less the case for African Americans than whites, especially in the last decades of the twentieth century, when African American buying power was finally recognized—and courted via the commodification of black history and culture (Malcolm X baseball cap, anyone?).

This quatrain is a particularly useful one for illustrating the way the blues provides the formal glue that holds together both the fragment and the quatrain, on one level, and the lyric and the epic, on the other. The fragment is a particularly apt and resonant unit for *Muse & Drudge*, because it links Sappho's poetry to the experiences of Sapphire and her sisters. Elisabeth Frost and others have discussed in detail the way the poem's opening line—"Sapphire's lyre styles"—conflates the ancient Greek poet, founder of the Western lyric tradition, and the sometimes derogatory, sometimes reclaimed image of Sapphire, archetype of the black woman who don't take no shit (Frost 157). But in addition to this imaginative merging of ancient lyric and modern blues styles, the line invites us to see the fragment as another, *formal* point of connection. All we have today of Sappho's poetry are fragments; according to Rayor, "only one definitely complete poem remains" of the nine collections of Sappho's work that existed in her day (2). Likewise, though for reasons different in their particulars, the experiences of black women during the Middle Passage and the era of slavery exist for us only in fragments, for the most part—pieces from which some of us long to construct a whole narrative.[25]

We cannot—and this is one of the sources of the blues that inform the poem. Mullen does not encourage the fantasy that these lost subjectivities can be accessed, even as she recognizes—and perhaps shares in—the longing for it. Her decision to cut-and-paste fragments together into quatrains honors this desire for a coherent narrative of black women's subjectivity. The quatrain is, among other things, the structural unit of the ballad, a poetic form long associated with narrative and folk culture; it is now received as a written form, but its origins (like the ancient forms of both lyric and epic, like the blues) are in oral culture, including song.[26] *Muse & Drudge*, with its page-upon-page of four-quatrain sets, thus offers at least the *appearance* of continuity. However, aware that the African American desire for knowable origins has underwritten some problematic kinds of recourse to African cultures over the years under the banner of black cultural nationalism, Mullen insists upon frustrating that desire even as she gestures toward it. She deploys the fragment in this effort in order to, as Mitchum Huehls has put it, "disrupt syntax, making it difficult to determine if the relations between words, phrases, and sections of the poem are causal, apposite, contiguous, or contingent" (40). In other words, the fragments in *Muse & Drudge* do not come together seamlessly; rather, they resist fluid readings and require readers, as we have seen, to double and triple back through parts of a quatrain before they can begin to unpack its multiple significations.

The blues helps to hold these fractured fragments together in more than one way. First of all, the quatrain has a deeply rooted connection to the blues. Though blues songs (and blues poems) are commonly associated with a stanza composed of two repeating lines followed by a third rhyming line, that was not the original form of the blues stanza.[27] As Baraka (Jones) explains in his influential study *Blues People*: "Very early blues did not have the 'classic' twelve-bar, three-line, AAB structure . . . [but rather] utilized the structure of the early English ballad" (62). In "The Weary Blues," Langston Hughes, who brought the blues into poetry, works with both this quatrain-based, eight-bar blues and the more familiar three-line form. The blues-inflected quatrain is perfect for Mullen's purposes, because unlike the ballad quatrain, it is not tied to the presumption of a linear narrative. Stanzas in a blues song are more likely to circle around a theme, elaborating on it through the accretion of divergent examples, than to spin out a tale in the way the folk ballads typically do.[28] As Sterling Brown, another excellent blues poet and literary scholar, has said: "The blues are often repetitious, inconsecutive, with sudden changes from tragedy to farce" ("Blues" 292)—an extremely apt description of the incorrigible wildness of *Muse & Drudge*. And, indeed, in the "dry bones" quatrain, Mullen's use of the fragment embraces and enables humor in such a way that it is essential to and inextricable from the political critique available in the stanza. The humor is pointed, but also provides the kind of emotional release that is characteristic of the blues, encapsulated in the old expression that one is "laughing to keep from crying."[29]

The blues connects not only the fragment and the quatrain in *Muse & Drudge*, but also the lyric mode (in which the quatrain participates) and the epic mode. Mullen takes the liberties of the blues singer to accumulate stanza after stanza without the imperative to build upon a plot. Rather, her 320 quatrains—each already potentially a collection of multiple voices, each voice an *I* that carries with it the suggestion of a large community[30]—represent large swathes of the experience of black (predominantly African American) women over the past few centuries. Mullen's strategy avoids essentializing black women, by bringing in voices that speak of and to widely differing paths, problems, and pleasures, often conflicting. No single (stereo)type of black woman is permitted to represent or speak for all others. An example of this juxtaposition of difference can be drawn from the stanzas already discussed. As Davis points out in her study of blues and black feminism, during the period from around Reconstruction through the first few decades of the twentieth century, the spirituals (and hymns) were "God's music," while the blues (and jazz) were "the Devil's music." The household that listened to one often did not listen to the other (6–7).[31] But Mullen, taking no sides, offers voices that speak of each. While the line "'tain't nobody's pidgin" alludes not only to a blues song, but also a blues lifestyle of liberated sexuality and a culture of drinking, the line "dry bones in the valley" references a song that comes out of a church-going tradition that could be intolerant of blues living. Of course, there would have been some speakers who could utter both lines with similar authority and enthusiasm (after all, "If I go to church on Sunday / Then cabaret all day Monday / Ain't nobody's business if I do"), and that represents yet another experience of black womanhood the poem comprehends.

This chapter has drawn particular attention to the blues, as all scholars and readers of *Muse & Drudge* must necessarily do, given its importance to the text, but a wide variety of musical traditions lend their language and cultures to Mullen's text. I have only scraped the surface of references to religious music—including spirituals, hymns, and gospel songs—despite its important place in the poem. Jazz is another musical focal point of this text (and closely related to the blues), as is hip-hop.[32] But she also references ragtime ("cut a rug in ragtime"), rhythm 'n blues ("scratch a goofered grapevine telegraph" refers in part to the song "Heard It through the Grapevine," popularized by Marvin Gaye), Trinidadian calypso ("last chance apocalypso"), and even the songs that accompany young girls' hand-clapping and jump-rope games ("Miz Mary takes a mack truck in / trade for her slick black Cadillac") (18, 9, 65, 16).[33] A particularly poignant stanza turns a Christmas carol, "Joy to the World," into a blues:

> dead to the world
> let earth receive her piece
> let every dark room repair her heart
> let nature and heaven give her release (39)

This stanza concludes a page of quatrains dealing with a common theme: black women's sexuality. The first quatrain deals primarily with unplanned pregnancy, the second with infertility, and the third with the way African Americans' investment in respectability (especially black women's sexual propriety) can lead to extreme social censure ("the souls ain't got a stray word / for the woman who's wayward"). The fourth quatrain, quoted here, seems to continue almost directly from the third, as the "wayward" woman need only be known or rumored to have been sexually active outside of marriage to become, in an earlier era, effectively "dead to the world" of social respectability.[34] This ideology of respectability (considered in some detail in chapter 2) would construct such a death as very like an actual, physical death, insofar as the woman's hopes of "marrying well" and gaining the financial benefits supposed to accompany married life were over.

Mullen proceeds to wring a powerful commentary out of the carol "Joy to the World" by sonically warping the lines to evoke the very opposite of a joyous welcome for an honored male figure. "Let earth receive her king" becomes "let earth receive her piece"; here, the image is, at best, one of the body's burial, but, less generously, reduces the woman to a "piece" of ass. Slant rhyming the carol's "heart" and "prepare" with "dark" and "repair," Mullen invites us to imagine the woman's reception by the world to be so painful that she finds solace and healing in the invisibility darkness brings. Though this "dark room" might be a metaphor for a coffin, it might also, in a more hopeful vein, signify the dim lighting of the scene of sexual activity, where lovemaking might "repair her heart." The quatrain maintains its ambiguity through the last line, in which the possibility of "release" might suggest the end of life as an end to suffering or, just as imaginably, a sexual release that might be consolation for the loss of social respectability. By the end of the quatrain, we are left to wonder if we should have heard "piece [of the action]," or even "peace," in line 2. In this way, Mullen sketches the dilemma of black respectability for black women, while arguably making available a reading that suggests that the pleasures of the "crime" might outweigh the pain of the "punishment."

WITH A SENSE OF how Mullen's black aesthetics shape the function of the quatrains as lyric eruptions at the individual level and the level of the page, we can return now to the question of the long form. *Muse & Drudge* is an epic because the scope of black women's blues is epic. The (mis)representation of black women in folk and popular culture, as well as the way black women represent themselves in light of the other images that circulate so powerfully about them: this is the poem's territory, and it covers a vast amount of ground, temporally and otherwise. To begin with the temporal, some stanzas' allusions send us back into the era of slavery: such as the line "rumba with the chains removed" (9), which recalls the dance's confining connection to the coffle. Or, in a second example, "money's mammy mentions / some chit chat" (55), which offers, among other things, an ironic and alliterative reminder that "money" (as a metonym for a rich person), in the pre-bellum South, typically did have a "mammy"—though this romanticized *and* maligned figure did not emerge in popular culture until after emancipation. Mullen also includes references to African ethnic groups, thus bringing a much longer history of civilization than the U.S.'s into focus, as well as extending the geographical scope encompassed by the poem.

In this stanza, for example:

black-eyed pearl
around the world girl
somebody's anybody's
yo-yo fulani (40)

Mullen concludes by citing the Fulani people, an ethnic group that resides across several nation-states in West Africa. This reference culminates a list of terms, all deeply compressed, that might be associated in multiple ways with black female identity. To my eye and ear, the first line collapses "black-eyed pea" (in the plural, a lucky soul food dish; in the singular, perhaps, an endearment), "black-eyed susans" (a flower, but also the title of Mary Helen Washington's important 1975 anthology of African American women's fiction), and "mama's pearl" (a Jackson 5 hit song of seduction). These largely positive associations take on an ominous quality when compressed, however, as Mullen's line calls up an image of domestic violence and the archetype of the abusive partner who, in one breath, calls his lover a "pearl" and, in the next breath, punches her in the eye. Line 2 modifies the title of LL Cool J's rap "Around the Way Girl," in which he describes his desire for a regular girl from the 'hood. Mullen's twist on the phrase calls attention to the fact that black women not only inhabit neighborhoods all over the world, but that we travel, too, and might be desired for our cosmopolitanism as much as for our homey familiarity. She continues the allusion to contemporary hip-hop culture with a slightly distorted quotation of a common call for audience participation—"Somebody, anybody, everybody scream!"—which, as a call-and-response trope, connects hundreds of years of African American culture back to the African cultures not entirely erased during the Middle Passage.[35] At the same time, the possessive forms of these words signify painfully on at least two kinds of troubling claims to ownership of black women's bodies (the particular injustice of being "somebody's" slave and the general indignity of being "anybody's" whore).

Thus, part of the work this stanza does is to crystallize for readers how the black woman, as represented in (African) American culture, is forced to "yo-yo" (another pun on hip-hop jargon) between a deeply circumscribed, stereotypical "authentic" African "ethnic" identity and a different "authentic" African American "urban" identity. Moreover, both of these identities are consistently linked, even by African American men, to her status as the object of male desire—whether she's his jewel or his girl-next-door. (The possessives in line 3 *look* gender-neutral, but the voice of hip-hop emceeing is, as commentators often note, overwhelmingly male, so that masculinist—indeed, sexist—context frames the line.) Yet, even as Mullen invokes these stereotypes, she challenges, modifies, and pokes holes in them with her powerful wordplay. This stanza suggests the temporal scope—and gestures toward the range of mutually contradictory representations of black womanhood—that the poem as a whole elaborates.

It also indicates something of the international scope of black women's experience as a concern of *Muse & Drudge*. Along with the Fulani, Mullen references the Yoruba, Dogon, Ashanti, Benin, and Dahomey peoples and cultures, along with symbolically significant African countries (Egypt, Ethiopia, and Liberia) and Africa as a continent. She insists that we see African American women's identity as extending beyond the boundaries of the U.S. Her interrogation of the relationship of nationalism to (black women's) identity is not limited to African nations (pre- or post-colonial), but also considers our neighbor to the south, Mexico:

> how a border orders disorder
> how the children looked
> whose mothers worked
> in the maquiladora (10)

Growing up in Ft. Worth, Texas, Mullen came in contact with Chicanos (and the Spanish language) on a regular basis: when she and her sister were in downtown Ft. Worth, riding on the buses, for example, or visiting their grandmother, whose next-door neighbors were Mexican American ("Solo" 651). Though Ft. Worth is a few hours away from the U.S.-Mexico border, Mullen had opportunities to become conscious as a youngster of "how a border orders disorder," in one sense, by organizing people along the lines of nationality—and, not unrelatedly, along racial and economic lines.

The remainder of the stanza underscores the relationship of race and class to this particular border, by drawing our attention to the phenotype (how they "looked") of the children whose mothers labor in the exploitative conditions of the maquiladoras. This image is placed in implicit contrast to the image of children on the U.S. side of the border, whose skin tone and features entitle them and their mothers to enjoy savings on products assembled in Mexican maquiladoras for U.S. companies— savings generated by paying the Mexican "mothers" 25 percent of the U.S. wage for the same work. But we must not miss Mullen's pun: a border also orders, or demands, disorder, by creating conflicts, symbolizing and enacting distrust and injustice, and even, literally, dividing families. If we question the racist assumptions that underlie the maquiladora system, the logic (or "order") of the system falls apart. Moreover, if the order this border is supposed to provide is in part a racial division, increasingly it defeats its own purpose. The population of Texas, and the U.S. as a whole, becomes less and less white, as Mexican immigrants, having "looked" across the border at our economic privilege, physically cross it in search of the wages and standard of living that same border works to deny them in Mexico. By including this critique, as well as other stanzas referencing Cuba, for example, and written in whole or in part in Spanish, Mullen claims Chicano and Latino cultures and concerns as part of African American women's experience—whether by firsthand observation of and relationships with Chicanos, like Mullen herself, or even more directly, as many Latinas from places like Cuba, the Dominican Republic, and elsewhere in the West Indies are racially black.[36]

The geographical and racial scope of the poem extends at times even farther afield, to invoke Asian and Asian American cultures. In a stanza that takes up the common blues theme of domestic violence, a speaker asks "where to sleep in stormy weather" (10); this scenario of a woman on the run reverses the story told in the lyrics to "Stormy Weather" of the singer's empty-home loneliness after her man leaves her. The speaker in the second line responds: "Patel hotel with swell hot plate" (10) suggesting that any woman who has been beaten until "friends don't even recognize my face" (10) will need a cheap place to which to escape.[37] The "Patel hotel" (or motel) is a shorthand for family-owned and –run establishments offering inexpensive rooms, which became highly common business ventures of East Indian immigrants, particularly in the 1960s and 1970s, when they moved in significant numbers to the U.S. to escape political unrest in East Africa (Dublish).[38] The disturbing double meaning of "swell" is reinforced by the stanza's third line, "women's shelter under a sweater," which implies the attempt to hide the physical evidence of abuse (10).

Another instance of Mullen connecting black and Indian cultures appears in the lines: "crow quill and India / put th'ink in think" (50). The "crow"—one of the many birds that contribute to an "African motif" Mullen threaded through the poem—supplies its ebony-colored feather as a quill for dark, black India ink ("An Interview" 414). This ink was being produced in India in the fourth century BCE, and thus is associated with an ancient tradition of writing, of literacy. Mullen, whose interest in the literary traditions of African cultures informs her scholarly and creative work, carefully suggests an ancient relationship between "blackness," writing, and the intellect, to counter the stereotypical representations of African cultures as "uncivilized," lacking in history, and "ignorant"—allegations made in part because these cultures were supposedly nonliterate.[39]

We move even farther East in the following quatrain, which proceeds predominantly by assonance and rhyme. The speaker apostrophizes:

moon, whoever knew you
had a high IQ until tonight

so high and mighty bright
poets salute you with haiku (40)

Mullen's deeply enjambed opening couplet first seems to invite a reading that exposes the assumed relationship among intelligence, visibility,
and lightness or whiteness, and between those qualities and the moon's
worthiness as a subject of poetry, laying this ideology—by whose
(il)logic brown- and dark-skinned black women have been particularly
devalued—open to challenge. At the same time, the first line break facilitates an alternate reading that arguably poses such a challenge, by
reminding us of bodies of knowledge that can be acquired without recourse to formal education. During slavery, for instance, one measure of
intelligence—in the absence of opportunities for formal education—
would have been the acquisition of knowledge necessary for survival.
Thus, "whoever knew" the moon, its cycles, and particularly when it
would be "new"—that is, dark—understood when it was safest to flee
north toward safety. The sonic equivalence between "high IQ" and
"haiku" enables the reader to think critically about the relative value of
visible beauty, objectified as the subject of a poem, and the intelligence
necessary to write in this seemingly simple Japanese form, which actually
calls for astute observation and subtle description of nature. We are reminded that Richard Wright wrote haiku in the late 1950s and that Sonia
Sanchez was writing what she later called "blues haiku," even during the
height of the Black Arts Movement. Mullen's quatrain thus helps us to
see significant points of connection between Asian- and African-based
cultures.[40]

RECALLING WRIGHT'S AND Sanchez's poetry leads me to the next
element of my argument about the epic scope of *Muse & Drudge*. Along
with temporal and geo-cultural expansiveness, Mullen's poem brings to
light the formal breadth of the primary literary tradition black women
have helped create. The scholarship on *Muse & Drudge* to date has focused significantly on blues culture and black vernacular language as
sources upon which Mullen draws in her sampling and quotation processes. That focus, however, has not erased, but has obscured, the influence of black *literary* influences upon the poem's structure and content.
Such an outcome would be predictable, based on the analysis of scholar
Tony Bolden, who has remarked (after Stephen Henderson) that "privileged histories of literature have consistently rendered the black author

invisible" (33). To bring the relationship of *Muse & Drudge* to the African American literary tradition into somewhat clearer focus, it is important to place Mullen in the context of blues *poets*, as well as blues singers. Mullen herself, in a short essay on *Muse & Drudge*, has stated:

> Of course I follow in the tradition of poets, including Paul Lawrence [sic] Dunbar, James Weldon Johnson, Langston Hughes, Sterling Brown, Margaret Walker, Etheridge Knight, and Gwendolyn Brooks, who often worked with humble, common, and 'folksy' materials, such as proverbs, prayers, folk sermons, lullabies, nursery rhymes and children's lore, blues, ballads, jokes, raps, riddles, and toasts. ("Kinky" 166)

This single sentence suggests an alternative (not substitute, but complementary) genealogy for Mullen's penchant for repurposing popular culture and folklore. We might consider Hughes's influence on Mullen's work as representative of this genealogy. As the first poet to bring the blues into poetry, he confronted without any models the problem of producing, in the silence of the page, a quality of voice that would be recognizably "the blues" (Chinitz 182). Even though the strategy he settled upon led him to write poems that are, quite effectively, as plain-spoken as Mullen's are lexically explosive, his work solved for her (and the many other blues poets who have written in the wake of his first forays into blues poems) the dilemma of how to transform aspects of the oral tradition into written form. David Chinitz argues that Hughes's tactic was not to *imitate* blues lyrics, but to make subtle and sparing use of poetic devices (nuances of enjambment and typography) in combination with a purposefully restrained diction, in order to convey character and emotion without coming off as "poetic" (in the sense of "artificial") (182–86). In other words, Hughes used artifice to achieve "authenticity."

Mullen's goal is not to re-create authentic-sounding blues voices, but rather to sample and quote blues voices in ways that highlight and interrogate their operation as re-presentations of black women's expressions and subjectivity. But we can see her in certain stanzas trusting a relatively plain diction to carry the ironies of her allusions and juxtapositions, as in the stanza that begins with language from a Hughes poem (3). Hughes's poem "I Dream a World," associated with exemplary African American women via its service as the title to Brian Lanker's book of gorgeous photographs, describes a time and place in which race and class oppression will no longer "sap . . . the soul" (Hughes, *Collected* 311). Mullen's simple, unadorned language brings a Hughesian blues realism to counter the fantasy of a post-oppression world of "sweet freedom" for all that his non-blues poem sets out in highly poetic, rhymed, metered quatrains. Mullen's quatrain, by contrast, points to the fact that the soul, perhaps, can rest in a dream world, but some actual work will be required to bring it about. Behind her quatrain, we can hear faintly—as encouragement and as acknowledgment—the lyrics to the spiritual: "Walk together children, / Don't you get weary." As the lyric *I* of this borrowed language imports an originally male speaker's voice into the mix of black women's blues voices, we will want to recall Hughes's own willingness to write blues poems whose speakers were women, such as his "Midwinter Blues" and "Young Gal's Blues." Hughes's recourse to speakers who were clearly identified as not literally himself (though possibly providing him with a socially permissible way for him to voice his own desire for men) lays some of the groundwork upon which Mullen could build her poem of non-autobiographical lines. Mullen may also have absorbed strategies employed in *Muse & Drudge* from reading Hughes's own polyvocal long poem of collective expression, *Montage of a Dream Deferred*.

To point to Hughes as a forerunner for Mullen's work is not to take anything away from the inventiveness of her poem, but rather to add further detail to the backdrop against which her innovations take shape. This backdrop includes Stein to quite a significant degree, and similarly Melvin Tolson, both influences she has acknowledged and who represent feminist and African American traditions of poetic modernism and experimentation that are widely or increasingly understood as "avant-garde." But it must also include modernist innovators like Hughes, whose experiments and artistic identity are so deeply rooted in African American culture and literature that their aesthetic daring is less visible to many readers than their "blackness." Aldon Nielsen makes this point precisely in his discussion of the poets in the Society of Umbra, a group of predominantly African American innovators who met, workshopped, and published together in the Lower East Side of New York City from approximately 1962 to 1965. Contextualizing the Umbra poets' aesthetics in relation to progressions within jazz musicianship, Nielsen writes:

> The radical poetics of Umbra writers like [Oliver] Pitcher and [Norman] Pritchard were no more lacking in precedent in black writing than Sun Ra's transmutations of the vocabularies of the big band were unprecedented in the black orchestral traditions; in each genre the innovators and outsiders were working with materials they had gathered from *inside* the tradition, but were working them in new ways. (*Black* 114–15)

I would underline this point by noting that Lorenzo Thomas—one of the poets who, by her own estimate, has most deeply influenced Mullen— was also an Umbra poet.

This is an appropriate note upon which to broaden our focus from African American poetry's formal influence upon *Muse & Drudge* to con- sider other roles African American literature plays within the poem— appropriate because Mullen gives the Umbra poets a nod in one quatrain:

> slumming umbra alums
> lost some of their parts
> getting a start
> in the department of far art (49)

Mullen appears to have constructed her playful sounding lines with her mentor Lorenzo Thomas's discussion of the significance of the Umbra writers (his own powerful work modestly set aside in his account of the group) in mind. In his historically and analytically rich book *Extraordi- nary Measures: Afrocentric Modernism and Twentieth-Century American Poetry*, Thomas devotes a chapter to Umbra as a group of writers who bridged the Afro-modernist aesthetics of the first half of the century with the Black Arts Movement cultural nationalism that took off just as Um- bra ceased to function. The description of Umbra "alums" as "slumming" could be playfully signifying upon Thomas's remark that these poets were able to pass down the older writers' cultural and political values because they "had questioned and conferred with these sages as part of an ordi- nary ghetto upbringing" (141).

Mullen thus emphasizes the point Thomas is making about the ex- istence of a vibrant and deeply politicized aesthetic that was being nur- tured within African American culture for decades and thus was readily available for BAM poets and theorists to draw from in the mid-sixties as their movement got underway. It is difficult for me to know how, and in how many ways, to read the pun-ready line about them having "lost some of their parts," but the last two lines could be an oblique reference to the degree to which spiritual values arising out of "various 'Eastern' or 'orien- tal' disciplines" were provided to, and passed down by, the Umbra poets, according to Thomas. He explains that these "far arts" constituted "a cul- tural alternative . . . that was investigated by the young artists" of BAM (140). While suggesting "far Eastern" in that sense, the phrase could also be heard as a sonic substitution for the popular phrase "far out," which Thomas also evokes for me in describing Umbra poet "A. B. Spellman's profoundly interior landscapes of the far edge of Manhattan, so distant from safety and sanity" (121). It may be less important to know precisely what Mullen's allusions here reference than to note that her treatment of Umbra in the quatrain seems to be affectionate and teasing, as opposed to cuttingly critical, and appears to form part of a network of allusions in *Muse & Drudge* that sketch out some of Mullen's most influential African American literary antecedents.

Another example takes us back to the stylistic kinship between Mullen's and Hurston's ways of blending the vernacular and "standard" American English, noted earlier in this chapter. Mullen inscribes her debt to and admiration of Hurston in *Muse & Drudge* through multiple references to her literary forerunner. There are at least two quotations taken verbatim from Hurston's collection of African American folklore, *Mules and Men*: "standing in my tracks / stepping back on my abstract" and "on the other side of far" (*Muse* 53, 40).[41] Another fragment, "muse of the world," offers a telling twist on a character's reference to the black woman as "the mule of the world" in Hurston's *Their Eyes Were Watching God*, as Frost has noted (163). The representation of black women as both "muse" and "mule"—dichotomous and equally (if differently) problematic, one-dimensional stereotypes—that this substitution highlights and troubles is also at play in the poem's title, of course. *Muse & Drudge* thus conjoins the line from Hurston's novel with the title of her anthropological work, impressing upon us the interconnectedness of the oral (Hurston's study constitutes her ear-witness account of African American speech) and the literary (we have access to these vernacular riches, to some degree, only because Hurston recorded them and wove them into her creative writing). But rather than offering this linkage as evidence of the primacy of the oral in African American culture, as many BAM theorists presumably would argue, Mullen emphasizes rather the interdependency of the speakerly and the writerly, by stashing her sonic echoes of Hurston ("mute and dubbed," "mules and drugs") in a poem that must be *seen* to be *heard*—and vice versa—in both senses of both words (*Muse* 42, 74).

Another important literary influence alluded to in *Muse & Drudge* is Gwendolyn Brooks. This quatrain samples, among other things, a poem from Brooks's first collection of poems, *A Street in Bronzeville*:

Ethiopian breakdown
underbelly tussle
lose the facts just keep the hustle
leave your fine-tooth comb at home (33)

Mullen's interrogation of diametrically opposed, yet mutually constituting roles available to black women, discussed above in connection with Hurston, is also brought into play in this stanza via her allusion to Brooks's "Sadie and Maud." That poem, also composed primarily of quatrains, begins:

> Maud went to college.
> Sadie stayed at home.
> Sadie scraped life
> With a fine-tooth comb (*Blacks* 32).

Brooks contrasts the two sisters over the course of the poem's five stanzas, revealing the kind of gendered catch-22 that black women of her era had to confront.[42] Just looking at the first stanza, we might begin to assume that Maud, whose decision to go off and pursue an education does not conform with typical mid-century gender norms still grounded on the separate-spheres ideology, is going to be portrayed at a disadvantage to her sister. If "a woman's place is in the home," Sadie's behavior must be appropriate; indeed, the conclusion of this quatrain and the next one, as well, suggest that Sadie lived a full, rich life. But the epithet "chit," applied to Sadie in the second quatrain (and signifying a "saucy," "pert," or "impudent" young woman), is our first clue that the poem may not be quite that simple. Brooks's third stanza (whose two "extra" lines repeat lines 3 and 4, with a slight variation, as if an inverted blues stanza were erupting in the middle of a traditional ballad) tells us that Sadie's "fine-tooth comb" scraped up two daughters, but no husband, to everyone's "shame" but her own. Maud and Sadie have switched places. But as quickly as it grants Maud the position of approbation, the poem shifts the terms again. Sadie's daughters, having inherited their mother's zesty approach to living, "str[ike] out from home," apparently unwilling to accept the confines of the domestic realm upon their activities. Yet, although their behavior is perhaps even less socially acceptable than their mother's, it is Maud whose choices are punished within the poem; she becomes "a thin brown mouse," properly at home, perhaps, but alone, her respectability having not earned her the purported reward of marriage and family. The African American woman is damned if she does and damned if she doesn't (though those who *do* would appear to come out slightly ahead in Brooks's estimate).

Mullen's allusion capitalizes on Brooks's having worked through (or over?) this lose-lose dichotomy. Her quick-moving quatrain tosses out, in the first line, a reference to a dance called the "Ethiopian breakdown," described in *A Dictionary of Jamaican English* as "a noisy, rollicking dance of rustic origin."[43] Line 3 references another dance, "the hustle," popular among African Americans during the 1970s (and associated with a song of the same title written and recorded by Van McCoy). But apropos of the fact that African (and African American) dance has long been constructed as evidence of black hypersexuality, the dance theme of this stanza also signifies sexual activity. "To hustle" means to act energetically and aggressively, but also to engage in illicit, money-making practices; one's "hustle" might, for instance, be prostitution. The second line's otherwise cryptic "underbelly tussle" becomes, if not clear, certainly illuminated in this context: "underbelly" as literal location or as a metaphor for that which is hidden and vulnerable readily suggests genitalia, and the phrase as a whole, considered in light of a theme of sexualized dance, could easily be a synonym for the "horizontal boogie." Of course, in this reading, we come to these lines already armed with an understanding that the fourth line's allusion to Brooks references sexuality. So what do we make of the directives of lines 3 and 4? They strike me as the same sort of contradictory imperatives that Sadie and Maud had to choose between. Without reducing either line to paraphrased prose, we might nonetheless note that line 3 ("lose the facts just keep the hustle") seems to counsel against Maud's course of pursuing education and eschewing sexuality, while line 4 ("leave your fine-tooth comb at home") seems to counsel against Sadie's staying at home with said comb *and* against her daughters' leaving home with it. Thus, we have Mullen not just sampling, but remixing Brooks, taking her predecessor's ironic modernist narrative about the impossible box in which black women's sexuality is placed and recasting the paradigm in postmodernist fragments that poke fun at it, in an effort to poke holes in it.

Another Brooks reference brings us full circle, in a sense, to "The Anniad." It arises in a stanza that is more about the materiality of language than allusion, a type of stanza that appears with some frequency in *Muse & Drudge*.[44] Each of the quatrain's four lines is composed of loosely anagrammatic or sonic play on the refrain to the antiwar anthem "Down by the Riverside":

no moors steady whores
studs warn no mares
blurred rubble slew of vowels
stutter war no more (46)

"Ain't gonna study war no more," the well-known lyrics announce. Mullen takes the last four words of that refrain and rearranges the phonemes for her own pleasure and purposes. The lines of her quatrain are neither sense nor nonsense, but something in between. The first line, "no moors steady whores," is certainly not intended as a generalization about the northern African and Arabic Muslims who once were called by that name. Yet the fact that both race and gender are invoked in the phrase can be no accident. That "studs warn no mares" may be true (though I couldn't swear to it), but that the specter of involuntary sexual intercourse looms behind the fragment is almost indisputable. The third line, which I read as two undemarcated phrases, stretches farthest away from the strict sounds of the original reference, but approaches it much more nearly in meaning. By this I mean that these phrases speak more directly to the consequences of war, which might be said, for instance, to produce "blurred rubble"—and, upon consideration of the pun in "slew," also to produce the long streams of vowels representing the screams of the wounded and dying. This line foregrounds the violence simmering below the surface of lines 1 and 2 and, additionally, makes available such associations as the construction of Moors as demonic, martial, and ruthless (think *Othello*), the concept of the war between the sexes (never as metaphorical as one would wish), and the way notions of gender and race have been used to underwrite and facilitate war for centuries upon centuries.

It may not be the case that Mullen had all of these specific ideas in mind in writing this stanza, but the allusion to Brooks in line 4 ratifies the reader in considering them. Rather than simply offer the fragment— "study war no more"—in a completely undistorted manner, Mullen employs substitution for one word: "study" becomes "stutter." Always one to slip in linguistic play, Mullen's replacement word, separated from "vowels" only by a line break, implies the consonants that are the bane of the stutterer's existence. But along with this wordplay, the substitution recalls for readers of "The Anniad" the description of how "tan man" is drafted into the army and taught to use a gun: "Names him. Tames him. Takes him off, / Throws to columns row on row. / Where he makes the rifles cough, / Stutter" (*Blacks* 102). Long after he has returned to the U.S. and to life as a civilian, "tan man" is "[h]earing still such eerie stutter" (102). I won't rehearse here the relationship of war to the critique of race and gender oppression Brooks's epic poem mobilizes, as it is thoroughly discussed in chapter 1, but I submit that Mullen's allusion to "The Anniad" in this quatrain invites us to reconsider the various ways those issues intersect, in hopes that we will "stutter war no more."

"The Anniad" demands that readers recognize the heroism in a young, working-class, African American woman's daring to dream that she might obtain the compensations, as well as the constraints, of her gender role, despite her race and class. That she seeks something other than honor on the battlefield is no sign that she faces fewer obstacles in her quest or is any less devoted to its pursuit. *Muse & Drudge* multiplies the heroism by incorporating the voices of scores of black women, each of whom represents countless more, all variously engaged in what is ultimately a single quest: for the right to self-determination, self-definition, three-dimensionality, full subjectivity. This quest is epic in its scope, having occupied black women's efforts to be seen as more or other than the flat, demeaning, often contradictory stereotypes that sum up black women variously as cheap labor, exotic hussies, punching bags, shrews, breeders, church ladies, asexual earth mothers, tragic victims, divas, cultural caretakers, and so on, depending on what label the context calls for—a struggle that has continued for hundreds of years.[45] Moreover, this quest is epic in its display of black women's heroism, insofar as simply surviving—let alone gaining some measure of control over—the (mis) representations of black womanhood constitutes an achievement. Mullen's poem, as we have seen, utilizes the productive frisson between the epic's comprehensive length and the lyric stanza's concentrated power to gather innumerable black women's voices and set them singing the blues. In the process of interrogating the nature of black women's subjectivity, she illuminates the rarely acknowledged breadth of black culture.

When we really take into account this aspect of Mullen's project, to which she has alluded repeatedly—that *Muse & Drudge* "is partly trying to enlarge [our sense of] what the black culture or the black tradition might be"—we run up against the limitations of terms like "mongrel," "hybrid," and "miscegenated" as descriptions of the eclecticism of this text ("Solo" 655–56).[46] Mullen is interested in the constructedness of identity, both in terms of the images and roles that have been imposed upon black people and in the ways in which, "[i]nstead of accepting our inherited legal status as nonpersons, or trying to become second-class white people, we've constructed, out of diverse materials, complex black identities" ("Conversation"). Thus she takes pains to emphasize that some references in the text mark cultural products to which she has always had access, while others point to material she has learned systematically through formal education (sometimes in white teachers' classrooms) or through autodidacticism.[47] For instance, Mullen had an organic relationship to the church and to spirituals and hymns, because her grandfather was a Baptist minister and, although she is no longer a religious person in the way that her family was, she grew up going to church (Mullen, "Interview" para. 29). Neither the blues nor jazz were played with any frequency in her childhood home (Mullen, "An Interview" 410). Thus her relationship to the blues culture and songs is belated, asserted (as a birthright), and learned. As she puts it:

> There were aspects of the blues that I never got until I was an adult, because that was considered basically gut-bucket, lowdown music in our household. We heard a lot of religious music. I collected my culture from books, from media, and to a certain extent from an actual oral tradition that I do participate in, but there were things missing that I have since gathered and collected. ("Solo" 669)

This experience of coming to certain black cultural literacies in the course of childhood while acquiring others in the course of a formally or informally pursued education is itself so common as to be constitutive of black culture.

Mullen's interest in the diversity and expansiveness of "blackness," however, is enshrouded by the terminology that is frequently applied to her text, which comes out of the discourse of scientific racism. Though this terminology is not being introduced for racist purposes, it inevitably brings the baggage of biological racism to the new contexts in which it is being used. The language of "hybridity" and "miscegenation," for example, obscures the global range of cultural influences that comprise "blackness" and reduces the text's diversity to dichotomized, faintly transgressive mixtures of ("black" and "white") cultural references. It encourages readings like the one by Joel Bettridge that fixes upon the lines "just as I am I come / knee bent and body bowed / this here's sorrow's home" as "effectively join[ing] the predominantly white Presbyterian experience with the black slave song and spiritual" (*Muse* 80; Bettridge 222). I am sure that the hymn "Just as I Am" was a part of Mullen's black Southern Baptist culture, just as it was an integral part of my own black, southern, religious culture; the fact of its white Presbyterian origins is, though not irrelevant, beside the point. Mullen does not claim that every reference between the covers of *Muse & Drudge* is to cultural material that *originates* with African and African American peoples. To the contrary, she acknowledges that "a line that I heard in a blues song someone else has heard in a country western song" ("An Interview" 408). She goes on to say: "Most of what I'm using doesn't really belong to any one person or any one group. Some material I think of as African American, and I will go somewhere else and find out that it is Irish, or German, or Italian! I think that it's mine. And I realize that I have to share it" (408).

But to separate references that resonate with nonblack readers from those that don't, calling only the latter "black cultural references," is in some ways to misread the whole poem. Mullen's understanding of African American culture is that it encompasses—on a nonexclusive basis—everything that African American people have experienced and made use of for their own cultural purposes. Her text, then, constructed upon that understanding, constitutes a fragmented reflection of how wide-ranging and variegated black cultural references are. Ultimately, the fact that some of those references also belong to or resonate with white audiences (and Latino audiences, and so on) is not evidence of cultural crossbreeding constructed *by* the text, as much as it is the result of multifarious, multidirectional cultural boundary crossings that *precede* the text. They function within the poem as invitations to a variety of audiences[48]—audiences that are invited to gain a more expansive understanding of black culture precisely through the realization that black culture comprises cultural products they might have formerly conceived of as exclusively their own.

The term "mongrel," offered as a way of describing *Muse & Drudge* by Cal Bedient in an early interview with Mullen, etymologically retains a sense of the multiplicity the text embodies. But to use this word to distinguish Mullen's poem from other African American texts—or other American texts—again misses her point. Consider the exchange between Bedient and Mullen:

> BEDIENT: The language in your poem has, of course, a mongrel aspect. There are different registers of English. Do you think of it as *a white/black text* in some ways?
>
> MULLEN: A lot has been said of how *American* culture is a miscegenated culture, how it is a product of a mixing and mingling of diverse races and cultures and languages, and I would agree with that. I would say that, yes, my text is deliberately a multi-voiced text, a text that *tries to express the actual diversity of my own experience* living here, exposed to different cultures. "Mongrel" comes from "among." Among others. We are among; we are not alone. We are all mongrels. ("Solo" 652; emphasis added)

Even after acknowledging the multiplicity of the text, Bedient immediately takes recourse to a racial dichotomy in attempting to flesh out what the "mongrel aspect" of the poem signifies. But Mullen, while accepting that many cultural critics and others have used (and continue to use) racialized, dichotomizing terminology to discuss the cultural multiplicity that defines American culture, nonetheless insists upon the "actual diversity" that has shaped her subjectivity. While *Muse & Drudge* is a poem about black experiences and black cultures, one that intentionally and aggressively foregrounds the multiplicity of both, the "amongness" that the term "mongrel" refers to is, in her view, a characteristic not only of black culture, but of "American culture," not only of her text, but of all American texts. Her black aesthetic strategies, however, call for her to make that "amongness" more legible in *Muse & Drudge* than it typically is in texts by authors across the racial/ethnic spectrum. Where some texts are invested in concealing the degree of cultural multiplicity that informs them, hers evidences a commitment to highlighting it—and, moreover, to disturbing the one-dimensional images that have masked and cloaked the wide inclusivity of black culture, in general, and of black women's identities, in particular.

Tony Bolden, in his study *Afro-Blue: Improvisations in African American Poetry and Culture*, offers this assessment of blues poetry:

> African American resistance poets, that is, blues poets, engage in expressive acts of cultural resistance. . . . I want to emphasize that "resistance poetry" here refers to a poetry that demonstrates an identification with the repressed colonized culture by its revision of vernacular forms. Like blues musicians, blues poets use these forms to counter (mis)representations, describing and responding to black experiences in styles that challenge conventional definitions of poetry, resisting ideological domination. (37)

Bolden only mentions Mullen's *Muse & Drudge* in passing, in the conclusion of his book. But in light of his understanding of the genre of blues poetry, I suspect he would agree with me that her poem will come to be seen as one of the most important and innovative blues poems of the twentieth century. Situated in the zone of overlap between the structures, ethos, and themes of the blues and blues poetry and the conventional concerns and tropes of the epic genre (after Brooks), Mullen's innovative black aesthetics generate an African American blues epic. To locate her innovations within black aesthetics is neither to deny the influence of Language poetry upon her poetics nor to erase the differences between her politics and the dominant BAM ideologies, both of which she readily acknowledges. Rather, it is within her specific context—as a late-twentieth-century poet indebted to both the Black Arts and Language poetry movements for the space in which to address and interrogate (respectively) the representation and subjectivity of black women—that her poem's form of "cultural resistance" is fully legible as black aesthetic work. Just as with Brooks, whose epic in rhyme royal stanzas becomes recognizable as black aesthetic writing when seen in the light of the mid-century context in which she wrote (while her poetic politics remain largely invisible beneath the retroactive glare of BAM priorities), Mullen's innovations must be historicized and culturally contextualized to be fully appreciated.

> restless born-agains
> outlaw beat machines
> yet the drums roll on
> let the churchy femmes say amen (54)

EXAMINING THREE unique poems in the African American tradition—to date, the only three long poems by African American women composed entirely in stanzaic forms—we have had the occasion to consider how three women of different generations and with widely differing goals and contexts for their work have used aesthetic practice to confront the racialized expectations they saw or anticipated from their various audiences. These three instances of black aesthetics, as I am using the term, exemplify possibilities for innovative, aesthetic resistance to racist or racial constraints that fall outside the rigidly prescriptive boundaries of the Black Aesthetic, that is, the narrow concept that has come to stand in for a wider range of BAM-era aesthetic stances. In particular, Brooks's, Sanchez's, and Mullen's works expose and challenge the masculinist and, relatedly, heterosexist norms embedded in the traditional epic genre, the Movement's ideology, and American society generally. Their revisionist epics feature quests that turn on concerns facing black women and gay men, in the first instance, even as the poems make claims for the broad racial (and/or cross-cultural) significance of those concerns. Thus, in addition to treating the innovations of three formally and politically complicated long poems, part I of this study foregrounds and analyzes the gendered character of black aesthetics, as well as those aspects of it dealing necessarily with sexuality and class.

Turning now to part II, *Renegade Poetics* employs this nuanced understanding of black aesthetics in examining the work of three African American poets whose writing centers on the subject of nature. As a thematic category, "nature poetry" and its latter-day incarnations (or close kin) "environmental poetry" and "ecopoetry" have long been constructed as an almost exclusively white tradition. When African American poets write about the human *in* or *as* nature, they risk marginalization in relation to that long thematic tradition and, simultaneously, to the African American tradition, which has placed the urban experience at its center since as early as the New Negro Renaissance. The chapters in part II consider the work of Anne Spencer, Ed Roberson, and Will Alexander, each of whom focuses on nature in their work in different ways: Spencer writes about the Virginia landscape she inhabits, especially the garden in her backyard; Roberson writes about the common ground of wildernesses (in Alaska, the Amazon, and the like), rural spaces, and American cities; and Alexander moves back and forth between the possibilities for life on Earth and the possibilities of life elsewhere in the universe. Even though our starting point is in a racialized thematic, we will find the attention we have learned to pay to gender and other such categories important for our considerations of these poets' black aesthetics; we will also find our interest in formal innovation well rewarded by attention to their varied approaches to negotiating the racial politics of this poetic terrain.

PART II

THE BLACKENING SUN, THAT STANDARD OF CLARITY
The Nature of Black Aesthetics

FOUR

PROTEST/POETRY
Anne Spencer's Garden of "Raceless" Verse

JUST AS AESTHETICS are culturally specific—and consequently are gendered and raced—so is nature. Or, to be more precise: "nature," which is to say that the culturally constructed idea we have in mind when we use this term bears the inscriptions of race, gender, class, and other hierarchies and paradigms that have likewise been set in place to organize the world and distribute (or hoard) power. Many of the familiar (and false) binaries that structure these paradigms—male/female, mind/body, white/black, active/passive, rational/emotional, and so forth—can be mapped onto the binary that divides *culture* (or the realm of the human) from *nature*. In each case, that is, the term on the right side of the divide represents that which is to be dominated and controlled, that which is to serve and be of use to its Other. When African American poets engage nature in their poetry, they risk not only marginalization of the sorts I described at the end of part I, but also the reinforcement of an association between black bodies and passive nature that has worked against African Americans for centuries. What could motivate an African American poet to take these risks? Each of the chapters in part II of *Renegade Poetics* will engage this question with regard to a different poet, beginning here with Anne Spencer.

Spencer is an under-studied figure of the New Negro Renaissance whose life and work present valuable challenges to the modes of reading and canon-formation that have shaped the tradition of African American poetry in recent decades. Her poetry was regularly featured in anthologies of African American poetry and writing that appeared during the Renaissance—including James Weldon Johnson's *The Book of American Negro Poetry*, Countee Cullen's *Caroling Dusk*, and Alain Locke's *The New Negro*—and continued to be reprinted afterward, consistently, through the 1950s. Editors and critics such as Johnson, Cullen, Robert Kerlin, and Jessie Fauset praised her work for its "complexness," "cool precision," "originality," and "diamond clearness," respectively.[1] As late as 1950—the year Gwendolyn Brooks was awarded the Pulitzer Prize—Herman Dreer recorded in the headnote to Spencer's work in his anthology *American*

Literature by Negro Authors, that "many regard [her] as the greatest of the Negro women poets" (47).

But by 1971, when *Cavalcade: Negro American Writing from 1760 to the Present* was published, she was singled out for a much different reason. Specifically, the *Cavalcade*'s editors list Spencer—along with William Stanley Braithwaite and Frank Yerby—as an example of those "Negro writers" who "write like whites," insofar as "[t]he entire stock of their referents is white, Anglo-Saxon derived" (xvii).[2] Braithwaite, whose literary critical contributions to the *Crisis* and *The New Negro* anthology "mark[ed] him clearly as a philosophical mentor of the Harlem Renaissance," in Lorenzo Thomas's assessment, did nonetheless avoid racial expression in his own poetry (Thomas 72). And Yerby, indeed, made a crossover career of writing historical novels with white protagonists, but only after the attempt to publish his protest novel failed utterly—and he is noted for having used his popular fiction to quietly debunk romantic myths about Southern plantation culture and slavery. But even less than these two is Spencer deserving of such a sweeping, categorical charge. One assumes that the *Cavalcade* editors were not impressed by the racial politics of the poem "Lady, Lady," which Locke had selected to represent her work in *The New Negro*. The piece is Spencer's tribute to a woman who earned her livelihood washing others' clothes. Refusing to respect or reinforce the typical race and class distinctions signified by the term "lady," the poem's first two stanzas describe unmistakably the physical markers of the woman's status as black ("Dark as night withholding a star") and as a laborer ("your hands, / ... / Bleached poor white in a sudsy tub"). The final stanza venerates the woman's heart as a "darksome place / ... / Where the good God sits to spangle through" (Greene 179). Though by no means a poem *about* the political, its politics are still clearly characteristic of Renaissance writers' efforts to counter the negative, racist constructions of black people so prevalent in dominant social discourse by instead depicting black phenotypes and black ways of being as beautiful (well in advance of the popularization of the "black is beautiful" mantra). And, in any case, the "referent" of Spencer's "Lady, Lady" is certainly not "Anglo-Saxon derived" (Davis and Redding xvii).

If only a poem with an unforgiving critique of white supremacy could shield Spencer from the accusation of writing "raceless" poetry, one would imagine that her piece "White Things" should suffice. First published in the *Crisis* in 1923, it offers a scathing condemnation of the "white things" that "stole out from a silvered world—somewhere," only to use "their wand of power" to "blanch" all the "colorful things" of the world—the "greenly grassed" plains and the "red hills darkened with pine"—and to "turn . . . the blood in a ruby rose / To a poor white poppy-flower" (Greene 191). The first stanza's indictment of European colonialism is followed by a second stanza that unabashedly identifies the "white things" as "hell"-spawned "ghoul[s]" who will stop at nothing in their quest to turn the world white: "They pyred a race of black, black men, / And burned them to ashes white; then, / Laughing, a young one claimed a skull" (Greene 192). The last quoted line recalls the well-documented practice of whites taking souvenirs of a lynching from among the physical remains of the dead.[3] Spencer later confirmed for her biographer, J. Lee Greene, that "White Things" had been inspired by a lynching that particularly "infuriated" her: the 1918 lynching of Mary Turner, a pregnant woman, whose womb was sliced open so her persecutors could crush the unborn baby under their boots (Greene 129–31). Spencer, who once famously claimed that she had "no civilized articulation for the things [she] hate[s]," was nevertheless moved by the account she read of this atrocity to sharpen her pencil to a fine point.[4] That her more frequent decision was to leave her pencil unsharpened might be explained in part by an assertion she makes in her biography: that "White Things" was censored before publication in order to remove a straightforward reference to "white men" (Greene 140).

I cannot help but wonder whether similar editorial caution prevented anthologists during that period from seeking to include "White Things" along with other less fiercely critical poems—or whether Spencer herself, taking the *Crisis* editors' advice to heart (they apparently believed the reference to "white men" to be "untimely and unwise . . . for a new black writer dependent on others for publication"), thereafter refused to give permission to anyone seeking to reprint it (Greene 140). The poem is so exquisitely wrought that it is hard to imagine a reason other than censorship or self-censorship for it not to have become as much a staple of those early and mid-century anthologies as some of her other strongest works. In any case, to be fair to the editors of *Cavalcade*, it must be noted that "White Things," unlike many of Spencer's Renaissance-era publications, had not (as far as I have been able to discover) been reprinted between its initial appearance in the *Crisis* in 1923 and the year when *Cavalcade* was initially released. Spencer never published a collection of her poetry, which might also have preserved the visibility of this poem (along with many others). Thus, the anthology's editors would have had to do some careful digging to find the poem, which they surely would have appreciated as an expression of "the experiential reality of blackness" produced, as they assert, by "most" African American writers (Davis and Redding xvii).[5] But while the influential 1971 anthology's assessment of Spencer's work may well have been written in ignorance of the existence of "White Things," Spencer's reputation has never fully recovered from the damage done to it by such editors and scholars of African American literature who, employing critical lenses focused expressly on poetry of protest, revolution, or cultural celebration, could not see her typical subjects and innovative stylistic maneuvers as connected to that "experiential reality of blackness."

It is ironic and unfortunate that the marginalization of Spencer was heightened during the era of the Black Arts Movement, when African American writers were once again, but even more insistently, asserting the relationship between black art and the political struggle against racism. During the New Negro Renaissance, Locke and James Weldon Johnson had framed that relationship in terms of the status of art as the measure of a people's worth and intellect, hoping that the exhibition of undeniable artistic genius across a generation of writers would "prove the key to that reevaluation of the Negro which must precede or accompany any considerable further betterment of race relationships" (Locke, "New Negro" 15). Johnson argued similarly, in the Preface to the First Edition of his *The Book of American Negro Poetry*: "The status of the Negro in the United States is more a question of national mental attitude toward the race than of actual conditions. And nothing will do more to change that mental attitude and raise his status than a demonstration of intellectual parity by the Negro through the production of literature and art" (9).

W. E. B. Du Bois, taking a slightly different tack, insisted in the late 1920s that "all art is propaganda" and called for art presenting the Negro in a positive light in order to counterbalance all the negative propaganda about blacks that was consistently produced by white American artists ("Criteria" 66). But by the 1960s, in the face of the failure of such artistic accomplishments as Richard Wright's *Native Son*, Gwendolyn Brooks's *Annie Allen*, and James Baldwin's *Go Tell It on the Mountain*—not to mention the amazing output of Renaissance-era writers from Hughes to Hurston—to move whites away from a supremacist stance, a different relationship was being articulated. BAM theorists insisted that black art be a part of an active, unyielding political struggle for power, teaching and mobilizing the people who would collectively seize their rights and their due. Had either Spencer's work or life been more fully known by them, she might well have been a figure of great interest to the young artists and activists of that moment.

Arguably more than, or at least in different ways than, most Renaissance-era writers, Spencer participated actively through most of her adult life in individual and collective efforts to gain civil rights and equal treatment for African Americans. One reason for this difference is that, unlike the majority of the most celebrated writers of the New Negro Renaissance, Spencer did not live in Harlem, in any part of the somewhat less rigidly segregated North and Midwest, or out of a suitcase in a flurry of cosmopolitan, international comings-and-goings, but in deeply racist Lynchburg, Virginia.[6] There, she put her antiracist politics into action on an individual basis, for example, by refusing to ride on segregated public transportation. Rather, she would walk the mile from her house to the downtown area, pay for a taxi when she could, or—to the horror of her scandalized neighbors—hitch a ride on a passing grocery wagon, something no "respectable lady" of the period would do. On the rare occasion when she found herself with no choice but to take the trolley, she defied the Jim Crow laws by planting herself firmly in a "whites only" seat and refusing to move until she reached her destination, regardless of the conductor's verbal abuse. At least once she followed this action up with an unexpected visit to the office of the trolley company manager, to whom she vented her outrage at her treatment. His nearly immediate response—"You must be that Ed Spencer's wife"—suggests how notorious she was in Lynchburg for protesting against discriminatory practices (Greene 88–89).

Another way she gained notoriety was through a successful battle fought on a collective level. Though she despised segregation in schools as well, she thought it the epitome of unfairness that students forced to attend a "black high school" were taught mostly, if not wholly, by white teachers, leaving black teachers jobless. Sometime in 1918 or 1919, she organized a letter-writing campaign within the local black community that so bombarded local decision-makers with expressions of indignation, that they replaced the white teachers with black ones beginning in the very next school year, 1919–20 (Greene 87–88).

Another of her community-based forms of activism served as the gateway to her participation in the literary aspect of the New Negro Renaissance. According to her biography, Spencer was one of a group of African Americans in the small city who, during that same post–World War I moment, began organizing committees intended to address the social, economic, and legal challenges faced by the people of their race. The "human relations committee," to which she belonged, proposed to establish a local chapter of the National Association for the Advancement of Colored People (NAACP), which induced the national organization to send its field secretary to Lynchburg to assist their efforts. The man holding this position at that time was none other than James Weldon Johnson, who, because the hotels in town did not serve blacks, ended up spending a few nights at the Spencers' home. Some sheets of her poetry lying about caught his eye, and he insisted that she consider sending them out to journal and magazine editors. With his support, her first publication, a poem called "Before the Feast of Shushan," appeared in the February 1920 issue of the *Crisis*.

That piece, like the majority of her poems, does not take up racial politics or black culture as its overt subject matter or primary theme. As Spencer would later write to Johnson, with whom she became close friends, "I react to life more as a human being than as a Negro being but I admit the latter is 1927 model. The Tom-Tom *forced* into poetry seems a sad state to me" (Johnson Papers; emphasis in original). This statement comes on the heels of an assertion of her unwillingness to have her poems entered into one of the *Crisis*'s regular literary contests, reflecting her awareness and critique of the market for a commodified black poetry that dealt in exoticism and primitivism, which a number of her literary contemporaries seemed willing, to some degree, to exploit. She is surely signifying on Langston Hughes's 1926 essay, "The Negro Artist and the Racial Mountain," in which he proclaims the "younger Negro artists['] . . . inten[t] to express [their] individual dark-skinned selves without fear or shame," adding that "[t]he tom-tom cries and the tom-tom laughs" (59). But her emphasis on the word "*forced*" suggests that it is only feeling *compelled* to express a "dark-skinned self" to which she objects.[7] Along those lines, we might imagine that she'd have objected to certain Black Arts Movement articulations of black aesthetics, which prescribed for black poets, among other things, a "primary duty . . . to speak to the spiritual and cultural needs of Black people," to quote Larry Neal ("Black Arts" 62).

However, while the word "duty" in this context might well have raised Spencer's hackles, I argue that it is only by taking a limited, ahistorical view of "the spiritual and cultural needs of Black people," a view that also fails to account for the particularities of place and region, that her critics have constructed Spencer's work as "raceless." I begin with the recognition that Spencer believed fiercely in equality and acted upon that belief by working to effect change in her personal and public life, and I propose that her poetry—like the other aesthetic practice for which she was widely known, her gardening—*participates in that work*, rather than stands apart from it. Spencer's garden, which extended from the back of her house all the way to the next street over, included paths through flower beds, a wisteria pergola, and a grape arbor; shaded seating around a cement pool; and the little cottage, Edankraal, that served as her writing studio and library. Commonly, Spencer criticism understands her garden as both a primary source of the imagery she uses in her poetry and, like her poetry, a space of beauty and refuge from the oppressive society in which she lived and performed her civil rights work. But I argue that Spencer used both her poetry and her garden as spaces where she could think about and experiment with ways of conceptualizing and articulating the operation of the social world—and to do so specifically in terms of her growing understanding of the interactions among things within the natural world and between herself and nature. What she learned from years of childhood spent amusing herself in solitude outdoors in rural West Virginia and from later decades devoted to designing and maintaining her garden informed her thinking about the dynamics among individuals and groups of people.[8] She worked out her ideas by putting them into play in poems, testing them out imaginatively and experimenting with language and formal devices.

MY ARGUMENT EXTENDS the important work of black feminist scholars of the period, such as (Akasha) Gloria Hull, Deborah McDowell, Cheryl Wall, and Maureen Honey. Their work foregrounds and problematizes the dismissive, gendered assumptions that see poetry by Renaissance-era women, including Spencer, as "genteel" and "feminine," but not "black," in its employment of conventional Romantic themes of love and nature. Black feminist scholars have contextualized Renaissance women's poetry, pointing to the specific challenges that women writers faced in that period, including the biases held by the predominantly male editors and critics and the constraints of family and respectability upon women's mobility (and thus their access to social networks that facilitated publishing, obtaining the financial support needed to write, and publicizing one's work).[9] The ideology of respectability presented a particularly ironic double bind. As I noted in chapter 2, black women's emphasis on propriety began during the post-Reconstruction period as a defense against the imputations of hypersexuality and promiscuity regularly made against them; the defensive strategy, however, drew a boundary around black women's sexuality and social behavior that functioned as both shield and prison.[10] Among other things, the adoption of this ideology by the black community limited the subjects which black women poets could properly take up, even as their "failure" to tackle more "masculine" subjects left them vulnerable to the accusation that they were out of step with the times. I am also indebted to black feminist scholarship—especially Honey's important conjoining of critical and anthological efforts in her work on Renaissance women's poetry—for demonstrating the way poets like Georgia Douglas Johnson, Alice Dunbar-Nelson, Angelina Weld Grimké, and Mae Cowdery would "encode" conventional nature imagery with racial subtexts in order to circumvent the constraints of respectability.[11]

Spencer's own aesthetics are certainly illuminated by this attention to the way gender helped to shape these women poets' possibilities as writers. Her resistance to limiting gender conventions—affirmed for Spencer by the life and work of South African feminist Olive Schreiner, whom she greatly admired—included not only vocal advocacy for women's rights, but also wearing pants in public and defining her role as "housewife" in contrast to that of a "housekeeper" (Greene 141–42, 45).[12] Influenced by the understandings produced by (black) feminist scholarship, critics writing during and since the 1970s have regularly pointed to Spencer's poems concerning sexism as evidence (in addition to "White Things") that she does not entirely shun overt protest in her oeuvre.[13] Moreover, her recurring garden imagery cannot be understood as merely decorative, in the wake of interventions like Honey's (xxxix–xlviii). But as important as it is to acknowledge her feminist aesthetics, only if we also account for the materialist thrust of her work can we fully appreciate Spencer's achievements as a poet. Hers is a black feminist aesthetic that emerges uniquely out of her distinct priorities as a "social heretic" challenging both racist and sexist oppression in the small Southern city of Lynchburg (Greene 98). In other words, we must never lose sight of Spencer's garden as a material place, if we hope to take an accurate measure of its role in the black feminist aesthetics underwriting her poetry. In Spencer's life, the garden cannot be reduced to a symbol; her relationship to the out-of-doors, as a girl, and to the garden, as a woman, involved deeply physical, hands-on encounters with the earth, its vegetation, and its creatures—not stereotypically "feminine" behavior, at least from a certain class perspective.[14]

This is also to say that we must remain conscious of her garden as an actual, rather than symbolic, space with regard to what is "black" about her aesthetics. It is through Spencer's intimate contact with and thoughtful observations of plant and animal life that she comes to understand the natural world as simultaneously a retreat from *and* a model of the social world. Consequently, much of Spencer's poetry responds to a different set of "spiritual and cultural needs of Black people" than Larry Neal might have had in mind in formulating his definition of the term. Her writing speaks to the need for spaces in which to turn over one's thoughts and process information about this deeply flawed society—not instead of protest poetry or poetry celebrating black people and black ways of being (because, as we have seen, her oeuvre contains examples of these), but in addition to, and in relation to, such work. Spencer invites her readers to enter a space in which they are not hailed immediately or insistently as raced subjects; a space that therefore *looks* "raceless," but is *for* black people (especially black women), in the first instance, at least; where readers are able to contemplate and analyze moral and metaphysical ideas that can inform the struggle for equality in which they are engaged.

Spencer's varied subjects and formal approaches mean that this claim plays out in a range of ways, so it should be useful to spend time with some examples. Her "Lines to a Nasturtium (A lover muses)," is an oft-anthologized poem that is typically pointed to as evidence of her "race-less" gentility—and of her aesthetic conventionality, another post-1960s characterization of Spencer's writing that I hope to complicate in this chapter. First appearing in October 1926, in a special issue of the journal *Palms* edited by Countee Cullen and devoted exclusively to poetry by African Americans, the poem was reprinted in Cullen's anthology *Caroling Dusk* in 1927:

> Flame-flower, Day-torch, Mauna Loa,
> I saw a daring bee, today, pause, and soar,
>> Into your flaming heart;
> Then did I hear crisp, crinkled laughter
> As the furies after tore him apart?
>> A bird, next, small and humming,
> Looked into your startled depths and fled. . . . .
> Surely, some dread sight, and dafter
>> Than human eyes as mine can see,
> Set the stricken air waves drumming
>> In his flight.
>
> Day-torch, Flame-flower, cool-hot Beauty,
> I cannot see, I cannot hear your flutey

Voice lure your loving swain,
But I know one other to whom you are in beauty
Born in vain:
Hair like the setting sun,
Her eyes a rising star,
Motions gracious as reeds by Babylon, bar
All your competing;
Hands like, how like, brown lilies sweet,
Cloth of gold were fair enough to touch her feet . . .
Ah, how the sense floods at my repeating,
As once in her fire-lit heart I felt the furies
Beating, beating. (Cullen 52)

Notably, as regards the issue of conventionality, this poem places Spencer among the very first women poets I have discovered to adopt an unframed, unmediated male persona. Her poetics are also unconventional in the ways they depart from the strictly traditional forms favored by the Romantic poets, to whom she and other Renaissance-era women poets are often compared. Spencer's particular brand of modernism here involves the use of metrically unpredictable but compelling rhythms; we find the predominant streams of iambs interspersed with clusters of feet that are emphatically trochaic or spondaic, in lines of irregular lengths. Spencer gives us a skillful blend of internal and end rhymes at varying intervals, such that rather than chiming heavily, they seem to float along the exuberant music of her language. She also takes an unusual, intuitive approach to such elements of typography as the indentation of lines, the duration of ellipses, and italicization. These modernist techniques, evocative of something other than the "Tom-Tom," do not mark the poem's aesthetics as "recognizably black," to be sure, but neither did Gwendolyn Brooks's modernist devices in "The Anniad"—and we learned from reading that poem (in chapter 1) that we must be willing to look beyond the "recognizably black" in search of black aesthetics.

Turning to the question of thematic conventionality, this poem—a lover's apostrophe to a flower—does, of course, engage the categories of "love poetry" and "nature poetry" with which Renaissance women poets are deeply (and dismissively) associated.[15] The concerns of this poem, however, are not wholly encapsulated by the categories of "nature" or "love," which function rather as the context for a meditation on power. The first stanza describes two interactions with the attractive nasturtium: one initiated by a bee and the other by a hummingbird, both creatures that

Spencer would regularly have observed taking nectar from her favorite flower (Frischkorn and Rainey 60). But the encounters in the poem are unusual. The bee is deemed "daring" for "soar[ing] / Into [the] flaming heart" of the flower and the speaker actually speculates as to whether the act has resulted in the bee's destruction. The hummingbird "[l]ook[s]," but does not dare to penetrate the flower's "startled depths," seeing, perhaps, some "dread sight" invisible to human eyes. The nasturtium is thus constructed as beautiful, but dangerous, by a poetic discourse steeped in caution, threat, risk, and fear; the references to its fiery, even volcanic, nature—"Flame-flower," "Mauna Loa"—serve as a warning, as well as a tribute to the nasturtium's vivid coloring. However, the allusion to "the furies" complicates the trope of dangerous beauty. According to Greek myth, which Spencer studied during her relatively brief education, the three Furies—goddesses of vengeance—punished criminals and other wrongdoers relentlessly and without mercy, pursuing their subjects to the ends of the earth until they were driven mad. The Furies were not indiscriminate in their work; they had specific, deserving targets. The implication, then, is that the bee and the hummingbird, in going about their accustomed, natural routine, are nonetheless committing some injustice. Given Spencer's preoccupation with resisting the racism and sexism she confronted in her hometown, her incorporation of injustice as a thematic element of the poem validates our inquiry into the poem's black feminist aesthetics.

The second stanza gives us the lover's assertion that there is a woman even more beautiful than the nasturtium. But the woman and flower have more than beauty in common; she also harbors "*the furies*" in "*her fire-lit heart*"—and he has felt them, "[b]eating, beating." The lover, then, is like the bird and the bee (the birds and the bees?) in having provoked the wrath of the furies. Using italicization to insist that we attend carefully to this penultimate line, the poem invites questions that begin to put flesh on Johnson's characterization of Spencer's work as "complex" (47). Are we to understand that the lover has, in effect, *violated* this woman, by "daring" to enter her "startled depths"? Is the lover exulting in his having "*felt the furies*" but—unlike the bee, perhaps—having come away from the experience unscathed? We start to see how Spencer's observations of nature lead to observations about the dynamics of power. We understand the role of insects and birds in the pollination of flowers to be natural and necessary. But by reimagining the visits of these highly mobile creatures to the flower as unwelcome (even promiscuous, one might say) and the nasturtium's immobility as a form of vulnerability, its "heart" ineffectively protected by its own *furi*-ous "beating," Spencer invites us to examine the ways in which behaviors constructed as natural may in fact simply be the prerogatives of the beneficiaries of an unequal distribution of social power. Put differently, a powerful person's "natural" actions may be experienced by the disempowered person as a crime—a crime that goes infuriatingly unpunished.

To further unpack the poem, we must recall that Spencer's interest in equality—and the scope of her aesthetics—concerns the problem of racism as well as sexism. The poem points most obviously to questions of gender, but if we have not already *assumed* the "racelessness" of Spencer's poetry, we might notice that the blazon in the second stanza unmistakably depicts a woman of color, presumably an African American woman. The comparisons of her attributes to "setting sun" and "rising star" align her beauty with nighttime darkness, a device common to work by Hughes and other poets of the era.[16] And though the horticulturally uninitiated (like myself) might not expect it, the brown lily, to which the woman's hands are compared, is indeed quite chocolate in color. Having established that the woman described in the poem is "colored," so to speak, we should note that the race of the *speaker* remains indeterminate. The poem thus opens up the issue of respectability from a different angle than that discussed earlier. We are reminded that black women's emphasis on respectability began in the post-Reconstruction period as a self-protective gesture, with which they defended themselves against charges of hypersexuality—a construction that functioned in dominant discourse to divert attention from the fact that white men could, and did, rape black women with virtual impunity.[17] Ida B. Wells was exiled from Memphis, Tennessee, in 1892, her newspaper office totally destroyed, for writing editorials that made this point and related ones about the power dynamics underwriting interracial sexuality and its construction in public discourse. Thirty years later, in the dawning of the New Negro Renaissance, lynchings of African Americans were still occurring at an average rate of one per week.[18] More than a concern for propriety might have led Spencer to treat such a subject in a "cryptic" fashion (J. Johnson, *Book* 45).

The implications of this reading of "Lines to a Nasturtium" recall one of the issues that arose in my discussion of Brooks's "The Anniad," in chapter 1: that masculinist constructions of the black community tend to obscure black aesthetic practices that take black women's experiences as their starting point. To point toward womanhood is too commonly equated with pointing away from blackness. Such gendered misconceptions would necessarily render Spencer's black aesthetics invisible, insofar as her poetic engagement with the concerns that preoccupied "the New Negro" frequently emerges from or focuses on issues and situations involving women's lives or women's equality. We saw this propensity of hers in the poems explicitly invoking race referenced earlier in this chapter. "Lady, Lady" treats the reinscription of "blackness" as beautiful and valuable in a portrait of a woman whose gender is only underscored by her identification as a washer of clothes. And "White Things," though it figures African Americans as "a race of black, black men," was inspired by a particular lynching made all the more insupportable for Spencer because of its outrage of black motherhood. It should not surprise us, then, that a poem that explicitly invokes gender, like "Lines to a Nasturtium," could have a significant racial subtext.

Indeed, the poem that began her publishing career, "Before the Feast of Shushan," treats similar issues using similar strategies, though its interest in power dynamics is unambiguous. Spencer is able to be more direct about the issue of power because she casts her examination of it in a historical, indeed, biblical setting. Though never subsequently included in reprintings of the poem, a parenthetical subtitle—"(Esther 1)"— appeared below the title in its initial publication in the *Crisis*, alerting readers to the poem's relationship to the Bible characters, Ahasuerus, king of Persia and its empire, and Vashti, his queen. Esther chapter 1 explains that Vashti lost favor with the king because she refused to appear before the court at his summons, her disobedience embarrassing him in the eyes of all the princes and nobles of his kingdom and all the other members of his court, who were gathered in the garden of his palace at Shushan for days of feasting. Advised by his counselors that Vashti's conduct, if unpunished, would set such a bad example for wives throughout his realm that chaos would surely ensue, Ahasuerus banished her from his presence and selected a new queen. Spencer thought to write a poem that would problematize this construction of appropriate marital relations (Greene 52).

Rather than writing a poem of "protest," per se, Spencer's black feminist aesthetics led her to employ a technique pioneered—or, certainly, perfected—by her favorite poet, Robert Browning: the dramatic monologue. A specific type of persona poem, the dramatic monologue *proper* is characterized, according to Robert Langbaum, by its creation of "a 'tension between sympathy and moral judgment,' so that 'we understand the speaker of the dramatic monologue by sympathizing with him, and yet by remaining aware of the moral judgment we have suspended for the sake of understanding' him" (qtd. in Radar 40). Spencer negotiates this careful balance by investing "the old beast" (as she once referred to

Ahasuerus [Greene 52]) with her own love of nature's beauty. Taking on his voice, she opens the poem with this stanza:

Garden of Shushan!
After Eden, all terrace, pool, and flower recollect thee:
Ye weavers in saffron and haze and Tyrian purple,
Tell yet what range in color wakes the eye;
Sorcerer, release the dreams born here when
Drowsy, shifting palm-shade enspells the brain;
And sound! Ye with harp and flute ne'er essay
Before these star-noted birds escaped from paradise awhile to
Stir all dark, and dear, and passionate desire till mine
Arms go out to be mocked by the softly kissing body of the wind—
Slave, send Vashti to her King! (Johnson, *Book* 213–14)

Speaking aloud, perhaps half to himself and half to those subjects and servants who must be at hand, Ahasuerus rhapsodizes about his palace garden, with its vibrantly colored flowers, soothing shade trees, and melodious birdsong, as second only to Eden. His endearing interest in these natural beauties is Spencer's invention; the garden in the Bible story is described entirely in terms of how it reflects the king's wealth—with fine fabric, precious metals, and costly marble—rather than as a *living* garden, like Spencer's own.

Spencer's purpose in foregrounding the king's estimation of the natural elements of the garden is twofold. Not only does it make him a three-dimensional, initially sympathetic character, it sets up the poem's structural logic, which turns, stanza by stanza, on the way Ahasuerus portrays nature. The second and third stanzas, for example, first, associate and, ultimately, conflate Queen Vashti with the natural world. The second stanza connects her regular visits to the garden with the setting of the sun, which "at each day's wane" casts its "fiery" light at such an angle as to "startle into flame" the palace towers. The king thus naturalizes Vashti's arrival each evening—treats it as cyclical, by associating it with sunset—though the first stanza's final line has already demonstrated that her appearance responds to his invitation-cum-command. The third stanza functions as a sort of real-time description by the king of how he is led to act in the face of the queen's "peerless beauty":

Cushioned at the Queen's feet and upon her knee
Finding glory for mine head,—still, nearly shamed

Am I, the King, to bend and kiss with sharp
Breath the olive-pink of sandaled toes between;
Or lift me high to the magnet of a gaze, dusky,
Like the pool when but the moon-ray strikes to its depth;
Or closer press to crush a grape 'gainst lips redder
Than the grape, a rose in the night of her hair;
Then—Sharon's Rose in my arms. (214)

Over the course of these lines, as King Ahasuerus moves from being prostrate at Vashti's feet to fully embracing her, the images composing the blazon of the queen move from a simile, likening her "gaze" to a "pool" in the moonlight, to a metaphorical identification of the darkness of her hair with "night," to a metonymic substitution in which Vashti is replaced entirely with the reference to "Sharon's Rose." The more closely identified with nature the queen is, the "closer" the king seems to "press" her to him, until he possesses her as completely as he does the trees and birds of his garden.

The moment when Queen Vashti becomes metonymically one with "Sharon's Rose"—both a symbol of perfection and an actual flowering plant—is the moment Spencer's structural strategy begins to pay off. As the king relates to the natural world, the reader understands, so will he relate to Vashti. The fourth stanza's first two lines—"And I am hard to force the petals wide; / And you are fast to suffer and be sad"—recall moments in the preceding stanzas that foreshadow his capacity for such violence and the attitude that underwrites it. The king's appreciation of nature, we see, is of a piece with the way the Ahasuerus of the Bible appreciates the fine things in *his* garden—what the things are (living creatures or gold and marble) is less important than that they are unparalleled, exquisitely expensive, and redound to his glory. To him, possession signifies control; when the wind "mock[s]" his empty arms (when nature cannot be forced to satisfy his desires), he turns his attention instantly to the people whose lives are under his sway. Spencer has him indict himself not only by revealing, with his self-interruption, the way Vashti functions for him as a kind of figure of the "natural" that he can summon at will, but also in the very language of his summons. Replacing the Bible's term "chamberlains," meaning "servants," with the word "slave," Spencer inevitably aligns Ahasuerus with the U.S. slaveholders whose memory, in 1922, was still painfully alive in her readers' minds.

Spencer concludes the poem by playing out the implications of the king's association of Vashti with nature. We hear Vashti's voice, ventriloquized by Ahasuerus, in the fourth stanza, where he repeats assertions she has made about how their relationship ought to work: "How says Vashti, love is both bread and wine; / How to the altar may not come to break and drink, / Hulky flesh nor fleshly spirit!" The thought of love being a "sacrament" that he dare not desecrate by reducing her body to its use value—as another means of displaying his power and privilege or satisfying his physical desire—clearly does "[a]maze" him. He expresses his astonished rejection of her proposition in a stanza composed entirely of assertions of his prerogatives as King of Persia. What is most important for our purposes is the telling way Spencer refigures some of the natural images of earlier stanzas in his pronouncements: living animals ("birds escaped from paradise") are reduced to "meat"; the "grape" one imagines plucked fresh from the vine has been distilled into "red wine, plenty, and when I thirst"—consumed for self-gratification, rather than as part of a spiritual ritual. It follows, then, that the king's view of Vashti, earlier equated with "Sharon's Rose," is equally sensualist and utilitarian: "Love is but desire and thy purpose fulfillment," he insists. Along with its implied condemnation of this kind of sexism, Spencer's poem argues that a person's ability to appreciate nature's inherent value constitutes a measure of his capacity for ethical relations with other people, an argument that anticipates similar claims made by people working in the fields of ecopoetics and ecocriticism.[19] Notice that once again, through nuanced images employed in the blazon (*"olive*-pink . . . toes," a "dusky . . . pool" by moonlight) and in the association of the queen with the coming of night, Spencer figures the woman of color as the object of sexist oppression—but, in this case, also as an articulately resistant subject, a woman who soon, during the feast of Shushan, as Esther 1 recounts, will refuse outright to answer her husband's summons.

IN SPENCER'S SLIM oeuvre of extant poems, there are several besides those already noted that engage race, if only by being titled for or dedicated to identifiably black people: "Rime for the Christmas Baby (At 48 Webster Place, Orange)," an epistolary poem to her friend Bess Alexander upon her delivery of a son; "We Remember / The Rev. Philip F. Morris / A Lott Carey Founder / —1923—," also an occasional poem, upon his death; "Black Man O' Mine"; "For E. A. S.," her husband, by his initials; "[Dear Langston]," another epistolary poem, written to Hughes; "Luther P. Jackson," a renowned scholar of African American history who cofounded with Carter G. Woodson the Association for the Study of Afro-American Life and History; "The Sévignés," whose central image is a monument to "Uncle Remus" in Natchitoches, Mississippi; "Grapes: Still-Life," an allegory of race told through images of grape varieties; "Dunbar," a short children's verse in the voice of the black poet; and, famously, "For Jim, Easter Eve," her elegy for James Weldon Johnson.[20] Not all of these poems were published during her lifetime, but they have been available in her literary biography, *Time's Unfading Garden*, since 1977, without uprooting the dominant critical narrative about her work's "raceless[ness]" (despite the interventions of scholars like Honey). It would nonetheless be misleading for me to suggest that black issues, culture, or people were the theme or even subtext of more than a third of her poems. I want to make clear that my argument is not that Spencer's black aesthetics can be read, across the board, in the language of her poems— though I have been pointing at how prevailing assumptions about the *absence* of black aesthetics in her work has rendered even her "recognizably black" elements invisible. Still, now, with an understanding that some of her poems that do not look like they are about race *in fact* treat race at the subtextual level, we are better equipped to think about how poems that do not in any way inscribe race in their language can nevertheless be *for* black readers, much like Sonia Sanchez's *Does Your House Have Lions?* is, addressing their "*spiritual* and cultural needs" (Neal 62; my emphasis).

That is, the struggles that black people were facing over the course of Spencer's writing life encompassed not only how to fight racism and end or circumscribe oppression, but also how to live lives that were not mired in bitterness and how to keep a moral compass in a society structured, de facto and de jure, as much upon inequity and injustice as upon freedom and democracy. Her more metaphysical poetry engages the garden, and the natural world in general, as a space through which to think about strategies for living well and *rightly* (in a religious, but not dogmatic, sense). Such poems often consider the role of artistic practices like poetry and gardening (and their products, if you will—poems and gardens) in creating the conditions for a fulfilling life, even in an environment defined by racial and sexual oppression. Spencer makes plain the connections she sees between gardens and (black) human lives in an unpublished, uncompleted draft essay entitled "Love and Gardens."[21]

This prose piece begins with a line from an unidentified gardening book, almost dismissed by Spencer as banal, but instead taken as the basis for a meditation on the conditions that "colored" children, like flowers, need to grow and thrive: "Flowers grow for those who love them, and the secret of success is in the worker." Despite its "apparent triteness," this gardening advice leads her into a consideration of our lives and the love we share with "Kith & Kin" as aspects of the "one kind of love & one kind of garden" that exist here on Earth—these being but a "shadow" of the "Love" shown us by the "great Gardener" and His Eden. But these earthly aspects of love and gardens need not be poor substitutes for their divine models: "[A]s for the kind of garden that we know, we may have Eden if we so will. Because objective gardens are but Empiric symbols of their antitypes, the green places in the universal soul." With this vision of utopian possibility, Spencer prefaces the concerns of the rest of the essay: the ways that parents and, to a lesser extent, teachers are responsible for raising the kind of children who will in turn shape the kind of world in which we want to live. As she puts it: "Parents *must* instill into their children the peaceful civilization of the next hundred years[.] If we hate war & love peace. [If we] desire pure government for the masses. If we desire brave spirits and dauntless hearts that can live above prejudice and wrong. Let us train our children with a tedious care for little things." She immediately follows these ambitious goals with the suggestion that "we who are here in Ly'b'g, and colored" work together to establish "a child's welfare society or a Big Brother & Big Sister league." If these concrete propositions sound a bit deflating after the lofty aspirations to engender "pure government for the masses," they reflect her knowledge as a gardener who slowly, over the course of forty or fifty years, turned a small plot for vegetables by her back porch into a lush, 7,800-square-foot, four-"room" garden (Frischkorn and Rainey 27–29). One must proceed with even the largest project one step at a time—and, in gardening on the scale Spencer undertook, there are a number of steps that must be taken *before* one can even plant the first seed. As with creating a garden, so with creating a world.

Her poem "Substitution" is an ars poetica on the possibilities of creating a world via imagination, the poet's imagination, in particular. This Shakespearean sonnet, first published in Cullen's *Caroling Dusk*, is by definition more formally conventional than the irregular, nonce patterns she creates for "Lines to a Nasturtium" or the sweeping free verse lines with which she accommodates the egotistic voice of King Ahasuerus in "Before the Feast of Shushan."[22] But it claims for the poet a power that both enlarges the sonnet and exceeds it:

> Is Life itself but many ways of thought,
> Does *thinking* furl the poets' pleiades,
> Is in His slightest convolution wrought
> These mantled worlds and their men-freighted seas?

He thinks—and being comes to ardent things:
The splendor of the day-spent sun, love's birth,—
Or dreams a little, while creation swings
The circle of His mind and Time's full girth . . .
As here within this noisy peopled room
My thought leans forward . . . quick! you're lifted clear
Of brick and frame to moonlit garden bloom,—
Absurdly easy, now, our walking, dear,
Talking, my leaning close to touch your face . . .
His All-Mind bids us keep this sacred place! (Cullen 48)

A bit in advance of some of the theoretical movements along similar lines
that are so familiar to intellectuals today, the speaker of Spencer's poem
considers seriously that the "worlds" we experience may be just as much
the creation of our *"thinking"* as God's "thought." Though it is perhaps
a concession to the pressures of the tight sonnet rhyme scheme, interestingly, the poet's creative powers *precede* God's in this meditation—as
though, in first recognizing that "poets'" minds drew the constellations
in the sky, the speaker is then able to understand divine creation as the
product of a tiny whorl of God's brain, or "All-Mind."

Spencer wields the power of language—the medium of "thought"—
subtly, but impressively, in the first lines of the second quatrain. God's
thinking brings "ardent things" into "being," the speaker asserts, and offers examples that call forth two different meanings of the adjective: the
"sun" is "ardent" in the sense of glowing brightly, while "love's birth" is
"ardent" in the sense of being passionate. The multiplicity of meaning is
part of the way language and thought create a world that is textured and
full of possibility. "[D]reams," too, are said to have the power to shape
"Life," suggesting that the unconscious as well as the conscious mind is
creative and, further, evoking the sense of "dreams" as hopes, which resonates through the African American literary tradition as a reference to
the hope of freedom and equality. If God's dreams can spin the galaxy
around, perhaps the poet's mind can move two "ardent" beings from a
"noisy peopled room" to a more "sacred place." The sestet enacts this possibility, in language that represents the speaker's "thought" as capable of
independent motion: "My thought leans forward," exerts itself, and without further ado, affects the removal of the speaker and addressee from a
social world, contained within "brick and frame," placing them in the natural setting of the "moonlit garden." In this little Eden, the two are free to
walk and talk together, to be intimately close to one another—something

apparently impossible in the setting of which the speaker's "thought" has "lifted [them] clear." Ultimately, this latter point may be more important to the poem than the former. That is, the poem seems to be less about the fulfillment of the desires of lovers than about the distinction between a world in which love is not possible and a world in which it is. If our "thought" has created the "noisy peopled room" that has no room for rambling, quiet conversation, or intimacy, the poem argues, it can also create a "sacred place" in which love and other flowers can "bloom."

In the poem's final line, Spencer again offers some productive linguistic ambiguity: "His All-Mind bids us keep this sacred place!" We might initially hear the verb in this sentence as calling for the lovers to remain in this world the poet's imagination has created—to "keep (to)" it, with metrical constraint requiring the syntactic compression that elides the preposition. Alternatively, given that this is an exhortation from God, effectively, we might hear "keep" in the religious sense: they must "keep this sacred place" as one might "keep the Sabbath," by treating it as a duty. But the third and, arguably, most important signification of the word is that of caring for, or maintaining, as in to "keep a garden." Spencer uses a noun form of the word ("keeper") in precisely this sense, in this short, untitled poem:

> God never planted a garden
> But He placed a keeper there;
> And the keeper ever razed the ground
> And built a city where
> God cannot walk at the eve of day,
> Nor take the morning air. (Greene 182)

"Substitution" suggests (as "Love and Gardens" argues explicitly) that we who embrace the power of the imagination and of creativity can plant gardens, much as God does—but it is our responsibility to "keep" them, for His pleasure (she might say), but also for our own sake. "God never planted a garden" gives voice to her belief that we humans have made a mess of every place where we have set foot on this planet. But this traditional pastoral trope—setting the natural, peaceful garden in opposition to the artificial, unhealthy city—in the context of Spencer's life and oeuvre, must also be understood to encompass a condemnation of the racist, sexist, and other unjust (and artificial) limitations that the social world places upon people's lives.

Greene's biography explains that, although it is nowhere visible in the poem itself, the "noisy peopled room" to which Spencer refers recalls for her the "courtroom . . . where she witnessed the trial of a black preacher accused of murder[ing]" a young girl "out of passion" (102). Greene does not specify the race of the murder victim, but he does indicate that the trial was "farcical"; in any case, if a black man, accused of a crime of any sort, was facing the "justice" of a Southern court of law in the 1920s (or earlier), we may be certain that race was at stake—and given the nature of the crime, gender was as well. That Spencer retrospectively keys the poem to this moment supports my reading of it as a poem in which she doubly models her philosophy of the kinds of work—physical and imaginative—that must be undertaken by those who share her commitment to social equality (especially the black community in which she lived and worked). The poem enacts what poetry can do: namely, provide a space for envisioning the kind of world (or "sacred place") one wants to inhabit. It doubles as testimony to our ability to create such a world by representing that world as a "garden" that we must "keep"—marking gardening, like poetry, as an artistic practice that serves as a model for how to create "the green places in the universal soul" (Anne Spencer Papers, "Love and Gardens").

IN 1929, ONE OF Spencer's very few published prose pieces appeared in the *Crisis*: a review of her friend Georgia Douglas Johnson's third book of poems, *An Autumn Love Cycle*. Of the five paragraphs comprising the review, Spencer devotes the first two primarily to venting her frustration over the pressures racism put on African American poetry. An extended quote is called for:

> Within the last ten years, Georgia Douglas Johnson has, through her publishers, brought out three volumes of lyrics, most of which employ— next to food—the oldest theme in the world, and would exquisitely complement a musical setting, here, too, in this united estate of America, where it is decidedly against the law,—Dred Scott, Monroe Doctrine or, maybe, some unwritten cartel of Marque and Reprisal,—for any person of color to write of love without hypothecating atavistic jungle tones: the rumble of tom-tom, voodoo ebo, fetish of sagebrush and high spliced palm tree—all the primal universal passions often solely associated with Africa,—
>
> Pardon, I did intend writing about Mrs. Johnson's latest book, *An Autumn Love Cycle*, but any digression is logical in an atmosphere where even an offering on the shrine of Parnassus must meet the agony challenge: Aha! It is white. . . . How important! Lo, it is black! Alas! (87)

In her characteristically witty and bluntly playful prose, Spencer constructs Johnson's book as an anomaly and, virtually, an act of courage. She spends the first few lines of the review's Faulknerian-before-the-fact opening sentence fragment making an elegantly oblique allusion to Shakespeare's *Twelfth Night* ("If music be the food of love, play on"), thus simultaneously displaying her credentials as a reviewer and placing Johnson's love poetry in a long, valued tradition of literature on "the oldest theme in the world." As Spencer casts it, Johnson has dared to write about love without cloth the theme in the primitivist racial garb so popular with many (white) readers—an act that must be against some U.S. law.[23] Spencer takes the occasion of the review to offer a brief critical analysis of how racism had shaped the reception of African American writing during the Renaissance period. The first paragraph, with its disdainful list of primitivist images alluding to poems such as Cullen's "Heritage," among others, criticizes the market forces encouraging African American writers to write in a clearly racially marked way; however, Spencer should not be understood as condemning all poetry that deals in themes and subjects particular to African American culture, across the board. Her point, as she makes clear early in the subsequent paragraph, is rather that African American poets are caught in a catch-22: on the one hand, racial images that corroborate certain white stereotypes of blackness are especially marketable; but, on the other hand, any writing that is "black" is—"Alas!"—clearly not, as she says, "important."

This dilemma exacerbated for Spencer the challenges of writing as a black woman and "social heretic" in the small southern city of Lynchburg, Virginia. She points at her problem in the biographical statement she wrote for Cullen's *Caroling Dusk*, which concludes: "I write about some of the things I love. But have no civilized articulation for the things I hate" (47). These sentences are often quoted as support for reading Spencer's poetry as "raceless"; according to this reasoning, her love for nature and her garden find expression in her poems and her hatred of racism remains unarticulated therein.[24] Certainly, an *uncivilized* articulation of her critique of racism and sexism, in her poetry, would have made her family's existence in Lynchburg a good deal less comfortable—without, perhaps, the offsetting chance of effecting positive change in the life of her community, as when the letter-writing campaign she organized led to the hiring of black teachers. But given Spencer's penchant for hyperbolic, tongue-in-cheek humor in her prose (on display even in the short excerpt from her book review), we might be safe in not taking her assertion *too* literally. Moreover, the conflation of "the things I love" almost wholly with nature ignores the immediately following claim, with which she concludes her biographical statement: "I proudly love being a Negro woman—its [sic] so involved and interesting. *We* are the PROBLEM— the great national game of TABOO" (47). "Being a Negro woman" is one "of the things [she] love[d]," and she did indeed write about it, in ways that at times shed light on "[h]ow . . . it feel[s] to be a problem," to refer-ence and reframe her friend W. E. B. Du Bois's famous question, as she arguably does herself.[25] If "the PROBLEM" is "the color line," African American women—their bodies, to be precise—were situated at, made to constitute, that line (initially by the law that made slave status a matri-lineal legacy). Spencer both respects and transgresses the "TABOO" against referencing this "PROBLEM" in "Lines to a Nasturtium," as I read it.

That poem represents perhaps the most striking example of Spen-cer's need for and discovery of a "civilized" language with which to cre-ate poetry about the ways in which the things she loved and the things she hated were bound up together—and the ways she thought about the struggle to disentangle them. She found in her knowledge of the natural world a language for thinking about race and racism (as inflected by gen-der and sexism) and the potential means of eradicating those forms of oppression that was then unprecedented within the (African) American tradition. By taking the workings of the natural world not as symbols, but as signs, Spencer discovered a way to make poetry a space for addressing her "spiritual and cultural needs" and, by extension, those of other Afri-can Americans like her. She writes about her understanding of nature as a poetic language in this untitled poem:

> Earth, I thank you
> for the pleasure of your language
> You've had a hard time
> bringing it to me
> from the ground
> to grunt thru the noun
> To all the way
> feeling   seeing   smelling   touching
> —awareness
> I am here! (Greene 197)

This poem points to nature as an organic process of becoming that is (like) the way new ideas take shape in language (the verbs of change sometimes having a difficult time of breaking "thru the noun" of some hegemonic order). The speaker—Spencer—learns from watching seeds "grunt" their way into mature plants how to articulate in her poems the fact that "I am here!"

Ultimately, I regard Spencer's black aesthetics as innovative not only for the fresh rhythmic choices she made in her free verse pieces, her deeply compressed lines, or her bold adoption of male personas—though these elements of her aesthetics also distinguish her from her predecessors and many of her peers. Still, her signal innovation is taking images of the natural world—living images grounded in the patterns of flora and fauna she had observed daily for years, rather than in static Romantic tropes— and politicizing them. She uses them not to protest oppression, but to interrogate its character, providing readers a range of aestheticized ways of conceptualizing the racial and gender politics that permeate American society. Spencer's work thus manifests a black aesthetics that responds to needs in addition to those of denouncing racism and producing positive depictions of blacks, needs that are no less vital for African Americans. It also challenges us to further reconsider constructions of the New Negro Renaissance, recalling that Afro-modernity in the South was not predicated upon a wholesale removal from the natural world to an urban-industrial one, but was signaled instead, perhaps, by the precious acquisition of a garden of one's own.

FIVE

BLACK AND GREEN
On the Nature of Ed Roberson's Poetics

AS MY DISCUSSION OF Anne Spencer's work demonstrated, when we talk or write about "nature" in the context of the U.S., race, gender, and class issues are deeply implicated. The focus in Spencer's poetry on gardens has been alternately dismissed and defended on the grounds of gender, as critics either condescendingly excused New Negro Renaissance women poets for choosing "genteel" subjects or pointed out the ways appearing to conform to feminine norms could accommodate "coded" treatment of purportedly masculine topics. At the same time, her poetry foregrounding flora and fauna has been characterized as "race-less," a discourse that supports the equation between black nationalism and the black male figure, on the one hand, and the one between African American experience and urban life that begins around World War I and becomes increasingly prevalent over the twentieth century. Spencer's black aesthetics are gendered, like those of the poets I discussed in part I, but where Brooks, Sanchez, and Mullen open the masculinist tradition of the epic for the concerns of those excluded from masculinity (women and gays), Spencer shows us how the feminized theme of nature can be the locus of powerful critiques of both racism and sexism.

Unlike Spencer, Ed Roberson has not seen his poetry sidelined because of his gender. But like her, Roberson has chosen to negotiate the perceived distance between "black poetry" and "nature poetry." This perception of dichotomy between the two categories—which has only recently begun to break down and thus characterizes the context in which Roberson has written for the bulk of his career—turns largely on a related, long-standing dichotomy between "political poetry" and "nature poetry." From the perspective of the literary establishment, the former is typically seen as a lesser, degraded type of work in comparison to poetry taking up the time-honored theme of nature; at the same time, from the perspective of an embattled African American community (literary and otherwise), greatly influenced by the aesthetics privileged by the Black Arts Movement, poetry that is not political is often seen as not relevant to the needs of the people. African American poets with an inclination to feature nonhuman aspects of nature prominently in their work have accordingly faced a decision entailing, as constructed, questions of ethics and identity.

Lucille Clifton's "surely i am able to write poems" enacts this dilemma, for example. Her would-be nature poem's flowing lines of landscape description falter when she comes to the image of "'trees wav[ing] their knotted branches,'" because she discovers abruptly, "under that poem," there "always" seems to be "an other poem" (ll. 8, 10–11). What remains unspoken in the poem is the unbidden, but irrepressible association for Clifton of knots and trees with lynching, revealing how the landscape itself is racialized and why this makes writing poems about "nature" potentially a different matter for those who have been "othered" in American society. Nikki Giovanni's 1968 poem "For Saundra" performs this type of dilemma, though its ending differs from Clifton's in a way that reflects the distinct times in which the two poems were written (Clifton's was published in 2004) and the poets' somewhat diverging emphases. Finding that the paucity of opportunities to observe nature in Harlem foiled her efforts to describe it in a poem, Giovanni's speaker wonders whether she'd be better off to "clean [her] gun," because "perhaps these are not poetic / times / at all" (322). Despite the differences between the poems, both make the point that certain aspects of African American experience—historically and contemporarily—present obstacles to the creation of nature poetry by African American poets.[1]

But the political issues that African American poets address are almost always bound up with one or more of the themes considered properly "poetic," including love, loss, family, beauty, and, indeed, nature. Taking even Amiri Baraka's (in)famously provocative poem "Black Art" as an example, we can easily identify loss (of power, of cultural unity) as a central concern, and we note that the poem constitutes, in a sense, an argument for seeing certain kinds of violence as acts of racial self-love (142–43).[2] Moreover, the opening lines call for poems to be worthwhile in the way that "teeth or trees or lemons piled / on a step" are: which is to say, arguably, by being *natural* and necessary to one's survival (ll. 2–3). The inability or unwillingness of many critics to grant this level of abstraction to poems grounded in African American opposition to national and global racism (and sexism and classism) suggests that underlying the concerns about the appropriate subjects of poetry is a deeper resistance to politics as inherently antithetical to art and aesthetics. Harryette Mullen has observed that "[w]hether one's perspective is the white-dominated mainstream of U.S. poetry, or the white-dominated avant-garde, whose U.S.

members see themselves as part of a historically international aesthetic tendency, the work of black poets tends to be excluded or marginalized in relation to some other practice of poetry that is regarded as more purely concerned with aesthetic matters" ("Incessant" 207–08). The insistence upon protecting poetry's aesthetic purity from the (racialized) taint of political issues and sociohistorical contexts can be seen as a futile—if ideologically powerful—attempt to construct a binary opposition between inextricably related categories.[3] The dichotomization of "political poetry" and "nature poetry" should be understood as a particular instantiation of the larger divide that has been articulated between politics and aesthetics.

In her poem, Clifton defends herself against criticism of the rarity in her oeuvre of poems intended primarily to celebrate the beauties of nature. It calls our attention to the fact that American racism has politicized the landscape in ways that seem inescapable to the poet whose current social condition consistently points toward the history beneath its picturesque surfaces. The poem skillfully suggests that the language almost in and of itself begins to exhume the memory of lynching, a history that the typical nature poem buries "under" its images of beauty. In other words, the political associations embedded in both our language and our landscapes create inescapable connections between "nature poetry" and "political poetry"—not only, but perhaps especially, in the eyes of readers and writers who are constructed as "other" to the normative American.

Thus, between oft-imposed stereotypes and frequently embraced ideologies, the "African American nature poet" has come to be seen by most as an anomaly—if he or she is seen at all. As a result, critical invisibility has been too nearly Ed Roberson's fate for the whole three decades of his career. Beginning in 1970, with the release of *When Thy King Is a Boy*, Roberson has published nine books of conceptually challenging, syntactically complex poems. Like Spencer, he assigns the natural world a conspicuous centrality throughout his work. He consistently draws upon nature, as theme and as image, perhaps more than any other source of subject or metaphor. Even the cover art of his books announces this preoccupation unmistakably, nearly all of them featuring outdoor images such as seashores, cliffs, open plains, and vast, cloud-thick skies. And, though it need not follow directly from this that Roberson would be largely ignored by the critical establishment, I find it striking that the scholarship on his work, to date, consists primarily of a tiny group of recently published essays, a smattering of book reviews, and the brief introductions to two of the collections. This level of scholarly neglect is all the more incredible in light of the evidence of his poetry's recognized merit: even his earliest books were released by a well-respected publisher (University of Pittsburgh Press); two of the later collections are prize-winning (in the National Poetry Series and the Iowa Poetry Prize competitions); and one of those, *Atmosphere Conditions*, was also shortlisted for the Academy of American Poets' Lenore Marshall Poetry Prize, which is awarded for the best book of poetry published in a given year. Roberson himself received a Lila Wallace Reader's Digest Writers' Award in 1998 and the Poetry Society of America's Shelley Memorial Award in 2008.

Of course, it would be an oversimplification to say that Roberson's pervasive attention to nature is the sole reason that he has been understudied by critics of African American and American poetry alike. His aesthetic—a demanding, disjunctive, associative style of moving among ideas and images—and his race have also presumably been factors contributing to his being neglected by critics working in both traditions, whether formalist, modernist, or postmodernist in their preferences. In an essay published in 2000, George Hart accurately asserted that "[p]ost-modernist poetry does not find much acceptance or generate much interest among readers of nature poetry and ecologically oriented critics" (315); this exclusion of innovative poetics from "the green canon" is exacerbated in Roberson's case by the equally conspicuous absence of African American poets in collections and criticism of nature poetry and nature writing more broadly.[4] The relationship of "nature" poetry to "experimental" poetry, on one hand, and to African American ("political") poetry, on the other, has changed markedly in the past few years, however, as I have been working on this study.

As the study of environment and literature has become a field unto itself, bringing the terms "ecocriticism" and "ecopoetics," among others, into common usage, it has also grown to accommodate a diverging (and sometimes competing) set of texts, foci, and methodologies under its umbrella. Some of these privilege avant-garde aesthetics (as evidenced by the poetry found in the journal *ecopoetics* and the essays collected in *The Eco Language Reader*, edited by Jonathan Skinner and Brenda Iijima, respectively); others privilege the perspectives of African Americans and other people of color (manifested, for example, in the poetry anthology *Black Nature*, edited by Camille Dungy, and the essay collection *The Environmental Justice Reader*, edited by Joni Adamson, Mei Mei Evans, and Rachel Stein). Overlap between the constituencies of the two groups represented by these publications—if not their contributors—constitutes the third leg of the triangle that has begun to bring Roberson's work into focus.[5]

Still, the criticism on Roberson has not caught up to these shifts (in part because it has about forty years of catching up to do), and I would argue that what makes his work so fascinating is the intersection in his poetry of precisely the three factors that combined to render Roberson invisible for so long: his subject, his aesthetics, and his racial identity. Roberson confutes the dilemma I have discussed here: the false dichotomy that says poets, especially African American poets, have to choose between writing about nature and writing about sociopolitical subjects.[6] This is not to criticize Clifton and others who rightfully identify and understandably respond to the powerful ideology that normalizes the racially inflected nature/politics binary. Nonetheless, I see it as equally important for us to pay attention to the ways Roberson's poetry negates the supposed opposition between the natural world and the sociopolitical (human) world. Specifically, he uses his distinctive poetics, including an unpredictably disrupted and disruptive hypotactic phrasing, to illustrate not merely the interrelation, but the *identity*, of the natural and the political realms. His subject position as an African American conduces to the urgency and shape of this project.

To better understand the significance of Roberson's work, we must situate it, briefly, with regard to the expanding "green canon," particularly British Romantic poetry and the contemporary American poetry that continues and diverges from that tradition under any number of potential banners, including "nature poetry," "environmental poetry," "green poetry," "ecopoetry," and "ecopoetics."[7] In this rough schema, Romantic poetry, written notably by such poets as William Wordsworth, Percy Bysshe Shelley, and John Keats, responded philosophically and aesthetically to the social tumults of the French and Industrial revolutions by turning a nostalgic eye toward the shrinking English countryside. From the disturbing chaos and growing unfamiliarity of new societal arrangements brought rapidly into place, these paradigmatic poets (like Henry David Thoreau, in the later period of American Romanticism) sought refuge and spiritual nurturance in visiting and contemplating those places that were relatively unpeopled: the tangled woods, the austere mountains, the depthless lakes. This was a different nature than the neatly cultivated gardens on the classical model that had previously been preferred; "nature" for the Romantic poets was "wild" and "spontaneous," even as it represented "the simple" and, implicitly, the primitive (Lovejoy 13). Max Oelschlaeger describes their philosophical position in this way:

> [T]hey believed that God's presence was revealed through an aesthetic awareness of nature's beauty. . . . The poetic view of nature gravitated to-

ward its wild and mysterious aspects, the felt qualitative rather than measured quantitative dimensions of experience known through immediate
contact rather than through [scientific] experimentation. Feeling instead
of thinking, and concrete emotion rather than abstract conception, were
the essence of the Romantic awareness of nature. (99)

Through immersion in nature, one obtained divine guidance and could
be healed of the spiritual sickness produced by the unhealthy instabil-
ity and increasing materialism of industrialized human society. Nature
is glorified in this tradition, but in opposition—and in service—to the
human. In this, the Romantic poets were of their era: if natural resources
were there for the use of industry in production, the natural realm served
the poet in his search for (human) Self through the contemplation of the
(natural) Other.

There are strong traces of this Romanticism in some contemporary
American poetry featuring "nature," as Bernard Quetchenbach, among
others, would have it (2). The lineage of this "neoromantic" poetry can
be seen in its tendency to consider "the physical creation as significant in
its own right, essentially independent of human culture" (Bryson 2–7;
Quetchenbach 8). Even as one moves along the spectrum toward writers
of environmentally aware, ecologically grounded poetry—from Mary
Oliver toward Gary Snyder, for example—one still finds the work reiterating the dichotomy between the so-called natural and human worlds,
despite the poets' recognition of its artificiality and their rejection of the
Romantic poets' subject/object (Self/Other) relationship to nature.
Subscribing to an ecological model grounded in the interdependence of
culture and nature, rather than casting humans as master over (or even
steward of) the natural realm, nonetheless maintains a binary framework. These poets, whose work is sometimes called "ecopoetry," can be
distinguished from another group of poets whose embrace of the very
similar term "ecopoetics" is meant to signify a very different aesthetic approach to environmentally engaged poetry. Poets in the avant-garde community creating such work have gathered under the latter term (though
sometimes as dissidents), claiming it for those who are critical of the way
"the environmental movement . . . has protected a fairly received notion
of 'eco' from the proddings and complications, and enrichments, of an
investigative poetics" (Skinner 7). Some poets and theorists writing under this heading tend to draw an equation between avant-garde poetics
(for its radical openness), environmental awareness (interdisciplinarity
manifested via poetic process), and political efficacy (work that does not

reinforce the status quo) and, moreover, to exclude from "ecopoetics" any ecologically oriented poetry that does not evidence a particular set of aesthetic/political values.[8] From this angle, these proponents of "ecopoetics" are ironically reminiscent of those participants in the BAM who similarly advocated a particular, politicized, potentially transformative aesthetics as the grounds for inclusion in a category of poetry—in that case, "black poetry."[9]

Roberson's poetry is most like the work in this category of "ecopoetics," though it retains a greater affiliation with the lyric than much of the work published in *ecopoetics* or the 2008 special feature on "Ecopoetics" in *HOW2*, a journal devoted to innovative writing by women. However, its challenging syntactic structures, communicated in part through idiosyncratic visual cues, mark it as innovative in ways uniquely his own, but influenced by BAM poets, poets publishing in LeRoi and Hettie Jones's *Yugen*, Black Mountain poets, and other experimentalist African American poets who, like Roberson himself, were "changed by," but not full participants in the Movement, such as Clarence Major and A. B. Spellman (Roberson, "structure" 765). In terms of its take on nature, in particular, I argue that, as an oeuvre, Roberson's work is especially important and unusual insofar as it consistently deconstructs the concept of an opposition between human culture and the natural world, to the point of destabilizing the fundamental dualism that underlies representations of them as two parts of a whole.

Roberson's poetry successfully mounts this challenge to our ways of thinking in part because it is neither primarily concerned with a critique of the negative impact of human societies upon the environment nor is it devoted to a Romantic idealization of nature's awesome beauties. As different as they may otherwise be, both of these frameworks rely upon the same division between human activities and other goings-on on the globe. Roberson's poems instead construct a world out of his experiences and concerns in which the urban and domestic spaces created by humankind are part and parcel of the various kinds of spaces created by other forces, animate and inanimate, across the earth. He studies the ecosystem of the Alaskan wilderness with the same perceptive attention he gives to the ecosystems of Pittsburgh, where he grew up, or central New Jersey, where he lived and worked for decades. His poems describe such environments with insightful detail, using a range of innovative and time-tested poetic techniques to portray the earth's workings without excepting humans and our habitats from it.

Significantly, Roberson's approach to nature poetry is a very conscious one, partly grounded in his desire to respond to the same racist ideology that inspired Clifton's poem. In an interview with Kathleen Crown, Roberson explains, "I wanted to hit something with the nature poem. In the sixties, people were saying that black folks didn't write nature poems. As a matter of fact, Nikki Giovanni has a hilarious nature poem. But they were always saying, black folks don't have this, black folks don't have that" (Roberson, "Down" 679). As already discussed in this study, of course, some of the "people . . . saying that black folks didn't write nature poems" were black folks. What was implicit during the New Negro Renaissance of the 1920s and 1930s became programmatic, for some, during the 1960s and 1970s Black Arts Movement: that modern, progressive blackness could and should be equated with the black culture that developed in urban, industrial areas like Harlem, Chicago, and Newark. The Black Aesthetic that has become most familiar to scholars and readers rejected poetic contemplation of trees or meadows as falling outside of "the black experience" or, more damning, as delusional in the face of the political urgencies facing black people.

That said, Roberson's intent in writing poems like "The Nature Poem" (in *Etai-Eken*) was explicitly to challenge the racism underlying both the view that African American experience could not be effectively mapped onto the "universal" theme of nature *and* the view that African American poetry was "simple," as opposed to being multilayered and, moreover, containing levels of philosophical abstraction ("Down" 661, 679–80). If such poems also spoke back to African Americans who turned what racists viewed as lack into a badge of honor, all the better. In fewer than twenty lines, "The Nature Poem" manages to gather a wide range of images including a pencil, a setting sun, Dorothy's house from *The Wizard of Oz*, and black panthers (at once the two-legged and the four-legged variety) and make a claim for them all as nature. He speaks with obvious (and merited) satisfaction about another self-described "nature poem"— "Properties," a section from his long poem "The Aerialist Narratives"—in which, he says, "I'm describing black folks' history but I'm actually describing water going through different states—water as liquid, water as steam" ("Down" 661). With "Properties," he reports, he was able "to make a nature poem that would actually *be* black folks' history" ("Down" 661; emphasis in original).

Although one scholar has warned that "the identification of the human and the nonhuman" is not necessary (and may be antithetical) to an environmental ethic (Gilcrest 6), I see significant value in Roberson's "postmodernist attempt . . . to reveal that nature is culture and culture nature" (Hart 320).[10] To preserve such binaries as human/nonhuman, especially when this distinction was for long years used to justify the enslavement of African (American)s as chattel, is to undergird an ideology that is dangerous, at best.[11] African American poets, like Clifton, have consistently questioned such binaries and the kinds of violence they underwrite. Roberson's work dismisses the divide between human and nonhuman ecosystems outright, in at least two ways. First, his poetry keeps an eye trained on the politicization of "the natural." By this I mean two things: on one hand, the ways the places we see (or don't) and beings we encounter (or don't) are constructed in political terms and, on the other hand, the ways behaviors that have been shaped by custom, culture, expediency, and other politically informed motivations are deemed "natural." Second, his poetry calls attention repeatedly to the ways in which our species is subject to the same "natural laws" as all other beings on the planet. In the remainder of this chapter, I offer and analyze some contextualized examples from Roberson's poetry that illustrate these points. In so doing, I flesh out the significance of race in the creation and interpretation of his particular type of ecopoetics and demonstrate the ways in which his particular brand of black aesthetics both calls for and facilitates his efforts to portray an undivided (natural) world.

IRONICALLY, ROBERSON'S poems remind us how much we have racialized not just our cities and other developed spaces, but the whole globe, because he writes so frequently and concretely about locations, creatures, and the like that are raced "white" or, at the very least, that are not coded "black." Though African American poetry is not generally associated with nature poetry, as I have noted, there are nonetheless a few "recognizably black" modes of writing about what we call "nature" within the African American tradition, the most common of which focuses on the agrarian South. Jean Toomer's *Cane* is exemplary of this mode of black nature writing, which tends to emphasize the deep connection African Americans have had to the land, in part a legacy of U.S. plantation slavery. In *Cane*, the black women seem to grow out of the soil like tomato vines and black men take shape through the back-breaking labor of the plow. Langston Hughes, though usually associated with the ultraurban space of Harlem, has written vividly and skillfully about the landscape of rural Kansas, the state where he grew up. His novel *Not without Laughter* can be seen as an offshoot of the tradition Toomer's work represents, insofar as the land and weather play a major role in the survival of the African American community he depicts. Elizabeth Schultz's essay on the novel discusses the way Hughes draws upon the weather, seasons, and agricultural work common in his childhood environment to symbolize his critique of white economic exploitation of blacks and to mediate his protagonist's sexual coming-of-age story in a manner acceptable to his conservative middle-class readership.

Another common type of "recognizably black" nature writing might aptly be called "Afro-Romantic" writing. By this I refer to the romanticized portrayals of African landscapes typified by Countee Cullen's poem "Heritage." This type of writing emerges from a longing for a connection to Africa that would mitigate the psychic and social damage caused initially by the Middle Passage and perpetuated by African Americans' status as second-class or marginalized citizens of the U.S.; it also manifests a desire to counter the negative constructions of Africa in Western ideology. The tendency of Cullen's poem to paint the picture of Africa with the broad brush of stereotypically exotic (and not particularly fact-based) images—"Copper sun," "Jungle star," or "Spicy grove, cinnamon tree"—characterizes the Afro-Romantic category of work (157–58).[12]

By contrast to both of these more familiar modes of African American nature writing, Roberson often features wilderness in his poems, especially the cold, icy, "white" wilderness of Alaska, as well as the Andean and Amazonian wilds of South America. His relationship to the land is not primarily that of the agricultural laborer (or the descendent of such laborers), nor that of the exile yearning for an impossible return to the motherland, but that of the adventurer and the student of biology and other natural sciences. Even the briefest sketch of Roberson's biography makes clear that the path that led him to writing ecologically grounded poetry unfolded organically. In college, he focused on limnology (the study of lakes and other freshwater bodies) and held a work-study job on a "game preserve and research station" in a remote, wooded area of northern Pennsylvania (Roberson, "structure" 766; Roberson, "Down" 655). These experiences led him to travel, and within the span of approximately four years, Roberson had been to explore and research in Alaska (Afognak Island, in particular), Bermuda, Peru, and Ecuador ("Down" 656). His travels included "a visit . . . to West Africa, and two climbing trips in 1963 and 1975 with the Explorer's Club of Pittsburgh to the . . . Andes and to the Amazon jungle" in South America (Edwards, "Black" 624). Pursuits such as wilderness hiking adventures and limnography are not popularly associated with African Americans or even blacks more generally—despite the achievement of Matthew Henson as one among the first group of people to reach the North Pole. By writing poetry that

draws upon his experiences of places and roles in which he does not "belong," Roberson not only challenges persisting racial stereotypes (such
as those that make him a seemingly unlikely candidate for exploring the
Amazon), but also provokes us to awareness of the racialization, and thus
politicization, of what we think of as the nonhuman world.

These places Roberson has explored and studied are not densely
populated or heavily developed (for residential, commercial, or industrial purposes). Yet he often writes about them in ways that deemphasize
their remove from the urban or domestic spaces more familiar to most
of us (a mode at least partly facilitated by what Lawrence Buell would
call his "place-attachments," which in Roberson's case are unusually diverse and wide-ranging).[13] For example, in "kenai lake alaska," a poem
from *When Thy King Is a Boy*, Roberson uses unstable present and past
tenses, hypotactic sentence fragments, and indentation to share with the
reader his fitfully palimpsestic vision of Kenai Lake over the streets of
Pittsburgh. The poem begins with description of the Alaskan landscape
that unfolds as if it were present before the poet's eyes, only to shift with
an indented stanza to the poet's recollection of his presence in an urban
environment:

lakes so long that they upend into
some ridged wave   there in that moment
tall enough to crest the sun's last rays
when all the other waters lay in darkness.
valleys deep enough the clouds that set
their rainfeet in the bottom grass can stare
only the broadways that the gamest eagles
dare   face to face to watch themselves
        upon the mountain
fine as a fog drop   work their way again
(as in a dream before their own huge eye)
        into a thunderhead . . .

        what was i remembering
        the avenue extends across the street
        and goes uphill only a couple of blocks. (12)

Roberson drops us right in the middle of a vision of lakes, mountains,
valleys, eagles, and clouds—a vision that refigures the mundane propor-
tions of the cityscape into the sublime scale of the Kenai Peninsula's ter-

rain. The complicated syntax slows us down to a pace appropriate to the majesty of this memory and leads us into a feeling of disorientation at the stanza shift that is not unlike the speaker's.

We, like the speaker, see the Alaskan scene superimposed upon the Pittsburgh scene—but not to construct them as opposites. Though the differences between the two scenes are foregrounded at the beginning, the poem moves steadily away from a romanticized portrayal of the Kenai Lake area. The next two stanzas reveal that first the gold rush and later the U.S. army brought men to the work in these mountains. Rather than finding themselves in an Edenic situation, men from both groups faced intense dangers. One danger for the original miners was "the current   monster" that might suddenly "swallow the ship" waiting to carry the mined gold to market (13). Six decades later, the soldiers on leave who drove down from their camps to work the same mines encountered terrifying isolation:

> i got really scared
> to think that i had been gone months
> someone could be really sick and days
> someone back home be hurt and days
> i could die and days
> days would pass before the flood of incidents ran off
> and left my body days old anywhere. (14)

Rather than set up a dichotomy between natural paradise and urban menace, Roberson depicts both places as sites of troubles that encourage drinking and other escapist behavior. He also connects and likens the two locations through aural imagery. Ostensibly sitting in a bar, the speaker again becomes disoriented. He begins, inexplicably, to experience the bar as a "boat" that is "rock[ing]," and says: "down in this hold the animals lean out their stalls / and roar / and now / it comes / to me. (the music) i remember" (13). The roaring of the animals, which appear to sense the dangerous shift of the lake's current, forms a mental and emotional link with the music playing in the bar—music that may well be the fearful and angry "roar" of human animals, descendents of Africans who also suffered through storms in the hold of a boat. The final image, the speaker's anxious need to "back . . . away / from whatever hole   i hear opening in the floor," echoes the poem's earlier reference to the lake's destruction of the ore-laden boats as "gold . . . thrown in / to the same old hole" (14, 13). The poem teaches us to see the political implications of the ways some humans respond to our environments: the fear, greed, and thoughtlessness lead to similarly exploitative situations, whether we are plundering gold from the mountains of Alaska or "black gold" from sub-Saharan Africa. By eschewing the requirements of linear narrative for a more fluid poetics, Roberson is able to deconstruct the natural/urban dichotomy, drawing not just parallels, but connections.

Indeed, one of the marks of Roberson's status as a nature poet is the extent to which his innovative poetics emerges from his experience and study of the way elements and creatures move through the world. The idea that Roberson's poetics might have, in part, such a source reminded me of Brenda Hillman's 2001 collection of poems, *Cascadia*, and her "poetic statement" about writing them.[14] *Cascadia*'s poems are spatially uninhibited and syntactically complex, using the margins of the page and parataxis to communicate interconnections across great distances and vast periods of time. They address changes in the lives of people and in the land called California, likening the process of recovering from drug addiction to the intense shifts in the earth's crust that produced the Coast Ranges. About her "California Geological Syntax," she writes: "The use of 'unnatural syntax' can be seen to come from 'nature.' . . . The rocks that form the crusty edges of California started in the obscure south and are inching up the coastline on their own plate at their own pace like a different tradition. It's not mainland granite—it is its own movement. But it's still granite" ("Twelve" 279). Hillman's engagement of five thousand years of geology in the form of *Cascadia*'s poems highlights the potential for meaningful variance in a nature-based approach to form.

Roberson had been thinking in analogous terms in 1970, I am persuaded, when he published "kenai lake alaska" and the other poems in *When Thy King Is a Boy*. An ars poetica that appears toward the end of the collection, entitled "jacket," makes explicit his recourse to natural models for his formal and syntactic choices. It begins:

> many of these poems attempt to make
> happen to words   that which happens
> to lines
>
>   in an optical illusion
> many of these lines have.   that.
>
> kind of architecture of
> things which live   in the sea

they are built
,without a base
beginning above
the ordinary ground of the mind
and ending   there in
illusion (60)

The result of modeling one's poetics upon the "architecture of / things
which live   in the sea," he continues, is a kind of "concretize[d] . . .
suspension" that becomes so paradoxically "solid . . . that chaos is the real
ground" (60, 61). Roberson's employment of space within the line and
his nonstandard, inconsistent use of punctuation are two of the means
by which he can emphasize productive ambiguity in the language of his
poems and the sources upon which he draws. The chaotic terrain he
creates based on this natural, aquatic model becomes a place where, as
in "kenai lake," one can occupy Alaska, Pennsylvania, and West Africa
simultaneously.

The architecture of the sea is not the only "natural" structural model
operating in Roberson's poetry. In *Lucid Interval as Integral Music* (published first as a chapbook in 1985 and reprinted in 1995 in *Voices Cast Out
to Talk Us In*), a long poem made up of multiple numbered and/or titled
sections, Roberson writes the majority of the sections in a form he calls
"the lena / after my daughter" (*Voices* 5). One line short of a sonnet, its
music is nothing like rhymed iambic pentameter—rather its rhythms are
the "rhythms that an infant's limitations   period by need" (63). That
is to say, the endlessly varying line lengths and the shifting mix of hypotactic and paratactic phrasing are determined by the thoughts that can
coalesce, the words that can be jotted down, in the moments between his
fathering duties (63). As Crown has observed, Roberson makes us aware
that, by giving her name "to his book's aesthetics of fragment, suspension,
interruption, and accident," his "infant daughter does violence to verse—
breaking it with her needy demands and 'her [diaper] changing'—yet
she is the tune he picks up" ("Reading" 209). The challenging "unnatural
syntax" of *Lucid Interval* "can be seen to come from 'nature,'" as with Hillman's *Cascadia*. The phenomenon Roberson focuses on—his baby's cyclical needs—is of a different magnitude than the geological movements
that Hillman registers in her poems, but of the same general type. In both
cases, the rhythm is dictated by what we might call "natural law": human
intervention cannot control, but only negotiate—or, at best, influence—
the tempo at which these phenomena operate. As if to emphasize how

little power he has over his daughter's biology, Roberson casts her metaphorically in cosmic terms:

here she is I will have to
hold   on a minute tell you her line.

a scribble
the universe and planets holes and scribbles
pure
interruption . . . (*Voices* 5)

"[H]er line," he warns us, is "a scribble"—which is to say, nonlinear—but
not necessarily a diminutive one. The next line of the poem resituates her
scribble from the intimacy of the poet's desk in the domestic space to
the infinite reaches of outer space, where entities like black holes possess
a gravitational pull not unlike a baby's. If the Pencil Nebula can be said
to produce intergalactic "scribbles" ("Pencil Nebula" [NASA website]),
then for Roberson the infant is "pure interruption" in the manner of a
supernova, and "the lena" is a form that registers such discontinuities,
rather than masking them.

The superterranean realms of air and space are increasingly featured
in Roberson's work, as in his long poem "The Aerialist Narratives," also
published in *Voices Cast Out to Talk Us In*, and in the poem sequence
Atmosphere Conditions, published in 2000.[15] Two poems from the latter
collection—one featuring this cosmographic aspect of nature, another
returning us to terra firma and, more specifically, to Alaska—will help
me illustrate the second way that Roberson's work militates against the
nature/culture and nature poetry/political poetry dichotomies. Not only
does his poetry expose the politicization of areas purportedly outside the
political realm (as we saw in "kenai lake alaska"), it also reminds us how
"natural" our sociopolitical world is by resituating human interactions
within a larger context of "natural" phenomena, rather than distinguishing between these. By dismantling this nature/culture binary, Roberson
makes meaningless the injunction against writing "political poems" as
opposed to "nature poems." His political poems typically *are* nature poems (and vice versa), just as human society is a *part* of nature, rather than
adjacent to it.

This characterization of his poetry, however, cannot be used to justify
the dismissal of his work by those who dislike the stylistics often associated with the category "political poems." Rather, it gives the lie to the pre-

sumption that "political poetry" can be described in terms of any single style of writing. Edward Foster, in a review of *Voices*, offers the aesthetic pleasures of Roberson's work, like those of Nathaniel Mackey's work, as evidence that these writers' poetry surpasses that which typifies the category:

> Both are African-American writers whose work derives from the example and aesthetics of the Black Mountain School, and both are political poets insofar as the experience of being the outsider must inevitably affect one's language. But neither is *primarily* ideological; their poetry is not fundamentally prescriptive or didactic but lyrical and mythic. There is a much greater range of sensibility here than one expects in explicitly political verse. Politically driven poetry frequently acquires its power from being simply direct and unequivocal, but Roberson has much too complex a mind and sensibility for that . . . (4)

The assumption underwriting this praise for Roberson and Mackey at the expense of "political verse" is that, basically, "political" poems are typically "prescriptive or didactic," "direct and unequivocal"—and not "complex." To the contrary, these adjectives encompass only a small range of the writing that can be described as political. For instance, overtly political poems are often quite lyrical and deal in nuanced images rather than directives. (Yusef Komunyakaa's "'*You and I Are Disappearing*'" is a wonderful example of this, as is Anne Spencer's "Lines to a Nasturtium," examined in chapter 4.) Others use humor and subtext to great effect. (To begin with, think of Robert Hayden's "A Letter From Phillis Wheatley" or either of Langston Hughes's long poems, *Montage of a Dream Deferred* or *Ask Your Mama*.) Or, to take a different example, a very powerful kind of political critique can be made by raising questions and revealing ambiguities within debates that are too often constructed in terms of simple of oppositions. (Consider the Harryette Mullen poem, "Denigration," from which this study's title is derived.)

Nonetheless, Foster is right to note that Roberson is among those poets whose aesthetics value and produce formal innovations as well as emotional registers that incorporate rage and indignation without locking in on them. These qualities distinguish his work from a subset of political poetry that offers unmuted (and pointedly accurate) analysis of the social condition of African Americans; it likewise differentiates him from those "ecopoets" whose writings tend to focus their political critique on "human intervention in and instrumentalization of nature" (Slaymaker 130).

Roberson uses poetic techniques that frustrate oversimplified analyses of the operation of social and environmental systems, encouraging more nuanced understandings of our relationships with the world around us. His techniques include syntactic stammering and disruption and torrentially unpunctuated phrasing—all of which, paradoxically, require us to read and reread slowly, to consider multiple possible interpretations of lines and phrases.[16] Roberson's poetics enable him to construct complex relationships among human and nonhuman natural entities that are not merely metaphorical.

In the poem "The Wanderers," Roberson creates an intricate portrait of what homelessness means—on land and in the sky. The poem occupies nine pages, its stanzas located in varying relationships to the margins and to other stanzas, as indicated by indentation and the placement of horizontal dividing lines. It begins with four deeply indented stanzas:

> The raggedy meteor homeless
> their flashing unraveling
>
> Fortune.
>
> Wishes nullify each other in its falling
> shower.
>
> Mine   a step in the air dissolving. (*Atmosphere* 16)

Most meteors begin as meteoroid debris from a comet orbiting the sun. Meteors are the relatively small particles that have entered the earth's atmosphere and, in the process of being dragged to the ground by gravity, create enough friction to generate a glowing streak of light through the sky. Our society calls them "shooting stars"—though they are not stars at all—and there have been those among us who believe that these bright, unexpected wanderers are lucky, are to be wished upon. Roberson asks us to see them instead as "homeless" and their irregular trailing flames as "raggedy." Having thus evoked the image of the numerous homeless people walking the U.S. city streets, wearing (out) fraying, tattered clothes, Roberson is able to dismantle the romantic myth of there being something lucky about these bodies.

Like the human homeless, the meteors' existence—and thus their "Fortune"—is "unraveling" before our eyes. If we can now see that a meteor's *mis*fortune is said to be the basis upon which our desires become reality, we may recognize that the misfortune of the homeless people in urban centers throughout our nation also facilitates making the American dream come true for middle-class and wealthy members of our society. The "[w]ishes" of some are necessarily "nullify[ing]" the wishes of others: to the extent that we understand a surplus labor force to be a prerequisite for the maintenance of a capitalist economic system, we see it as inevitable that everyone who wishes it cannot be rich, or even financially secure. Roberson's use of idiosyncratic punctuation and capitalization in the first three lines invites us to identify and flesh out such commonalities between homeless bodies in the atmosphere and homeless bodies in the nation's cities.

The following section, separated from the above stanzas by a line cutting across the middle of the page, elaborates these themes. Roberson increases his use of punctuation, space, capitalization, and enjambment to fragment the lines, even as the meteor itself is fragmenting as it hurtles toward "The imposed ground" (16). The speaker articulates our unwillingness to recognize meteors and completely impoverished people for what they are: visible reminders of what it means to be *needed to be unnecessary.* He explains,

> It may be here   you don't want to
> see something through something
>
> else because you don't want to see it
> at all when it comes down
> to it (16)

Whether "here" is the crater created when a meteor "comes down / to it"—to the "imposed ground"—or the space the poem clears for us to focus on the human homeless, the speaker asserts that we are avoiding acknowledging the real intersections between these kinds of homelessness and our own lives. "Gravity," as an inexorable natural law, speaks in the "plainer language" required to pull us into the underlying significance of "what you call your metaphor" (16, 17).

Roberson pushes us past simple metaphorical relationships by conflating the "raggedy meteor" with a woman he sees in the subway:

> she was coming towards me
> through the deep erratic
> lighting of the subway tunnel

the hot pinks they wore sheaths in
in the fifties in and out
of the light the shape the hips
the small waist in the dress
up close she had no shoes
her caked feet swollen she
had ground sleep leaves in her hair
as she passed my face must have
augured her open she say
sometimes
it be's that way (18)

Roberson's alignment of the woman with the meteor is made explicit in a later section of the poem, when the speaker tells us: "... *and she's the star*" (23), a move that recycles, but arguably renews, the Romantic tradition of gendering nature as woman.[17] Roberson is calling our attention to the way we impose meaning on the world around us, by applying prescripted associations that are often wildly inaccurate or inappropriate. Looking at meteors, we fail to perceive "stars that wander   that fall / fire up and blow inside / out," but, rather, see opportunities for wishing; similarly, the silhouette of the woman is the ground upon which the speaker initially projects his culturally constructed fantasy. The unpunctuated phrasing washes us down the column of poetry with a rapidity that mimics the speed with which we fling assumptions and associations at the people and objects we encounter. Yet the tongue-twisting current of words ultimately forces us to go back and reread more carefully, in order to comprehend how the speaker's perception of the woman changes. If she is naturalized, it is not through simplistic similes, but through description of her very un–Thoreau-esque, unromanticized being-in-nature: feet "caked" with dirt, hair not *like* but containing "ground ... leaves." Roberson's poem strips away the illusions when he reveals what she looks like "up close," teaching a conceptual lesson that redeems his decision to gender the meteor feminine.

The woman's defensive remark ("sometimes / it be's that way"), rendered emphatic by the vernacular, constructs her homeless condition as randomly inevitable, not unlike the appearance of a meteor dragging its "raggedy" tail across the sky. But the poem goes on to refigure her comment as ironic, by inviting us to see that interconnected societal systems like racism and capitalism work together to create the conditions that force a portion of the population to live on the streets. The next section interrogates the notion of the cost of living, literalizing the idiom through (ex)plosive questioning:

> when location costs when
> race costs schools
> cost cost costs you
> your choice   what does this mean
> death does   to the price & not just of   real
>
> estate (20)

Roberson's enjambment makes the poem pay off even when one reads lines *against* the sense of the phrases: "cost cost costs you," taken on its own, stammers meaningfully, reinforcing the thrust of the phrases "schools / cost" and "cost costs you / your choice." Those who can pay the price of living as they desire, do so at others' expense. The poem describes the craters created by meteors' landings as "cups // that the surrounding change / falls into" (21), reconnecting the familiar request of the homeless for spare change with the crashing fall that has enabled someone else's rise. Meteors fall away from comets that have themselves been dislocated by a passing star and thrown into orbit around the sun. Whether in the atmosphere or on the earth, "homelessness" has its causes.

Like "The Wanderers," "Afognak" is a characteristically Robersonian poem, insofar as humans appear as a *part* of nature, rather than above or alongside of it. We are natural phenomena among natural phenomena. The poem's first four stanzas constitute, arguably, a single sentence that details the long-term aftermath of a volcanic explosion, during which the thick shower of ash that "settles" over the lake ultimately "purifies" it (*Atmosphere* 49). The speaker releases the description of this process in little disjointed phrases that revise the sense of the sentence as it develops, so that understandings (and temporary misunderstandings) accumulate, much like the dust expelled from the volcanoes. Just as "[t]here are islands," like Afognak (located off the southern coast of Alaska), that go through this sometimes violent, sometimes peaceful, but natural, inevitable process of change, "[t]here are fauna" that go through such processes, and "the humans / themselves" are "one" category within that group (49, 51). In the poem's final stanzas, Roberson represents our social structures as subject to dissolution and extinction in the same manner as any other natural phenomenon:

There are fauna   the humans
themselves one have fit
themselves into   systems

ideas   as niches
that give out   like races   churches
colorations of nations'

flags   mummifications
(wch if anyone's left to)   unfurl
dissolve   into that pool of mirror

thin air is   that yet
flies the blackening sun
that standard   of clarity (51)

Roberson's distinctive syntax, with its odd, piecemeal phrasing, enables him to portray the hypothesized social (r)evolution as an event that operates on the same principles as the volcanic eruption. The first stanza of this section uses line break, the absence of punctuation, and the presence or absence of spacing to locate humans inextricably within the ecology of the poem. On the same principles that govern the ecological systems around the volcano, we can see that the inevitable collapse and destruction of human institutions does the good service of extinguishing systems—of race, religion, and nationality—that are about to "give out," that have outlasted their beneficialness. Here, the political analysis does not displace the examination of the natural history of Afognak Island; rather the natural history *is* the political analysis. The poem concludes with an image of the sun, "blackening," perhaps, in the ash of an explosion like that of the volcanoes—by implication, a social explosion of people of color. The sun, however, is still flying, flag-like, as a "standard   of clarity." Whether or not we interpret that final line as ironic, the poem maintains its commitment to suspending the human within the natural and understanding the entire natural world on that basis.

I had completed the first draft of this take on Roberson's work well before the publication of his seventh collection, *City Eclogue*, in 2006. This volume, whose title alone supports the way I had been reading Roberson's oeuvre, clearly foregrounds the line of thinking that I argue he had pursued in his poetry since the publication of *When Thy King Is a Boy*, in 1970. I consider *City Eclogue* his masterwork, to date; it is and will likely remain one of the most important poems of the new century. Encompassing themes that span from the Civil Rights Movement sit-ins and gentrification to 9/11 and the aftermath of Hurricane Katrina, this collection (arguably a long poem) takes the long view on the (d)evolution of American cities. The poem "City Eclogue: Words for It" opens by acknowledging that many readers will hear the phrase "city eclogue" as an oxymoron—the "eclogue" being traditionally a pastoral poem, complete with shepherds extolling the beauties of their rural environment. "[Y]ou'd expect" for "beautifully flowering trees" to be the result of birds and seeds and soil coming together in a seemingly random way, the first stanza notes, when in fact city planners have drawn up a blueprint designating where trees should be planted by city workers who go from site to site by truck, with shovels in hand.

The second and third stanzas (below) explode the fallacy behind our assumptions, by calling attention to how language is policed in order to preserve the association between cities and artificiality:

> Where everyone is lying when it's said these words
> are not accurate, that this shit is not the flowering,
> that shit off the truck and not the gut
> bless of bird and animal dropping isn't somehow
>
> just as natural a distribution
> as the wild bloom   The trees are
> delivered in ordered speech   as is
> dirt mouth curse and graffiti
> to where the backed perches want them. (16)

These lines insist linguistically on what they argue for materially: that the beautiful and the ugly are inseparable, in urban ecosystems as in less populated ones. Roberson uses "shit" as abstracted slang ("this shit" to reference the whole process of city-arranged planting) only to repeat it in the following line in a way that reconnects it to its original referent (the "bird and animal dropping" that goes into the manure we use to fertilize the trees. There is an order to these systems of distribution that is beautiful, perhaps even divine, despite the rawness involved: in "gut / bless" we inevitably hear "god / bless," as well. The third stanza continues to extend and unfold this idea, reinvoking "shit" as profanity ("dirt mouth curse and graffiti"), but also as "ordered speech" that, like the trees, is delivered to the places where it is called for—for example, to the benches where people congregate and communicate. By naming them "backed perches," Roberson aligns the people of the city with the birds, who perch on the trees and leave their white and gray "graffiti" on the benches and cars and sidewalks below. All of it nature, at once lovely and ugly: "the stinking flower / the difficult fruit   bitter   complex" (17). The poem's final stanza references our penchant for trying to separate (and segregate) these qualities—"Committee cleanliness and its neat / districts for making nice nice and for making sin / may separate its pick of celebrant monsters"(17)—but the city, like any other organism, changes over time, in response to and in defiance of our regulations.

Roberson clearly writes out of a fascination with the processes by which life on earth sustains itself, and with as deep a compassion for the urban environment as for any other. Insofar as the term "urban" was one of the twentieth century's favorite code words for "blackness," a poem like "City Eclogue: Words for It," which refigures graffiti less as art than as a "flowering" that follows "naturally" from "the experience that thought up city," demands to be read for its politics (16). And given that the nature poetry *and* avant-garde poetry communities' devaluation of "political poetry" (narrowly defined) not infrequently entails the marginalization of African American poetry, on the assumption that the latter is usually also the former, Roberson's insistence that we read nature for politics and read the political as natural must be understood as the foundation of—the nature of—his black aesthetics.

THE NATURE WE come to know via Roberson's poetry—an all-encompassing nature, not shunted to one side of a binary's slash mark—may be singular in that sense, but at the same time, like Whitman, it is "large" and it "contain[s] multitudes." This is to say that by relinquishing the dualistic nature/culture framework, we gain a greater awareness of and appreciation for the diversity that exists, or has existed. In the title poem of his most recent collection, *To See the Earth Before the End of the World*, Roberson points to various "endings of the world": "the crash scene of species extinction," for example, or "the five minutes it takes for the plane to fall" (3). By constructing the end of the world as multiple, rather than a grand catastrophic event, he highlights the importance of each of "the world's death[s]," including "our small human extinction." To call it "small" is not to diminish its significance, from our own perspective, but to remind us that our perspective is a limited one. In a lecture given at Northwestern University, where he currently teaches creative writing, he explained the distinction this poem's—this book's—title sets up: "The world is not the same as the Earth. The world is *our* experience and the structure of that knowledge in which we live." "Earth" is what "you see from the satellites," he adds, but even that view that technology has provided humans in our most recent decades is part of our limited experience of nature. There is always an "unknowable hidden aspect" of nature for two reasons, he suggests: first, because we cannot get "outside" of it, we can never wholly objectify it; and, second, because there is a "mystery beyond words" located in all of nature that is "noncommunicative" (in our languages).[18]

The limit of the "nature poem," then, is our limit. Recognizing that our experience of earth is all that we can get into the poem, Roberson avoids the appropriative gesture that some ecopoets have embraced, that of attempting to "speak for" nature. In this, his black aesthetics can again be seen to inform his ecopoetics, offering the caution against "speaking for" the voiceless that African Americans—a historically silenced people— have learned the hard way.[19] Put differently, we might say that we can speak *as* nature, but only as situated within it—and here I am thinking of and extending Linda Russo's discussion of ecopoetics as "emplaced or environed writing," or "writing within" (2).[20] While Russo's focus is on the importance of the individual writer's primary locale, her bioregion, as the ground for "emplaced writing" (of which I am not being critical), Roberson's poem functions on a larger scale, categorically, spatially, and temporally, such that it is the place of the human species—Earth—over a period of time measured by the movement of glaciers that is at stake.

Roberson's background and orientation are such that the contemplation of Earth as a planet and people as a species are regular features of his poetry, as we have seen. Will Alexander, whose work I engage in the following chapter, takes this global scale and vast temporal scope almost as his starting point. His angle of approach to nature encompasses not only this planet, but the universe. Perhaps fittingly, then, he is more invested in a black aesthetic that is deeply grounded in diasporic influences than the other poets discussed herein. Alexander finds in surrealism a poetics that can accommodate the range and span of his interest in the cosmos. Yet we will find that for all of his differences from these other innovative poets, his black aesthetics contains significant points of connection with theirs.

SIX

WILL ALEXANDER'S SURREALIST NATURE
Toward a Diasporic Black Aesthetics

WILL ALEXANDER's fabulously idiosyncratic poetry poses a productive challenge for this project of redefining the concept of black aesthetics to encompass the wide variety of ways that African American poets have innovated formally in negotiating the relationship between U.S. racial politics and their art. The challenge lies in the fact that he discursively distances his poetry from the African American poetic tradition on occasion, while his poetry and his discussions of it both reveal an explicit debt to African ways of thinking and being that connect him to a variety of artists belonging to the African diaspora—including some located in the U.S. His multilayered relationship to "blackness" also entails his willingness to embrace artistic models from or intellectual affinities with the peoples and cultures of Asia, South America, and Europe, insofar as they can be reconciled with the values and principles in which his poetics and, indeed, his cosmology, are grounded. His complicated (but not ambivalent) engagement with African and African diasporic cultures and to the art and thought produced in a variety of non–Anglo-American contexts accounts for his having been virtually invisible within the African American poetry tradition—and being much celebrated, though not much written about, by predominantly white American avant-garde communities—across his nearly three decades of publishing.

This critical invisibility does not trouble him, which perhaps should not be surprising, given his self-described "alacrity for what the mechanically sighted call the invisible," with its implied rejection of any worthwhile distinction between that which can be seen with the physical eye and that which appears only to more discerning faculties. This exchange between Alexander and Harryette Mullen, in a 1997 interview, conveys his perspective:

MULLEN: How do you feel about the institutionalization of an African-American canon of literature . . . [and] the fact that the canon inevitably will exclude certain writers, such as yourself, while including others?

ALEXANDER: I don't need it. I'm what you could call a maroon. I'm a psychic maroon.

MULLEN: Marooned from the mainstream, as well as from any academically and pedagogically oriented canon?

ALEXANDER: Absolutely, from both. Both of them join up, at one point or another.

MULLEN: Do you feel marooned also from the avant-garde?

ALEXANDER: I'm not interested in that as some kind of activity to pursue . . . [or] some kind of movement. Not even a surrealist movement. ("Hauling" 401–02)

Alexander's lack of concern about his "maroon" status cannot be understood as a lack of commitment to his artistry; incredibly prolific, he has published six books of poetry, two books of fiction, and a book of essays, almost all within the last fifteen years. Moreover, he always has a huge stockpile of writing awaiting publication, as well as a number of projects in progress and in mind—this despite working a long line of blue-collar jobs to earn his livelihood (another factor that may have contributed to his critical invisibility). Thanks to the efforts of small, independent presses, Alexander has consistently been able to make his writing available to his modest, but devoted audience, and he seems content, otherwise, to be a literary ousider.[1] Nonetheless, those of us who take an interest in the shape, the inclusivity, of the African American tradition and/or the tradition of American avant-gardes may see his marginalization as a situation that bears correcting—not simply for the sake of his work, which acquires a clearer focus and greater resonance within the larger, non–U.S.-based contexts noted above, but also for the sake of the traditions that his work expands and illuminates.

It is particularly important to read Alexander into the tradition of innovative African American poetry that this study helps to trace, in part because, as Aldon Nielsen (one of the few scholars to take on the poet's oeuvre to date) has argued, Alexander's "highly politicized practice of a uniquely North American surrealism needs to be understood as an innovation within an ongoing revolution in black poetics" ("Will" 410). Significantly, Alexander's poetry, like that of Bob Kaufman, Jayne Cortez, and Ted Joans, foregrounds the monumental contribution of the Martinican poet Aimé Césaire to the poetic (and philosophical) practice of surrealism, an aesthetic that is broader than its "orthodox" (strictly Bretonian) stream.[2] Additionally, and specifically because of Césaire's influence on his surrealism, Alexander brings yet another form of Afri-

can American nature poetry into view; his is formally innovative, like Ed
Roberson's and Anne Spencer's, but its innovation takes a different form
than either of theirs. In the poem "Topoi," as a corrective to our taking
this biosphere for granted, Roberson writes, "The earth is the footprint
of life" (*To See* 12). While Spencer would likely have agreed, Alexander's
poetry prepares us to step off of the globe—in our imaginations, at least.
This chapter examines his fifth volume of poetry, *Exobiology as Goddess*
(2004), which is characteristic of Alexander's work insofar as it evidences
his poetic "predilection" for "the fluidic motion of the sidereal"—or as he
has also described it, his "verbal momentum always magnetized to the
uranic" ("My Interior Vita" 371). His interest in the stars (or we might
say the language of the stars) is given perhaps its fullest expression in
this book, whose title signifies that "exobiology"—the branch of biology
devoted to questions of life outside the earth's environment—will be
not simply central, but deified. In the process of working with this richly
textured text, I highlight the diasporic black aesthetics the volume (and
Alexander's work, generally) mines in lieu of the (U.S.) black nationalist
aesthetics from which much of the other work discussed in this study
takes off. This focus in turn clarifies the particularity and significance of
his unorthodox (heathen?) and nature-based surrealism, which has its
roots in the "black soil" of Martinique and Africa, among other places.[3]
As we will see, Alexander learns from Césaire how to bring an African
cosmology to life in a liberatory poetics that is all his own.

EXOBIOLOGY AS GODDESS is an 89-page exploration of sustained
possibility, a hypotactic suspension bridge between our planet and wherever else life might exist in the universe. It is composed of two long poems,
"Solea of the Simooms" and the title poem, which function together as an
extended meditation on the infinitely vast number of forms life has taken
and may take. While these are not questing poems—they do not recount
a search for extraterrestrial life so much as they affirm its potential—their
scope and willingness to imaginatively encounter manifestations of the
divine or the spiritual may recall for us the epic long poems of Brooks
and Sanchez discussed in part I. The opening lines introduce us to the
goddess who is the subject of Alexander's imaginal project:

Not some writhing in a tortuous canine province
nor some hallucinated witness starving in a broken endocrine manger
but Solea
the splendiferous dolorosos of Solea

> with her blind electrical surges
> with her transmundane penetration
> like a rain of green sorrows
> with their clairvoyant ethers
> become a cyclone of minerals (1)

One may read on in hopes of obtaining a clearer understanding of who or what Solea is, but be forewarned: no neat and tidy definition is forthcoming. The reader comes to comprehend Solea's infinite and divine scope only through a slow and repeated surrender to the poems' gorgeously impossible images, their mesmerizing pace, their intricate yet spacious syntax, their elusive lexicon, and their passionate voice. That voice is projected in *Exobiology* by an equally difficult to identify "I," a speaker that one learns relatively quickly is not Alexander—at least, not on any literal level. Only in the most metaphorical sense could a poet-speaker, a "Will Alexander," utter these lines:

> so if I form a perpendicular mass as regards her
> or if I form a condensation
> or a sudden Hydroxyl in her favour
> I will know
> that the gulfs burn
> the biopsies detach
> the nebulas roam . . . (4; ellipsis in original)

Alexander has described the non-autobiographical "I" of another of his poems as speaking "not . . . about me but about those other realities flowing through me" (*Singing* 253). This capacious and fluid "I" and Solea interact again and again in the volume, until the reader sees that their identities, whatever they are, are linked: if not mutually constituting, nonetheless fundamentally necessary to one another.

Painstaking work with dictionaries and encyclopedias is required of any reader of this text whose background in the sciences is not exceptional. A four-page glossary in the back of the volume functions primarily as a way station between the poems and the reference books, as the glossed terms are defined in terms that themselves must be looked up. On the first reading, one wavers between a constant anxiety that the significance of the poems is slipping past in some multisyllabic, Latinate word and a blissful sense that ignorance actually allows one to luxuriate more fully in the incantatory rhythms and weird beauty of the lines.

In subsequent readings, one discovers that both intuitions are accurate. The poems beg to be read aloud for attention to their sounds. But the reader who does not know, or take the time to discover, what words like "neutrino," "cephalopod," "Ishtar Terra," "Pre-Cambrian," and "orismology" mean will not be able to appreciate the poems' nuances, or even the volume's overall thrust (though a lot remains to be enjoyed in the middle ground). An equally, maybe more, important lexicon of cultural references, some of which are similarly obscure, at once increases and diminishes the strangeness of the scientific terms; I will come back to this aspect of the volume shortly.

But for the moment, I simply want to register, as a starting point, the unique vision, vast scope, and significance of nature in Alexander's book. His practice here is not to represent, via description, an observed nature (à la Spencer), nor is it to inscribe human ecosystems into the biosphere of which they are a part (as does Roberson). As he puts it: "I have never been drawn to provincial description, or the quiescent chemistry of a condensed domestic horizon" ("My Interior Vita" 371). Megan Simpson's engrossing and thoughtful essay "Will in the Wilderness" attempts to trace the points of connection between his earlier collection, *The Stratospheric Canticles* (1995), and the natural world as it is most commonly constructed: as a scene to be admired, as the non(sub)urban, outdoor setting of a range of leisure activities. She makes a strong case for those connections, particularly for how his defamiliarizing language enables the reader to see the familiar world of nature with new eyes.

But that construction of nature, the one most commonly found across the range of what might be called "ecopoetry," is decidedly not the nature evoked by the language of *Exobiology as Goddess*. Rather, Alexander's "uranic" orientation inclines him toward a poetics that seeks to express the beauty of nature as a dizzyingly complex, virtually incomprehensible collection of biological, chemical, and physical processes in action—a beauty akin to what is meant by mathematicians when they speak of the beauty of certain equations. The analogy is not exact, which is to say that Alexander's language cannot be equated to the language of the scientist, the exobiologist, as it were. He does not provide literal, technical descriptions of the processes to which the poems allude. Rather, he keeps an analytical perspective of nature perpetually in view by drawing heavily upon scientific nomenclature for the poems' nouns, but simultaneously repurposes that terminology for beauty and mystery by juxtaposing it with words from discourses of religion/mythology, linguistics, and the arts, as well as lay terms for natural phenomena. Almost miraculously,

Alexander makes terms like "Brachiopods," "Hydroxyl," and "Biome Distribution" take on a poetic charge by weaving them into lines and stanzas of heightened lyricism.[4]

Because his lexicons and syntax work together to make the language seem strange and new, one may be tempted to treat him as a poet whose aesthetics circulates within the orbit of Language poetry. Indeed, Simpson places Alexander within a category of "language-oriented African American poetry" in the opening of her essay—then devotes a long footnote to defending the classification, anticipating that he would reject it (117). More specifically, Simpson groups Alexander with Mullen and Nathaniel Mackey, not simply as experimental or innovative African American poets, but expressly as "Black American poets concerned with linguistic play and the philosophical/ideological effects of foregrounding the operations of language itself" (118). She justifies this move by arguing for a more inclusive way of understanding what it might mean to be "language-oriented," to wit:

> I use the term "language-oriented" to refer to a diverse body of contemporary writing marked by the related tendencies to blur the boundaries between the creative and the critical, draw attention to the role language plays in how we know the world by using it in other than transparently representational ways, and engage in radical linguistic play to suggest and discover alternative viewpoints and modes of knowing. (133)

Simpson's spirit of inclusivity is welcome; certainly, Alexander's poetry models and calls for the kind of openness her more permeable construction of "language-oriented" poetics involves. If there is a problem with her gesture, it is the extent to which the surrealist practices that Alexander riffs upon—which predate Language poetry as a movement and constituted an alternative strand of modernism to the Steinian strand that leads to Language poetry—are subsumed within (rather than brought together with) the field of language-oriented poetics, in her articulation.[5] By privileging the Language poetry tradition as a framework for thinking about his poetics, Simpson deemphasizes Alexander's affinities with the distinctly Caribbean surrealism that emerged from Césaire's and Léon Damas's poetic explorations of négritude. That Caribbean surrealism—by grounding its formulation of black subjectivity in the natural landscape of the (black) colony, rather than in the metropole, and embracing ancient African cosmology, with its interest in the skies beyond earth's atmosphere—points doubly to ways in which nature signifies in Alexander's work, especially in *Exobiology as Goddess*. Accordingly, that tradition is critical to my reading of his work as ecopoetry—and, relatedly, to my understanding of his black aesthetics.

THOUGH SURREALISM HAS been and continues to be practiced by poets in locations spanning the globe, I take the Bretonian stream of surrealism as the point of departure for my discussion of the surrealism of the Caribbean, because of its direct and documented relationship to Césaire's interest in the aesthetic (along with that of other black francophone poets studying in French universities in the 1930s) and because Alexander frequently cites it, along with the U.S.-based surrealism of Philip Lamantia, in his essays and interviews.[6] Bretonian surrealism has consistently been concerned with, among other things, transcending the false perception of "man" and "nature" as being in opposition to one another (Fowlie 107). The explosion of that dichotomy and similar commonly accepted "contradictions" ("life and death, the real and the imaginary, the past and the future, the communicable and the incommunicable," for example), achieved by using language in ways that purposefully defy logic, is central to the surrealist commitment to liberation of the imagination and, by extension, of mankind (Fowlie 106–07; Caws 18). But Aimé Césaire's desire for liberty emerges out of the specific circumstances of his status as a racialized colonial subject. He develops his sense of the liberatory power of unconventional language and images, in the first instance, from his reading of the very poets who also initially inspired the founders of surrealism—Baudelaire, Rimbaud, Mallarmé, Apollinaire, and Lautréamont—as much as from his acquaintance with surrealist writing itself (Césaire, "Poetry" 233–36, 239; Gregson Davis 14).[7] Having determined, in the process of writing his transformative poem *Cahier d'un retour au pays natal / Notebook of a Return to the Native Land*, how he could use such poetics in his effort "to bend French" for the purpose of articulating négritude, a few years later Césaire asserts the compatibility of the politics of his (black) aesthetics and the politics of the surrealist movement (Rosello 52; Arnold 88–89).[8] But Césairian surrealism remains distinct from the Bretonian version in a variety of ways, and while Césaire also expresses concern with resolving the opposition between "man" and "nature," the particular resonance of "nature" in his poetry and the specific images he uses constitute one of those distinctions.[9]

One basis for this distinction lies in the difference between the forms in which "nature" manifests itself in France and in Martinique. The vegetation and the (nonhuman) animal life on the Antillean island are dramatically dissimilar to their counterparts on the European continent. Unlike Jamaica Kincaid, who has railed in both fiction and memoir about how her colonial education focused on England's beloved daffodils rather than the flowers she grew up seeing in Antigua, Césaire was lucky enough to have a teacher, Dr. Eugène Revert, who understood and communicated to his students the importance of their knowing "the unique fauna and flora and . . . the peculiar geographical characteristics" of the tropical place in which they lived (Arnold 7). Such background was not normally acquired by Martinican students, whose curriculum prepared them to take the same standard examinations as students in the metropole (those covering the geography and vegetation of mainland France). Perhaps for this reason, this knowledge deeply informed Césaire's poetry, especially his *Notebook*, which readers in France often found off-putting (because unfamiliar to them) or dismissed as "exoticism"—evidence, ultimately, of their cultural imperialism (Arnold 91; Eshleman and Smith 1). The importance Césaire placed on Martinicans knowing local Martinican nature is underscored by the fact that *Tropiques*, the literary journal he helped to found and publish in the early 1940s, periodically ran pieces intended to disseminate this knowledge more widely among the people there (Arnold 91).

In acknowledging the connections between Césaire's writing and his own, Alexander points to the emphasis Césaire places on Martinican specificity as one reason to recognize that those connections are ultimately more spiritual than they are based on concrete similarities between the two oeuvres. He notes that the urban Los Angeles environment where he has spent nearly all of his life is not only different than Césaire's early childhood town of Basse-Pointe (or even Fort-de-France, where Césaire lived from adolescence onward), but it is a difference utterly necessary to his writing, which is grounded, not in southern California's ecology, but in L.A.'s libraries and universities. That is, the references to nonhuman nature that permeate Alexander's work point toward an "eclectic range" of information that, in a period before the widespread availability of the Internet, he could nonetheless easily access through the clusters of cultural and educational institutions characteristic of large cities (Alexander, "Will" 19).

But while his focus on nature is more universal (in at least two senses of the word) than local, Alexander is clearly sympathetic to Césaire's philosophy of nature, at times seeming to embody in his poetry or poetics some of the abstract principles to which Césaire gave voice in "Poetry and Knowledge." For example, Césaire writes: "Within us, all the ages of mankind. Within us, all humankind. Within us, animal, vegetable, mineral. Mankind is not only mankind. It is *universe*" (236; emphasis in original). A very similar understanding of the "primal unity" of the whole of creation appears to animate *Exobiology as Goddess*, which, as I will argue below, uses language—lexicon and syntax—in such a way as to minimize or even erase the boundaries between categories (temporal, spatial, typological) that we take for granted (236). One is further tempted to see Alexander's expressed preference for traveling via the imagination fueled by books, rather than the usual physical comings-and-goings, as a nod to Césaire's praise for the tree. For Césaire, the "superiority" of the tree to mankind is manifest in that it "is fixed, attachment and perseverance to essential nature"; paradoxically, its "stability . . . is also surrender. Surrender to the vital movement, to the creative élan" (237). Alexander has said that he can access this nonphysical, "vital movement" because the subconscious (the locus of the imagination), the "physical plane," and the "supra-plane" all "partake of one single substance"—a concept that again echoes Césaire's concept of the "knotty primal unity" of all things.[10] We might note an additional point of connection between both of these concepts and the surrealists' notion of "the *point sublime*," where the unity of the real and the "super-real" is visible (Caws 18).

The parallels between Alexander's and Césaire's aesthetics are most resonant, however, in their common (but apparently independent) recourse to ancient African metaphysics and cosmologies for non-Western approaches to understanding nature. Césaire, having read the African ethnography of Leo Frobenius during his studies in Paris, decides to weave certain themes and ideas about nature gathered therefrom into his *Notebook*, the magnificent long poem that, for all practical purposes, introduces "négritude" to the world. Gregson Davis's illuminating chapter on the poem, in his critical study of Césaire's oeuvre, identifies some of the ways the poet uses what he learns from Frobenius in illustrating the scope and significance of négritude and in constructing his speaker's journey into a full awareness of what his identity as a Martinican of African descent entails. If the speaker arrives back in Martinique filled with both bitterness and tenderness toward his native land, he comes to a clearer sense of "his birthright" through the powerful process of self-examination that the poem enacts (Gregson Davis 22). Part of that process is taking an honest account of what his African heritage includes and claiming it. From Frobenius, Césaire absorbs the idea of an African "*paideuma*," or "vital force" that identifies Ethiopian culture with "vegetal forms of life" (Eshleman and Smith 11). Thus, one of the ways he signals his reclamation of his people's African past is by figuring the speaker and other Martinicans as trees (an image we already saw him use above):

> From staring too long at trees I have
> become a tree and my long tree
> feet have dug in the ground large
> venom sacs high cities of bone
> from brooding too long on the Congo
> I have become a Congo resounding with
> forests and rivers (Césaire, *Notebook* 51)

As Davis argues, this passage performs an "aggressive 'racination'—the act of re-rooting black culture in its originary African soil" (37).

Not only in the *Notebook*, but throughout his poetry, Césaire figures himself and black Martinicans in terms of plant imagery, which, as noted, roots a deracinated people and mythologizes their ability to survive (Eshleman and Smith 11). In other instances, he draws upon African mythologies to signify the "sense of deep cultural difference" between the speaker and Europeans, as when he alludes to the "tadpoles hatched in me by my prodigious ancestry" (Césaire, *Notebook* 65). According to Davis, the tadpole image recalls an "Ancient Egyptian cosmogonic myth" of creation, which depicts "a watery primal mud from which life emerges in the form of amphibious, frog-like creatures" (49). These references do not signify easy celebration; in the passage quoted above, for example, the tree roots are associated with "venom sacs," and the lines immediately following those quoted reveal that the Congo contains, along with its "forests and rivers," a cracking "whip" and anger that drive "the boars of / putrefaction to the lovely wild edge / of the nostrils" (Césaire, *Notebook* 51). But however complicated the speaker's (and Césaire's) connection to Africa, it appears nonetheless to be a necessary one for Césaire, who sees in Africa's mythologies and cosmologies the useable symbols of a fertile past and a direction for the future.

Alexander is similarly invested in tapping into the knowledge and understandings of the world that developed and circulated in ancient African civilizations. In his interviews and essays, he repeatedly references ancient Egypt (or Kemet) and that culture's conception of a "visible world" and an "invisible world," both of which were contemplated not only by the prevailing religious paradigm, but also by the society's science ("Hauling" 404; "Will" 15).[11] Moreover, knowledge of the world was not divided into separate disciplines to be studied in isolation from one another; regardless of the focus of one's study, one undertook to understand it in relation to "the cosmos as a whole" ("Will" 15). This comprehensive "African world view" is not so much what Césaire's work, in its reliance upon Frobenius, offers directly as what Alexander submits it made possible: "By such opening as Négritude provided there was organic access to, say, the mathematical and astronomical genius of the Dogon people. Black people who 'knew of the rings of Saturn,' of 'the four principle moons of Jupiter,' of 'the rotundity of the Earth and its turning on its axis'" ("Caribbean" 144). Thus, Alexander draws a line through Césaire to the ancient cultures that made such wonderful and early advances in scientific knowledge without rejecting the unseen—indeed, made those advances *because* they did not reject the unseen, he implies in noting that "such peoples as the pygmies of the Ituri Forest . . . knew of nine moons of Saturn without any recourse to modern instrumentation" (144).[12] The Caribbean surrealism of Césaire (and Léon Damas, another influence Alexander acknowledges) can be seen, then, as a germinal point for Alexander's cosmology and poetics, in which nature takes a particularly "uranic" slant.[13]

ALEXANDER'S EMBRACE (and customization, we might say) of surrealism, then, has in common with Césaire's a recognition that it is a language practice, an artistic practice, intended to reveal the existence of a reality that is infinitely more expansive than the limited "real" that the majority of us perceive. It has in common with "language-oriented" avant-garde poetries an understanding of the conventions of language as constraining our ways of thinking and talking about—and thus experiencing and understanding—the world. But it is ultimately a more humanist vision, insofar as it conceives of the imagination as more powerful than language. For Alexander, a person whose imagination can encompass the three planes of existence—subconscious, conscious, and supraconscious—is able to use language in ways that reveal all those realities to others. Rather than seeing language as a system that "experimental" poetry might destabilize enough to expose the way it operates (upon us), Alexander points to language as a powerful instrument the poet can use to create change:

> My feeling is that language is capable of creating shifts in the human neural field, capable of transmuting behaviors and judgments. Humans conduct themselves through language, and, when the latter transmutes, the human transmutes. . . . [W]hen language is mined at [the] seminal

depth of poetic strata, chance can take on a more lasting significance. And I do not mean in a didactic manner, but in the way that osmosis transpires, allowing one to see areas of reality that here-to-fore had remained elided or obscured. ("My Interior Vita" 371)[14]

He describes being changed himself by reading the poetry of Bob Kaufman, for example, upon which occasion "an urgency, a vortex occurred within me, as if awakened to a new viridity" ("Footnotes" 121). Poetry is "alchemical," and surrealism is "an imaginative spark" that ignites the language and contributes to the "heat" that poetry requires ("Alchemy" 165; "Ambidextrous" 28). As I will discuss further later, this investment in poetry's potential to create change situates Alexander among a wide spectrum of African American poets with similar investments and whose poetics, differing in various ways not only from Alexander's but often from one another's, cannot all be reduced to didacticism. By the same token, I should note that the engagement of such writers as Jayne Cortez, Ted Joans, Henry Dumas, A. B. Spellman, Larry Neal, and Amiri Baraka with both surrealist practices *and* black cultural nationalism complicates the bright line Alexander draws here between "didactic" and "alchemical" uses of language.

The seeming invisibility of Africans and African cultures, of their value as anything other than labor or amusement, within "Western" societies in Europe and North America goes a long way to explaining the attraction of surrealism to both Alexander and Césaire. A poetics that not only admits of, but seeks to reveal, "areas of reality" that have been "elided or obscured" by pushing the already metaphorical language of poetry to new intensities of imagery offers certainly one avenue for exploring the empowering significance of African cultures and cosmologies like those discussed above. That surrealism originated with a group of poets who were "socially progressive" as well as "artistically iconoclastic" only adds to the draw (Gregson Davis 67). Alexander has highlighted, in particular, the "morality" of Breton's and other French surrealists' racial politics in comparison to the racism of U.S. high modernist poets during the same era:

There exists during the 1930's and 40's no sustained poetic attack against a Prussian-like apartheid, against the unbroken pact of the lynch law. . . . [T]here is Eliot strutting in his Anglican métier, and Williams with his colloquial insight into the "American Grain," but to both, the non-white always objectified, always considered as a trinket, as an exotic marsupial. Can one imagine them denouncing the American occupation of Haiti in the way, say, that the Surrealists denounced the French-Moroccan war in 1925? On the contrary, Stevens during this time praises the likes of Mussolini, and accedes him his right to envelop Ethiopia in the way that he sees fit. ("Above" 138)[15]

Surrealism, not repugnant in its ideological grounding, also appealed to Césaire insofar as "[i]t was like dynamite to the French language" (qtd. in Gregson Davis 72). It opened the way for him to break through the constraints of the (colonizer's) language upon his thinking, "to discover the fundamental African" (qtd. in Gregson Davis 73). Alexander has articulated a similar relationship between European languages and African identity (that is, black subjectivity), suggesting that the language of his surrealism is indebted—attuned—to this Césairian black aesthetic.[16]

This black aesthetic propels the innovative formal structures of both poets' work. For example, Brent Edwards has written about Césaire's striking combination of anaphora and negation in his *Notebook of a Return to the Native Land* as a way of placing surrealist imagery at the service of a construction of négritude as qualified, indeterminate, even contradictory—and he identifies the echoes of this strategy in Alexander's "anaphoric, interminable sentence structure" ("Aimé" 8–9, 12). Edwards gives us an example of Césaire's poetics in these lines (Edwards's translation):

> my negritude is not a stone, its deafness hurled against the clamor of
>   the day
> my negritude is not a leukoma of dead liquid over the earth's dead eye
> my negritude is neither tower nor cathedral
> it dives into the red flesh of the soil
> it dives into the ardent flesh of the sky
> it pierces the opaque prostration of its straight patience (Edwards,
>   "Aimé" 6)

Compare these lines from *Exobiology as Goddess* describing the protean Solea:

> her vocal ballet
> not corruptible as human scent
> not torn down to scale
> but as raw protracted renegade's miasma
> as percussive power as dalliance (10)

We can see the "syntax of influence," to use Edwards's phrase, upon Alexander's work. Alexander clearly shares Césaire's penchant for anaphora, using it virtually as the spine of the poems; it appears at least once on every page—and usually more than once. Here, we have two distinct instances of anaphora—the "not-not" and "as-as-as" clusters—woven into just a handful of lines. In another case, anaphora might structure an entire stanza, as in this tercet: "Solea as burst / Solea as diurnal / Solea as dissolved in dwarf electric flame" (*Exobiology* 60). Alexander also parallels Césaire in using structures of negation in his lines ("Aimé" 7).

But while the things that négritude is "not" fundamentally cohere as symbols or descriptions of the oppressive Western culture from which Césaire wishes to distance his identity, Alexander's negations remain disjointed, having nothing obviously in common besides their "not" being descriptive of Solea, her activities, or her close associate, "I," the speaker. Alexander's negations furthermore appear consistently within correlative conjunctions ("not . . . but") that link them to phrases that, by contrast, apparently *are* apt descriptions of the goddess. And where Césaire's syntax finally resolves into sections of complete sentences, Alexander's phrases continue to roll out as phrases, hypotactically, never definitively resolved into a sentence, unless (as Mullen has proposed concerning others of his works) the whole poem is one, long, unpunctuated sentence ("Collective" 422). Indeed, what I think of as Alexander's signature device, the most commonly recurring pattern in *Exobiology*—the adjective-adjective-"noun" pattern ("noun," because often his nouns are basically adjectives that have been nominalized)—has no real precedent in Césaire. Ultimately, given that Alexander's subject is not négritude and his syntax offers its own innovations, we must look beyond Césaire's example to account for the form of Alexander's black aesthetics, even as we note their common recourse to an African cultural legacy.

Alexander departs conceptually from Césaire, I would argue, to the extent that he understands ancient African civilizations as having produced not only a cultural legacy that should inform and empower African-descended people in the Americas, but also (even more importantly, perhaps) metaphysical and scientific knowledge that constituted the foundation of Greek and other European traditions of thought and learning. *Exobiology as Goddess* manifests this understanding in two ways. The first, more direct way that the book reveals the importance for Alexander of precolonial African cosmology is by figuring the complex scientific field of exobiology as an ancient Egyptian goddess. This move effectively reverses the Western practice of naming the heavenly bodies after the gods, goddesses, and other characters from Greek and Roman mythology. Whereas that practice basically reduces a complex of religious beliefs to the objects of scientific study, Alexander equates the practice of scientific study with divine activity; the goddess Solea represents at once the search for and the possibility of extraterrestrial life. The very name Alexander gives his goddess—"Solea"—doubly signifies his black aesthetics. It alludes, mutedly, but unmistakably, to the Andalusian region of Spain, where the Soleá form of Flamenco music originated.[17] Andalusia is a critical site on Alexander's diasporic map, because it was in that region that Moorish (Northern African) culture deeply and directly influenced European culture for several hundred years, beginning in the eighth century. He has made particular note of the "organization of knowledge," the "hundreds of bookstores," and the proto-universities established by the Moors in this region, crediting them with "actually creat[ing] the Renaissance in Europe"—a part of history that has been deliberately obscured, he argues, "because of their religion and their color" ("Will" 15). The name "Solea" is apt, then, not only for indexing the significance of this time and place of African cultural influence on Europe, but for identifying his goddess with the sun (ironically, via the Latin root "sol"), whose worship was prevalent and central in ancient Egypt and other parts of Africa.[18]

But these are not the sole links between the goddess of his text and (ancient) African peoples and cultures. The second way that Alexander reinforces this association is by describing Solea explicitly in terms of ancient Egypt: "she being the rise of an a-bodiless Kemet" (*Exobiology* 80). Similar links are forged between Solea and deities worshipped in Egypt beginning nearly three millennia BC:

> we meander through explosive fictive geography
> through de-activated tundra
> being the primordial link to "East/Central Africa"
> to the remnants of "Bast"
> of "Selket"
> of "Nepthys"
> of "Mut"
>
> & Solea like "Neith" (*Exobiology* 82)

Alexander, who is far from glossing every word or reference with which the reader might be unfamiliar, takes the trouble to note that the five names he mobilizes in this passage all belong to "Egyptian goddess" (93). He leaves it to the reader to uncover the nuances of his choices of these particular goddesses from among the nearly fifty goddesses who played a role in the culture during the centuries upon centuries of Egypt's predynastic and Early Dynastic periods and Old, Middle, and New Kingdoms. A quick survey reveals that: Bast was originally a sun goddess, the daughter of Ra; Selket, also a daughter of Ra, was a goddess of magic and of the burning wrath of the scorpion, who revitalized the dead upon their arrival in the afterlife; Nepthys, too, connects death (which she symbolizes) and life (as the comforter of women in labor); Mut, a grandmother figure, was patron of the sky and of mothers; and Neith was a warrior goddess who protected the dead against evil spirits. All five are associated with religious beliefs and practices that are related, at least symbolically, to the concerns of exobiology: the sun, the sky, the seemingly magical processes through which life is created, and, from a less celebratory standpoint, the rites of death. To these five are added, in the penultimate stanza, another ancient Egyptian goddess, Isis (who is also associated with mothers, magic, and life), as well as the Hindu goddess Devaki, who was the mother of Krishna.

The reference to Hinduism is not the only non-Egyptian/non-African allusion in the poem, of course; Alexander's imagination carries him all over the globe, as well as all over the universe. But the way *Exobiology* markedly layers reference upon reference to black cultures and "blackness" in its last several pages points to their significance for the book. In addition to the small pantheon of Egyptian goddesses noted above, for example, Alexander invokes "the tree of the Neters," using the glossary again to ensure that the reader is aware that this refers to Egyptian gods (84). Less obvious is the fact that even the Hindu goddess referenced constitutes an allusion to blackness, insofar as Devaki's son Krishna (sometimes referred to as the Supreme Being) is typically depicted as having black or blue skin, because his name in Sanskrit means "black" or "dark blue." Another reference that might not immediately be understood by readers as falling within this category appears on the penultimate page; Andromeda is a constellation (and a galaxy) named for a character from Greek mythology, but she is identified in the myth as an Ethiopian princess—a fact which often goes unnoted (88). On this same page, the speaker announces: "it is the Goddess & her phenotypic African form." Certainly, Solea has taken myriad forms through the course of this book—but none resolve as readily into an image one could easily visualize.

Alexander's reason for inviting us to associate Solea with Africa and African cultures is not reducible to a notion simply of black pride in the rich precolonial history of the continent (Hegel notwithstanding). Rather, the poems of *Exobiology as Goddess* embody the emphasis he places in his interviews and essays on the need for Western culture once again to learn from and, indeed, adopt ancient African cosmological approaches to knowledge. "Once again," he would say, as a reminder of the Hermeticism of Europe's Renaissance period that "went underground and went underground and went underground" at more or less the same moment marked by "the mounting fervor of the Inquisition and the beginning of the slave trade" ("Will" 15). *Exobiology* is not so much an argument for, as an embodiment of, ancient African cosmology, by which I mean to say that its formal innovations (some of which characterize Alexander's poetry generally) so powerfully model that cosmology that the reader is virtually compelled to inhabit that mode of thinking while reading the poems. This is precisely why his contribution to ecopoetics is so unusual and so critical: the assumptions upon which his work is based constitute a view of nature that does not even acknowledge the dualism that Western thinking about "nature" has long embraced. Roberson's poetry also enacts the all-inclusive singularity of nature, as we have seen in chapter 5, but remains grounded, so to speak, on Earth; Alexander takes up a cosmology and a poetics that, together, facilitate the exploration of a nature that is even more expansive for being even less tethered to our home planet.

If Kemetic cosmology seeks to comprehend the whole, rather than discrete parts, then Alexander's poetry uses unique syntactical structures calibrated for precisely that type of inquiry. Mullen posits that "Alexander's preference for hypotaxis rather than parataxis" is logical, given the vast "load of information and history" he tends to incorporate into his poems ("collective" 422). She cites Keith Tuma as having first focused critical attention upon "the agglutination of parts in Alexander's poems" (422). One function of his hypotactic syntax in *Exobiology* is to insist that the reader hold up references to periods from the earliest prehistoric eras ("the Ammonites") through the twentieth century ("Roberto Matta or Varo") for simultaneous consideration. Likewise, he can place the most mundane, localized items (a "pomegranate") alongside a star located 500 light years away ("Alpha Persei") (3, 14, 41, 68). The effect of steadily unreeling phrases that must be understood as syntactically connected (though not always in readily identifiable ways) is to impress upon the reader the potentially limitless scope of Solea, which is to say the possibilities of life in the universe.

For example, consider these two short stanzas that appear in the first few pages of "Solea of the Simooms":

her voice seems enveloped in blurred "paraxial rays"
conditioned by stellar antimonies
by spectral invisibility
by means of monstrous sibylline confetti

so that interactive mass
exists as a-positional dialectic
as maze across a floating microbe chart
being a cistern on fire with the light of miraculous causes (12–13)

A paraxial ray, I learned from a quick trip to the dictionary, is "a light ray that forms an angle of incidence so small that its value in radians is almost equal to its sine or its tangent" and antimony is "a toxic metallic element" whose symbol is Sb and which, if ingested, "may produce symptoms similar to those of acute arsenic poisoning." Alexander's syntax insists that to understand Solea's "voice" (an actual sound? a metaphor? and if so, for what, exactly?), we must be able to hold such "rays" and "antimonies" in connection, not only with one another, but also with a ghostly "invisibility" and a kind of prophetic "confetti." The specific connection his syntax makes between these items is, furthermore, open to multiple interpretations. Her voice "*seems*" to be "enveloped in blurred 'paraxial rays'"— though it might not be (emphasis mine). And does it also "seem" to be "conditioned by stellar antimonies"—as would be the case if "enveloped" and "conditioned" are in parallel construction—or do the paraxial rays alone have that honor? Does "seems" modify the whole rest of the stanza or just the rest of the first line? If the indeterminacy of this stanza were self-contained, we might be able to come to terms with it using the reading strategies we normally employ, but it is not. The following stanza's meaning depends upon this one: it begins with the phrase "so that," which relegates everything following to the status of a result of . . . whatever it is we decide is the upshot of the previous stanza. The second of the stanzas offers us a variety of scientific and theoretical terms—"mass," "a-positional dialectic," and "a floating microbe chart"—one or the other of which is equated with a "cistern" that, despite its watery associations, is at least metaphorically "on fire with the light of miraculous causes," bringing us into the discourse of religion. These different lexicons are yoked, without apology or explanation, by Alexander's "depthless fractional sentence," to borrow a phrase (that may or may not be self-reflexive) from the poem (6).

Again, what this means in terms of the book's focus on nature is that we are confronted with a much more scientific portrayal of nature than we typically meet with in "nature poetry" (like Spencer's) or even "ecopoetics" (like Roberson's), in the sense that, in Alexander's African worldview, neither "science" nor "nature" are compartmentalized: anything can appear in the poem as a part of nature and as a means of studying, understanding, and articulating it. The syntactic structure reinforces the volume's sublimely long view of the history of life on earth and its patient anticipation of the emergence or discovery of life outside of our biosphere. Where Césaire wrote that "[m]ankind is not only mankind. It is *universe*" ("Poetry" 236; emphasis in original), Alexander offers a far less anthropocentric view, while still acknowledging our deep and multiple interconnections with the stuff of the universe. *Exobiology* incorporates references to a variety of creatures that existed or began to exist millions of years ago, "forms which preceded human electrical formation," the speaker tells us (3). Early in "Solea of the Simooms," we are given this list—"the Ammonites / the Brachiopods / the Medusina"—which strikes my ears (thanks to years of Sunday school) like a series of tribes defeated by the children of Israel, but in fact names three aquatic life forms of increasingly ancient origins (from 65 to 600 million years ago). On this scale, human life is reduced to a blip, which is a significant element of the work of the poems. This sense of scale is critical to conveying to the reader the sublimity of life, which is located less in the advent of the Johnny-come-lately Homo sapiens, and more in the vast temporal scope of life on earth and the immeasurable potential for life to exist or come to exist (or have existed) somewhere within the near and far reaches of the universe.[19]

Thus it is important to recall that, even as Solea is a "Goddess," what her deity represents (or constitutes) is "Exobiology." Indeed, Solea ultimately comes into focus as nothing less than the potential for life, and the speaker—her consort, her disciple—often seems to be the raw material through which that potential can be realized: "I / the first explosion from space / I / the first genetic fluidity / who combines with Solea being the geo-electric of earth" (58). Solea, whose name alludes to our sun, Sol, is often described as "blazing" or "burning," while the "I" is more frequently (though not exclusively) associated with tangible items like "sudden igneous floods" or properties that work upon the tangible, such as "colloquial commitment to gravity" (72, 76, 61, 37). They are imagined as (re)productive, in gendered terms—as powerful, protean "Goddess" and her devotee, as "diamantine ballerina" and her virile "knight"—whose "mat[ing]" produces life itself (41, 24, 79, 47). The following passages will communicate the fantastic manner in which Alexander suggests the roles of and relationship between Solea and the speaker:

> I now exult
> the impregnation of new planes
> above Auriga
> above Bellatrix
> above the scorching of Canis Major[20]
>
> when our glimpses touch
> they are "ablaze with immaterial matter"
> with motionless impulse turning (35)
>   *   *   *
> so that our substance writhes
> between the x-ray at its minimum
> & the sound which combines at atmospheric dioxide
>
> I
> the woven corona of lightning
> & she
> the scope of ovarian transmission
>
> we combine as a precipice of morals
> always obsessed by blank progressive spasmodic (45–46)
>   *   *   *
> & I am he who has no amorphic to tell
> no arrangement mechanic with incubation & omega
>
> she is that which blows into disappearing nether vatics
> outside ensemble
> outside the link of the one singular existence
>
> yet Solea & I are linkage
> of the solar ore & the camel (74)

As these and the numerous additional instances I could quote demonstrate, both Solea and "I" are moving targets—or, more accurately, they can be named and described in such a wide range of ways—because they encompass the limitless field of exobiology. They contain paradox ("motionless . . . turning") and make manifest synesthesia (their "substance" located along an axis that begins in the visual field of the "x-ray" and ends in a potentially breathable sonic field of "atmospheric dioxide"). The initially heterosexual-seeming thrust of some of the language is complicated by the ways the images are fleshed out, so that the "I" is figured as the circular "corona" around the phallic "lightning" and the goddess Solea is associated with ovaries whose "scope" of "transmission" might align them more with masculine activity than feminine receptivity. The two figures "touch" and "combine" and "link" repeatedly, despite or because of the impossible contradictions they embody individually and engender together, and the result is the "impregnation of new planes." Wherever Solea and "I" come together, life—imagined as, say, the reciprocal heat of "solar ore & the camel"—is possible. *Exobiology as Goddess*, we might say, is a creation myth waiting to happen.

THOUGH WILL ALEXANDER's surrealist poetry could not be any more stylistically different from Octavia Butler's speculative fiction novels, I am convinced that both African American writers are drawn to the stars in their works in part because of the way the stars—beginning with the North Star—represent freedom in the African American tradition.[21] The protagonist of Butler's *Parable of the Sower*, Lauren Olamina, living in an utterly dystopic twenty-first-century world, determines that the possibility that humankind may be able to move away from earth and "take root among the stars" constitutes our salvation (84); though she doesn't use the word "exobiology," it is the study of the potential for life to exist or survive on other worlds that motivates her. But looking not only toward the future, but into the past as well, we recall that the stars helped guide the enslaved to the North and freedom from bondage. The slave narratives brought this significance of the stars into the African American literary tradition early on, and in keeping alive the history of enslavement, the literature (in poems, stories, novels, and more) has continued to allude to the relationship between the stars and freedom. Admittedly, Alexander's *Exobiology* does not cast the stars into that traditional relationship to (African American) freedom; indeed, as we have seen, Alexander considers himself a "psychic maroon" from the canon of African American literature. It is, rather, ancient African cosmologies and practices, long predating the era of the Atlantic slave trade, that primarily generate the resonance of the stars in his poems. But his engagement with surrealism—a poetics and a politics that "is concerned above all with *freedom*" (Rosemont 55; emphasis in original)—creates an important point of intersection between his African-oriented, diasporic black aesthetics and other forms of black aesthetics that characterize African American poetry more familiarly. In other words, ironically, his insistence upon liberation—the characteristic that makes surrealism so attractive to him—is what distances him from the canon of African American poetry *and* what connects him to it.

Alexander has been forthright about his critique of the kind of black poetry that foregrounds what he would call "acceptable didactics" ("New" 68)—acceptable not to him, that is, but to the social forces seeking to delimit work by African Americans. He associates this type of poetics specifically with the "African-American condition of poetry," citing Césaire as a counterexample, a black poet from outside the U.S. whose work showed Alexander that he need not accept the "limitation" that the "Black poetry" label tended to place upon one's work within the national boundaries ("Hauling" 397). He points to Melvin Tolson's unique and challenging modernist poetry as constituting for him an exception, so to speak, to the rule that "Black poetry" must confine itself to the "little area" that is given to it, which Alexander appears to conceive of fundamentally as protest poetry or overtly political poetry (397). Describing Tolson's situation upon the publication of *Harlem Gallery* in terms that he suggests would also apply in many ways to his own circumstances as a young poet in the same period, Alexander writes:

> I'm thinking of the dilemma faced by Melvin Tolson, circa 1965, his imagination deleted by anti-poetic debate. On the one hand, the myopia of the Anglo poetic establishment, and on the other, the didactic stridulation of the burgeoning Black Arts movement. His poetic complexity obscured, his splendor momentarily eclipsed by pervasive ideology. ("New" 67)

The "little area" to which African American poets have been confined, in his view, is characterized in part by an aesthetic "formula" composed of "the conventions, the themes, [and] the subject matter" that would seem to make black poetry worthy of (or, alternatively, safe for) publication ("Hauling" 398). But it is also a kind of "psychic confinement," insofar as the "formula" is grounded not only in externally imposed expectations for black aesthetics, but also in the poet's own felt need to "writ[e] on [the] ubiquitous repression," created by "Saxon institutional attack," using "the plain spoken speech of the hour" ("New" 67).

The dilemma Alexander identifies here as confronting Tolson (and himself) is fundamentally the same as that faced by all of the poets I discuss in this study. All of them—Brooks, Sanchez, Mullen, Spencer, and Roberson, like Alexander—have sought and successfully innovated strategies for escaping from the racially based limitations imposed directly or indirectly upon their poetry. (For example, one hears Alexander's condemnation of "the didactic stridulation of the burgeoning Black Arts movement" as an echo of Spencer's assessment during the New Negro Renaissance that "the Tom-Tom *forced* into poetry seems a sad state to me.")[22] Thus, while I subscribe wholeheartedly to Alexander's characterization of the problem, one of the knottier ones that black poets have dealt with in the production, dissemination, and reception of their work in the U.S., I have argued herein that a wider range of strategies should become visible as innovative *and* as black aesthetics than he and most others have typically deemed to be such. In a context like the one this study delineates, Alexander's renovation of surrealism can be understood precisely (though not exclusively) as a kind of quest for freedom that typifies the African American literary tradition, even as it draws much more upon African and African diasporic ideas and aesthetic models than African American ones for its power and direction.[23] At the same time, Alexander's inclusion in the African American tradition foregrounds and productively contextualizes the diasporic thread running through the black aesthetics of other African American poets, such as Sanchez and Mullen, just to draw two examples from the poets considered herein.

To avoid losing the nuances of difference in this moment of drawing connections, I might locate Alexander's quest for freedom under the heading of *freedom to,* as distinguished from the more common type, which I might call *freedom from.* Let the *from* suggest an orientation that keeps at least one eye on the "ubiquitous repression" that African Americans have met with in the U.S. for hundreds of years ("New" 67). *Freedom to* need not imply an indifference to that repression, but simply an orientation, an emphasis, on "bringing into view the expansional repertoire of Afro-American written expression," as Alexander has put it ("New" 67). Fascinatingly, Alexander's *freedom to* is a freedom in or through or by way of language—not in spite of the way language carries racial and cultural meaning, but because of it. For example, he argues specifically that the "psycho-emotional constant" of dealing with racism produces an "imagination always awash in elusive complexity" ("New" 67). But even more generative of what he calls "Afro-centric complexity" than resistance to racism, Alexander proposes, is the imaginal legacy inherited "from the 'oldest nation on record . . . the Nubian nation Ta Seti'" (67). He asserts the importance of this legacy in no uncertain terms: "[W]hen I use language I am thinking of its African applicability" (67). That is, part of the power of language (and thus of poetry), for Alexander, is its capacity to provide him access to ancient African ways of thinking and being that were purposefully stripped from the culture of Africans and their descendants in the Americas, and likewise stripped from, or suppressed in, the historical record of Africa.

As discussed earlier in this chapter, Alexander is drawn to surrealism because, like Césaire, he finds it "perfectly conjunctive with [his] understanding of an African world view" in that "[i]t deals with the visible and the invisible" ("Hauling" 404). Here, we can productively connect Alexander's emphasis on the ancient African cosmology informing his understanding of the poetic imagination to Mullen's discussion of the tradition of "visionary literacy" in African American literature. This tradition, which has its origins in the nineteenth-century spiritual autobiographies of such figures as Jarena Lee and Rebecca Cox Jackson, parallels the secular/political tradition of literacy that emerges out of the slave narratives (or, more properly, as Mullen indicates, the "ex-slave narratives") by people like Frederick Douglass and Olaudah Equiano. In her essay "African Signs and Spirit Writing," Mullen explains that "visionary literacy" is "a spiritual practice in which divine inspiration, associated with Judeo-Christian biblical tradition, is syncretically merged with African traditions of spirit possession" (673). While Alexander's work is not at all religious in the Christian sense, it could be usefully understood, I would argue, as a syncretic mixture of surrealism with what he calls his "animistic instinct" and associates with an African worldview ("New" 68). Thinking of his work in relation to this tradition not only underscores Alexander's own sense of his poetry as connected to an African or black experience of the world, but also provides us with an additional framework within which to consider the relationships between the visual and the linguistic that Alexander's work posits.

One such relationship that Alexander creates in *Exobiology as Goddess* lies in his consistent use of metaphors of language to describe Solea and the universe she inhabits. Here, I do not mean simply that he uses metaphorical language; rather, I point to the fact that he depicts Solea's many possible incarnations and contexts by using the terminology of linguistics, grammar, and writing metaphorically. He writes of "her electric punctuation" and "her fleeting sonar crystals / culled from intermolecular force / like verbal nitrogen writing / a draft" (2, 5). The speaker laments, "I can never seduce her as a noun / collected in the form of optic mineral branches"—perhaps because "she then exists / as verb in lowly typhoon water / as glyph in which scarps & layers are missing" (19, 48). Mullen explains in her essay that some African cultures valued certain "script for its cryptographic incomprehensibility and uniqueness, rather than its legibility or reproducibility," insofar as this writing represented the ineffable or constituted communications from the orisha, their deities, to be read figuratively, not literally ("African" 672). Given this expansive construction of writing, and recalling Alexander's recourse to the concept of "animism," we might conceive of *Exobiology*'s language metaphors as resonant efforts to represent the divinity of Solea, which constructs the natural world as *both* alive and speaking *and* as a text or "spirit script" that is, if not illegible, certainly cryptic. It is in this way, perhaps, that Alexander's work most clearly connects to other African American innovators (such as Mackey and Roberson) whose poetics Megan Simpson described as "language-oriented" (Simpson 117–18). Like them, his marginalization vis-à-vis the African American tradition can be attributed to the degree to which his work is more "writerly" than oral (Mullen, "African" 670–71). Moreover, like Mackey and Butler, Alexander emerges from what Mullen identifies as the "specifically African American culture marked by a productive tension between ... the sacred and the secular, aspects of everyday life that African cultures had worked to integrate seamlessly" (686). He can thus be understood as one of a number of African American "artists and writers who have preserved aspects of African and diasporic cultural consciousness in their syncretically visual and visionary works" (686). The fact that Alexander is also a visual artist, whose drawings and paintings grace the covers of his numerous books, is an additional factor informing this aspect of his writing.

Surrealism, then, by facilitating the use of language through which Alexander's syncretism functions, also facilitates Alexander's participation in this tradition of African American visionary writers. Rather than underscoring the distance between his poetry and African American poetry, it locates him in proximity to an alternative tradition that lies within, or significantly overlaps with, the increasingly inclusive and complicated picture of the African American tradition to which this study contributes. While Caribbean—specifically Césairian—surrealism has been indisputably important for Alexander's poetics (as this chapter has demonstrated), that diasporic influence must also be understood as precisely the point of connection between Alexander and other African American poets who are likewise the heirs of Césaire. Bob Kaufman, in particular (who perhaps signaled his own admiration for Césaire by claiming—falsely—that his mother was from Martinique), loomed large on Alexander's poetic landscape, for years drawing the younger poet "to North Beach as to some internal Mecca" in hopes of sighting him ("Footnotes" 123).[24] (It is fitting that he came closest to meeting Kaufman—who was holed away in the next room while Alexander read the just-typed original manuscript of "The Ancient Rain"—through Philip Lamantia, the other American surrealist Alexander consistently identifies as one of his influences.) Jayne Cortez, of course, is another African American surrealist poet whose name comes up consistently in the scholarship on Alexander and in the broader context of African American surrealists who have been significantly influenced by Césaire and Damas.[25]

But Alexander's connections to African American poetry via surrealism are even thicker than these chartings of influences would suggest. The introduction he provides for K. Curtis Lyle's 2003 collection of poetry, *Electric Church*, testifies to the existence of a *community* of African American surrealism in which Alexander's poetics were nurtured. In "Re-emergence from the Catacombs," Alexander begins by acknowledging Lyle as a significant mentor, whose "organic Surrealism" takes its cues from Amos Tutuola (Nigerian author of *The Palm-Wine Drinkard*), rather than Breton (1–2). It was Lyle's poetry, more so than Lamantia's or even Kaufman's, that brought home to Alexander "that it was possible to conduct oneself this way in English," precisely because Lyle was a homeboy, was "someone who had developed in the community in which I lived, in which I was questing for an ecstatic kind of language" (2). Alexander's reading of such international surrealist writers of color as Kaufman, Césaire, Octavio Paz, and Jean-Joseph Rabearivelo came alive through a long series of conversations with Lyle, who basically embodied the "international rhythmus" to which Alexander was aesthetically drawn (3). But, moreover, their poetic communion did not exist in a vacuum. Alexander goes on in the introduction to describe a large and vibrant network of like-minded artists coming to flower in South Central Los Angeles in the mid-1970s:

> At this time both Lyle and myself were members of an extended community which was not unlike the great Surrealist gatherings some sixty years earlier, or the utopian communes evinced by Fourier a century prior to Breton. One of our central hubs was the Broadway and Manchester local where the Los Angeles musicians Ray and Ernest Straughter operated a collective incense business. In essence it was an Afro-Surrealist hive frequented by poets, musicians, and fellow travelers. (3)

Alexander locates this "Afro-Surrealist hive" as not only geographically proximate to Watts, but as aesthetically proximate to—influenced by— the previous decade's artistic innovators, namely musicians Eric Dolphy, Charles Mingus, and Ornette Coleman, as well as Cortez and the poets in the Watts Writers Workshop (to which Lyle had belonged from its inception in the wake of the Watts uprising) (4).[26] Thus, even as Lyle's influence helped Alexander develop roots that were "growing . . . against the imaginal limitation expected of the Afro-American poet," it connected him directly to writers and musicians whose own art had developed within—and helped to develop—the Black Arts Movement (3).

That Alexander ultimately has modeled himself more along the lines of the quintessential loner, Bob Kaufman, than the community-oriented Jayne Cortez, does not negate the importance of this communal moment early in his career. Nor did it later inhibit him from gathering with an impressive and eclectic group of innovative African American poets in April 2000 for "Expanding the Repertoire," a three-day symposium convened to discuss "the mostly unattended question of the history and role of innovation in contemporary African American writing" (Gladman and Singleton 3). The essay that documents his remarks at that gathering, "A New Liberty of Expression," contains some of his most trenchant criticism of BAM ideology, even as it participates in the conference's project of elaborating and extending a specifically "black" avant-garde tradition with its emphasis on aesthetic freedom. That Alexander's surrealism thus constitutes and, indeed, facilitates his black aesthetics cannot be surprising. As Robin D. G. Kelley has argued in *Freedom Dreams: The Black Radical Imagination*, the "black artists with whom the surrealists identify suggest that a thorough understanding and an acceptance of the Marvelous existed in the lives of blacks and non-Western peoples—before Breton, before Rimbaud, before Lautréamont—in music, dance, speech, the plastic arts, and above all philosophy" (185). This black openness to the surreal is grounded, for Alexander, as for Césaire, in an African cosmology that foregrounds the divinity of, and our participation in, nature, locating Alexander in a rich (if historically invisible) arena of African American poetic innovation—a tradition of "green" black aesthetics—of which Anne Spencer and Ed Roberson are two equally potent examples.

BLACK AESTHETICS AT THE TURN
OF THE TWENTY-FIRST CENTURY

I HAVE NOT ARGUED that all poets who identify racially or culturally as black or African American employ black aesthetics in their writing. Just as there are no essential racial characteristics, it is not inevitable that an African American poet will negotiate race in the process of writing. But we should not be surprised to find that so many African American poets do. As Kimberlé Crenshaw has noted, "To say that a category such as race or gender is socially constructed is not to say that that category has no significance in our world. On the contrary, a large and continuing project for subordinated people . . . is thinking about the way in which power has clustered around certain categories and is exercised against others" (375). That project has been one in which most African American poets—across genders, sexualities, class backgrounds, and other such factors—have participated, to varying degrees and in a plethora of ways, since Phillis Wheatley was writing.

For this reason, it is important that we are able to work with a conceptualization of black aesthetics fluid enough to account for the wide variety of experiences, concerns, and poetics that African American poets have, but grounded enough in social and literary histories relevant to a given poet's work to provide the necessary analytical precision. Scholars and critics of poetic traditions that include or overlap with African American poetry need to be aware of the breadth of ways that "blackness" or racial politics may manifest themselves in work by African American poets. This is not to say that the lens of black aesthetics must always be employed—there are other ways of entering and unpacking black poets' writing, of course—or that it will repay the inquiry to the same degree in every instance. Rather, the point is to destabilize, to dismantle, the assumption that, if race is going to be significant to a poem by an African American, we will be able to tell at a glance. This reconsideration of black aesthetics is equally vital for scholars and critics who focus on African American poetry, as it will enrich the tradition, suggesting additional, illuminating ways of reading poets individually and in juxtaposition.

For example, I had not imagined, at this study's inception, that half of my work would be taken up with how innovative African American poets conceive of nature. While, as a Southerner, perhaps, I had long been particularly aware of the presence of landscapes and gardens and other such "outdoors" images in work by black poets, I was nonetheless surprised to discover that such images—and other more encompassing conceptions of nature—might be not just the backdrop for poems dealing with race, but the analytical hinge upon which three poets' metaphysical or cosmological understandings of the world might turn. Yet, my interest in the ways "blackness" functions in the poetry of Anne Spencer, Ed Roberson, and Will Alexander ultimately taught me how intricately and imaginatively each of them views nature. For Spencer, as for Alexander, the divine is implicated in nature; she parlays this understanding into a poetic examination of how people have replaced the various gardens with which God has entrusted them with cities, places that cannot accommodate the caring and mutual respect that is necessary for social equality. Roberson's nature is secular, but like Spencer's (though less metaphorically), it comprehends cities as well as landscapes more traditionally considered "natural," and understands that how people treat nonhuman nature is a good measure of how they will treat other people. Alexander's poems do not speak to racism—except insofar as their reclamation of ancient African cosmologies demonstrates an imaginal liberty that diminishes the psychic impact of oppression, even if it cannot eliminate its material effects. Engaging the poets' black aesthetics reveals how the complexity of their views of nature, conjoined with our multilayered racial history, calls for formal innovation.

The deep attention to form that the investigation into black aesthetics invites is as critical as the emphasis it places on historical context and individual identity. Criticism of African American poetry too often treats the art as if it can be reduced to antiracist slogans. Nathaniel Mackey has attributed this gesture to the "emphasis upon accessibility" in African American poetry, among other traditions (17). A quality highly valued by BAM poets and activists, who wanted poetry to appeal to large numbers of African Americans who were not habitual readers of poetry, "accessibility" tends to be conflated with simplicity. The assumption that African American poets intend to write "accessible" poetry, according to Mackey, leads to "shallow, simplistic readings that belabor the most obvious aspects of the writer's work and situation, readings that go something like this: 'So-and-so is a black writer. Black people are victims of racism. So-and-so's writing speaks out against racism'" (18). Part of the point here is that not all African American poets value "accessibility" as much as the Black Aesthetic has insisted we should. But we must also recognize that even poetry intended to be accessible may be multilayered.

The three poets whose epics I treat in part I illustrate this point beauti-fully, if we recognize that each of them is motivated by concerns about accessibility, though in atypical ways. Sonia Sanchez was interested in making her AIDS elegy accessible to a segment of her African American audience that is homophobic. Gwendolyn Brooks sought to write about the desires and hopes of an African American woman in such a way that it would be accessible to the white men who predominantly comprised the literary establishment. Harryette Mullen's challenge was to make the long, fragmented history and diverse experiences of African American women speak to people unfamiliar with black women's wide cultural ter-ritory *and* to make her fragmented form and multiplicitous "I"s speak to people unfamiliar with these poetic strategies. Their poems become leg-ible as innovative encounters between the epic and lyric modes—and as highly inventive forms of resistance to masculine biases in both the American and African American literary traditions—precisely because our inquiry concerns something more than confirming that they are op-posed to their own oppression.

If a more expansive and fluid conception of black aesthetics leads to a correspondingly more expansive and nuanced construction of the canon of African American poetry, it will be none too soon. The African American poets of the twenty-first century are writing not in a post-racial moment, but in a moment that is being called "post-racial" in the face of massive and increasingly violent evidence to the contrary. The meanings of race are more amorphous, and the operation of racism is more dif-ficult to articulate, even for those of us who know it when we see it, so to speak. Among these poets are women who are being encouraged to think of feminism (and the *need* for feminism) as "dead," and gays, lesbians, and other queer-identified people who may be exoticized or fetishized in one minute and reviled or utterly ignored in the next. The contradictions inherent in the gaps between the discursive registers and the facts are worthy of the most multifaceted and surprising poetry these poets can invent. Already books like Renee Gladman's *The Activist*, Thomas Say-ers Ellis's *Skin, Inc.*, Ronaldo Wilson's *Poems of the Black Object*, Claudia Rankine's *Don't Let Me Be Lonely*, and Douglas Kearney's *The Black Au-tomaton*, all deeply occupied with the traditions and histories cited in this study as well as with the twenty-first century's "new normal," are available as markers of the aesthetic range the new millennium is calling into being. We must reread the innovative black aesthetics of the past century along with them, as it will prepare us—as much as we can be prepared—to engage the textual re-visions of "blackness" in the next.

NOTES

INTRODUCTION

1. I borrow the phrase "recognizably black" from Aldon Nielsen, whose "This Ain't No Disco" in *The World in Time and Space*, edited by Edward Foster and Joseph Donahue, offers a provocative, incisive discussion of the role played by racialized expectations for the work of African American poets in the constitution of a canon of poetic innovation. His pointed commentary on the desire of certain audiences for "recognizably black" writing appears on page 539.

2. As David Lionel Smith observes in his sharp and useful essay "The Black Arts Movement and Its Critics," published in *American Literary History*, "The concept of 'the Black Aesthetic' has been integrally linked with the Black Arts Movement, yet even at the height of that movement, there was no real agreement about the meaning of this term" (94). Smith goes on to parse some of the competing uses of the term that obtained the most traction in the short- and long-term.

3. Mathes and Mae Gwendolyn Henderson together organized the conference "Don't Say Goodbye to the Porkpie Hat": Re-evaluating Larry Neal's Creative and Critical Vision of the Black Aesthetic, which was held at Brooklyn College in November 2006. I am quoting from unpublished writing Mathes produced in connection with this event.

4. The elements of the caricature of the BAM's black aesthetic are, in fact, grounded in rhetoric used by Black Arts theorists and critics at times; to point to the selective nature of the construction of BAM ideology that leads to this caricature, then, is not to suggest that it is baseless. To sample some BAM-era language that contributes to this limited understanding of the Black Aesthetic, we might begin with "Towards a Black Aesthetic," by Hoyt Fuller, editor of *Negro Digest/Black World*. With some sense of the irony, one hopes, Fuller quoted a white critic's enumeration of the qualities that constitute the "mystique of blackness"—those catchy, colorful, and cool ways of dressing, talking, walking, and being that made black men from Satchel Paige to Sammy Davis, Jr., to Duke Ellington the epitome of style—as a way of suggesting what a black aesthetic might entail. "Black critics," he continued, "have the responsibility of approaching the works of black writers assuming these qualities to be present" (204, 205).

Don L. Lee (later known as Haki Madhubuti) noted in "Toward a Definition," his own essay on defining a black aesthetic, that African Americans' sensibilities have been shaped, to their detriment, by "a white nationalist consciousness called Americanism that's really a refined, or unrefined, depending on your view-point, weak version of the European sensibility" (214). Thus, "to understand the aesthetic of black art or that which is uniquely black, we must start [by examining black music, because it] was least distorted and was not molded into that which is referred to as a pure product of European-American culture" (213). My point here is not to isolate and make straw men of these two important figures, but simply to provide examples of the kinds of language and discussions that have come to stand, in too much of the subsequent discourse about the BAM, for the entire range of ideas that were in play.

5. See, for example, "The Myth of a 'Negro Literature,'" by LeRoi Jones (Amiri Baraka), for a cogent (if merciless) argument for why African American music should be the foundation and jumping-off point for African American writing; by contrast, see Stephen Henderson's introduction to his *Understanding the New Black Poetry: Black Speech and Black Music as Poetic References* for a thoughtful, descriptive analysis of the presence of black vernacular speech and music as sources for the form and content of African American poetry.

6. Two essays in the collection *Modern Black Poets*, edited by Donald Gibson and published during the waning years of the Movement, immediately suggest this view of the politics of the black aesthetic, in both its positive and negative constructions, simply through their titles: "The Poetry of Three Revolutionists: Don L. Lee, Sonia Sanchez, and Nikki Giovanni," by R. Roderick Palmer, and "The New Poetry of Black Hate," by Arthur P. Davis.

7. Gayle devotes his 1971 essay, "Cultural Strangulation: Black Literature and the White Aesthetic," to tracing the history of the association of "black" and "blackness" with danger and evil in Western culture.

8. Black feminist critiques of the formulation that puts black women at the fork in the road, forced to choose between race and gender, are numerous. Among the relatively early examples that circulated widely both within the academy and popularly would be Toni Cade's 1969 essay, "On the Issue of Roles"; Audre Lorde's 1979 essay, "Sexism: An American Disease in Blackface"; and bell hooks's 1981 book, *Ain't I a Woman: Black Women and Feminism*. A particularly influential theoretical counter to this formulation was proposed by legal scholar Kimberlé Crenshaw in 1991, in "Mapping the Margins: Intersectionality, Identity Politics, and Violence against Women of Color."

9. Specifically on this phenomenon in BAM writing, see, for example, chapter 3 of Elisabeth Frost's *The Feminist Avant-Garde in American Poetry*; Karen Jackson Ford, *Gender and the Poetics of Excess* (190–92); and chapter 2 of Phillip Brian Harper's *Are We Not Men?* For a discussion of this issue as it impacts the African American tradition more broadly, see Barbara Smith's important intervention, "Toward a Black Feminist Criticism."

10. See Mullen's essays "African Signs and Spirit Writing" (especially pp. 670–71) and "Incessant Elusives" for articulations of her critique of Gates's theory and the *Norton Anthology* that lead to important explorations of writers

and alternative traditions within the African American tradition not easily accommodated by his work.

11. Jarena Lee and Rebecca Cox Jackson are two of the most familiar names from this lineage. See Mullen, "African Signs" (676).

12. My articulation here is influenced by Arlene Keizer's discussion of the relationship of black subjectivity to the genre of contemporary narratives of slavery. Her book, *Black Subjects*, argues that "through their representations of slaves, these [contemporary African American and Caribbean] writers have managed to destabilize blackness as a biological or cultural essence, while maintaining a sense of the integrity of creolized black cultures in the Americas and showing how black subjectivities are produced and contested within these cultures" (11).

13. Notably, BAM poets and thinkers such as Sanchez, Baraka, and Ishmael Reed, among others, taught some of the very earliest courses in black (and black women's) literature.

14. Clarence Major, a poet whose work might easily have been treated in this study, has stressed the importance of context to aesthetics: "Aesthetics aren't a set of abstractions existing outside historical circumstances and daily reality; they're always grounded in the needs and aims of specific artists and audiences, influenced by the social setting and context" ("I Follow My Eyes" in *Clarence Major and His Art*, 80).

15. Mackey more specifically describes othering as "black linguistic and musical practices that accent variance, variability"—an aesthetic counter to the social condition to which African Americans have been subjected, that of being kept "in their place" (266). The relationship I am drawing between my thinking and Mackey's does not equate black aesthetics with othering, but emphasizes that both notions describe actions, rather than outcomes, and that both point to the artist's interest in strategies or practices that liberate the work from confining, racially based expectations.

16. I take the quoted phrase from Stephen Henderson, who observes: "Since poetry is the most concentrated and the most allusive of the verbal arts, if there is such a commodity as 'blackness' in literature (and I assume that there is), it should somehow be found in concentrated or in residual form in the poetry" (*Understanding* 4). In Gates's discussion of the flaws in Henderson's theory of blackness, he seizes upon this phrase: "Had Henderson elaborated on 'residual form' in literary language, measured formally, structurally, or linguistically, he would have revolutionized black literary criticism" ("Preface" 157). While I am arguing, quite to the contrary, that the blackness of black aesthetics is not a feature of the literature, but—to one degree or another—a factor in the subjectivity of African American writers, I agree with Henderson that the compression and heightened attention to form required in poetry makes it a particularly productive genre in which to seek the traces of blackness and, thus, to pursue my project of redefining black aesthetics. I also agree with Gates that it is critical that we attend to the "residual form" of writers' black aesthetics in literature, if and when we find it—but,

further, I would assert that works in which we do not find it, or do not find much of it, are just as valuable and interesting to think about within the framework of the African American tradition as those that are laden with it.

17. In "After Language Poetry," Marjorie Perloff makes a strong case that the term "innovative" has been overused to the point of meaninglessness (15–16). Perloff's compelling objections are grounded in the sense in which the term signifies "newness," however, whereas Mullen's definition, which I borrow here, focuses rather on the exploratory spirit with which the poet approaches her craft.

18. John Keene kicked off the *jubilat* "African American Experimental Poetry Forum," published in 2009, with the provocative question: "Isn't all poetry experimental at some level?" (Hayes and Shockley 119).

19. This is not to say that I am avoiding temporal questions raised by this project; indeed, one of my goals for the following chapters is to thoroughly historicize the works they treat with relation to how both social and poetics matters are functioning contemporarily with the writing of those works. I mean to signal simply that debates about the relationship between "modernist" and "postmodern" as categories of writing, which are significantly connected to questions of periodization, are not central to this study.

20. Nielsen, who devotes a number of pages of his influential book *Black Chant* to the Society of Umbra and the work of poets who participated therein, points to the importance of the relationship between the two avant-gardes: "That so much of Umbra work was formally, as well as politically, radical is something that needs to be considered when we think about this group's importance to the Black Arts Movement, in which several Umbra writers were key figures" (114). The larger argument of his book emphasizes the need for fuller histories of innovative writing by African Americans. On the related point of the occlusion of African American contributions to and participation in the modernist project, see Geoffrey Jacques's recently published *A Change in the Weather*, which offers a book-length corrective to this cultural and scholarly blind spot.

21. It must be said that both Roberson and, to an even greater extent, Mullen have become much less marginal to the African American canon during the six or seven years in which I have been working on this project. However, it becomes no less important for us to analyze and understand the lines of thought and social forces that created the historical circumstances which prevented Roberson's work from gaining a significant audience between 1970 and the turn of the century and created such complicated divisions in the collective audience for Mullen's first few books.

22. Thus, Moten's incomparable study *In the Break*—though with a very different approach and to different ends than my work here—may also be seen as a kind of response to Thomas's provocation.

23. I am drawing upon Gregson Davis's discussion of this line, as well as using his translation (17).

24. I recognize that there is ongoing debate about how the "epic" and the "long

poem" are to be defined, individually and in relation to one another. See Bernstein, Friedman, Kamboureli, and Keller. My purpose here, however, is not primarily to weigh in on that debate, but to consider the ways these poets' innovative engagement with long form, including the deliberateness with which they invoke and exploit longstanding epic conventions, figures in their negotiation of a literary terrain full of obstacles for them.

25. Black men who have published long poems in stanzaic form include: Albery Whitman (*Twasinta's Seminoles; or Rape of Florida*, published in 1885, was written in Spenserian stanzas); Fred D'Aguiar (*Bloodlines*, written in terza rima); and Major Jackson ("Letter to Brooks," which, written in rhyme royal, is doubly an homage and appears in his second book, *Hoops*).

26. See, for example, *The African Epic Controversy* by Mugyabuso M. Mulokozi and *The Epic in Africa* by Isadore Okpewho. See also *The Female Homer* by Jeremy M. Downes and *Approaches to the Anglo and American Female Epic, 1621–1982*, edited by Bernard Schweizer.

27. Bakhtin's formulations are not my focus here; however, I would note that his text "Epic and Novel," in distinguishing the polyglossia of the novel from the static, monoglossia of the epic past, indirectly underscores the innovative nature of these three poets' elicitation of polyvocality from the interaction between lyric and epic verse. See, especially, pp. 12–15. Mae Henderson's conceptualization of black women's writing as "speaking in tongues" is an outgrowth of her own engagement with Bakhtin in relation to her work on gender and race in African American literature.

1. CHANGING THE SUBJECT

1. For example, Don L. Lee opined in his preface to her 1972 autobiography that Brooks intended "In the Mecca" to be an "epic of black humanity" (22). Melhem herself had identified both epic and mock-epic elements in "The Anniad," in her 1987 study, *Gwendolyn Brooks: Poetry and the Heroic Voice*. Other critics, writing before and after 1990, would similarly deem these poems as epics (or as epic to some degree). See, for example, Cheryl Clarke, *"After Mecca"*; Ann Folwell Stanford, "An Epic with a Difference," and Tracey L. Walters, "Gwendolyn Brooks' 'The Anniad' and the Indeterminacy of Genre."

2. Hortense Spillers has described the title "The Anniad" as a pun on the name of one or both of the well-known Greek texts (121).

3. In a 1982 in-depth profile, when asked if certain critics (the type who "would shriek and shudder" at the idea that Brooks hopes her poetry has been "useful") mattered to her, Brooks responded: "Absolutely not. They used to. I used to watch for reviews. Wanted to write poetry that would bowl them over. No longer" (Kufrin 50).

4. The existence of such stereotyping and its potential for negatively affecting the reception of her work in that era is undeniable, as reviews of her books and

comments from her editor and advance readers demonstrate. (See George Kent's *A Life of Gwendolyn Brooks*, which contains numerous references to such materials.) It is worth noting, however, that in one of her earliest interviews (with Paul M. Angle, a noted Illinois historian), she denies having experienced such negative effects: "You asked me if being a Negro has adversely affected my 'career.' . . . My answer continues to be no. . . . [W]hen I was thirteen, or twelve, I began sending manuscripts to magazines. . . . I can't say that the manuscripts came back because I was Negro; they came back because they were not good. That is my experience. Now, you might get different answers from other writers of my race, and properly so" (Brooks, *Report* 140).

5. This is not to deny the extent to which her heroine may also function as an everywoman, irrespective of race, as argued by Tracey Walters, for example (357).

6. We might refer to "The Anniad" as a "pocket epic," following Brian McHale's extension of the term from the British to the American tradition (xii, 99–101).

7. Jenny Goodman and D. H. Melhem are among those who understand Annie's whole life, from birth through womanhood, to constitute the epic journey (Goodman "Revisionary" 166; Melhem, *Gwendolyn* 56). My focus on "The Anniad" is motivated in part by the formal choices that distinguish it from the first and last sections of *Annie Allen* (concerning both its unique lyric stanzas and its sustained length as a single poem, rather than a sequence). But I also take seriously Brooks's titular cues; Annie's "Girlhood" and her "Womanhood" precede and follow what Brooks deems "The Anniad," or the portion of Annie's story that is likened to ancient epic.

8. Ann Folwell Stanford, for example, states bluntly that "Annie ultimately fails in her quest for love" (285).

9. Stanley Kunitz, writing for *Poetry*, called the collection "uneven" and laced his mainly enthusiastic praise with criticism of the "awkward locution" of a line here, the "totally out of key" use of a word there (11, 12). The *Nation*'s critic, Rolfe Humphries, decried her "streaks . . . of awkwardness, naïveté, when she seems to be carried away by the big word or the spectacular rhyme; when her ear, of a sudden, goes all to pieces" (8). Phyllis McGinley's *New York Times* review applauded Brooks's "sophistication of thought and phrase" and "vitality," and described "The Anniad" as "technically dazzling, . . . a surprising accomplishment in combining story-telling with lyric elegance"—but faulted "youth and editors" for the volume's "unevenness" (177).

10. McGinley's admiration for "The Anniad" is cited in the preceding footnote. By contrast, "The Anniad" is one of the poems Kunitz singles out for his criticism (referencing it not by name, but by briefly quoting from its lines), and one suspects that Humphries also has this poem especially in mind in his critique.

11. It is generative to think here of Mark McMorris's discussion of Edouard Glissant on the Afro-Caribbean transformation of Créole speech, in which "distinctions between noise and lexicon collapse" (42). Noting that the power of this

mode of voice was that the master class could not follow meaning into its labyrinths of sound, McMorris goes on to quote Kamau Braithwaite on this subject: "It was in language that the slave was perhaps most successfully imprisoned by his master and it was in his (mis-)use of it that he perhaps most effectively rebelled" (42). Though at one level, Brooks may be seen as speaking *to* the "master class," if you will, through her employment of its traditional poetic forms, we might also consider the excessive musicality of her language as inviting into her poem some of "the opacity of orality" that comes at a pitch their ears cannot fully comprehend (42). See, relatedly, my discussion of the "poetics of excess," later in this chapter.

12. Just to briefly survey some landmarks on the critical territory, Don L. Lee (now known as Haki Madhubuti) wrote in 1972 that "'The Anniad' requires unusual concentrated study," which contributes to his perception that the collection was "written for whites" (17). One of her oft-anthologized poems, "the sonnet-ballad," though "probably earth-shaking to some, leaves [him] completely dry" (17). Just a few years later, in 1979, Hortense Spillers calls "The Anniad" "a funny poem," "a mock-heroic journey" (121). She asserts that it "may be read as a workshop in Brooks's poetry" because of the way it "echoe[s]" and "anticipates" poems that precede and follow it—indicating that it is not so unusual in Brooks's oeuvre as others might suggest (121). In 1991, Henry Taylor calls the poem "a tour de force," despite (or because of) the fact that "paraphrase is often difficult," noting that "it is also difficult to resist being carried along on the sound waves, heedless of incomprehension" (260). He sees its "satire" of Annie's naïveté turn to sympathy in the final stanza (264); in a nuanced, but not insignificant distinction, Melhem deems the poem "a mock heroic, more compassionate than critical or satirical" (62). At the close of the century, Joanne V. Gabbin, while acknowledging the "highly developed and stylized form" of "The Anniad," pointedly claims—within the pages of a critical anthology devoted to African American poetry that takes its name from Brooks's work—that it "is treasured because of the poignant truth it reveals about the male-female relationship" (261). Quite recently, Jenny Goodman has argued that *Annie Allen*, as a volume, constitutes "a book-length response to the Western epic tradition," while retaining for "The Anniad" the status of a "mock-epic" section of the larger epic work (160, 166).

13. Brooks's understanding of these demographics was made clear in an interview with Ida Lewis in 1971. Lewis asked, "Who was the audience for black poets before? Who supported your readings, for example?" Brooks's reply: "Chiefly whites, of course." To underscore that this situation was not specific to herself, she added: "Blacks didn't seem to be buying our people's work in great quantity, not even Langston Hughes's books. It was whites who were reading and listening to us, salving their consciences" (Brooks, "My People" 61). Inez Cunningham Stark, whose writing workshop for young South Side poets steeped Brooks and the other workshop participants in (high) modernist aesthetics, would have been among those who personally embodied that white elite readership of African American poetry for Brooks.

14. See Keith Leonard, *Fettered Genius*, pp. 121–22.

15. Brooks, *Blacks* 99. All citations to *Annie Allen* are to the edition reprinted in Brooks's collection *Blacks* and are hereafter cited parenthetically in the text.

16. Houston Baker describes Booker T. Washington, in his autobiography *Up from Slavery*, coming to a similar assessment about the inaudibility of the epic in a black context (and he without facing the additional obstacle of dismissal on gendered grounds), as he attempts to establish for his (white) audience the vast implications of Reconstruction, when "a whole race [was] beginning to go to school for the first time" (qtd. in Baker, *Modernism* 27). Washington likewise addresses the audibility problem via the rhetorical device of repetition. Baker points out that the "repeated announcement of the subject in the passage, pre-fixed by the phrase 'as I have stated,' comes so hard upon the opening epic intentions that it appears the narrator knows that no one in his white audience will listen to sounds of an epic" (27).

17. In this poem, which appears in the "Notes from the Childhood and the Girlhood" section of the volume, the oversleeping Annie is awakened thusly: "Out then shrieked the mother-dear, / 'Be I to fetch and carry? / Get a broom to whish the doors / Or get a man to marry'" (Brooks, *Blacks* 90).

18. Claudia Tate reads "The Anniad" as a pointedly critical mock-epic whose most direct target is the "virtually inert" and emotionally "flattened" Annie—and only secondarily the society that produced her (146–50). Melhem finds the poem a much more "compassionate" mock-epic than Tate does, removing Annie from the hot seat and noting that the mock-epic's satiric mode "afford[s] a means of social criticism, protected from political or literary reprisals by not seeming to take itself too seriously" (63). Spillers, calling the poem "mock-heroic" and "parodic," similarly focuses on its use of irony as a tool of social criticism (121). A. Yemisi Jimoh and Tracey Walters both see elements of the epic and the mock-epic in the poem; they also see Brooks's relationship with her heroine as less directly critical than Tate does. Importantly, Walters sees this generic ambivalence in the poem as evidence of Brooks's effort to revise the traditional epic so that it can accommodate a woman's psychological battle, rather than the typical physical confrontation a male hero would face (356). Walters's perspective overlaps to a degree with that of Ann Folwell Stanford, who also sees the poem's main thrust to be a critique, not of Annie, but of the structural imbalance of power between men and women. But where Walters's reading places the poem in the position of straddling the epic/mock-epic divide, Stanford reads "The Anniad" unequivocally into the epic tradition, noting that the use of the genre's conventions to critique patriarchy makes this poem "an epic tale with a difference" (286). Ironically, Keith Leonard's reading of the poem draws upon Stanford's discussion of Annie's creativity to emphasize what he regards as the young woman's "feminine" heroism, but follows the lead of earlier scholars in calling the poem a mock-epic (139, 145, 147).

19. Brooks's own "Negro Hero"—the title and subject of a poem in *A Street in Bronzeville*, her first book—would be a more typical figure for the role, insofar as he (Dorie Miller) was in the military (though assigned, because of segregation,

to the position of mess attendant), was known for his physical prowess, and was celebrated for his lifesaving bravery during the bombing of Pearl Harbor (Brooks, *Blacks* 48; see "A People at War," National Archives and Record Administration).

20. Only two other scholars, one of whom is Brooks's biographer, have noted the similarities between Brooks's life and Annie's. See Stanford (284–85) and Kent (58, 245).

21. See Tate (141–42, 149–50); Spillers (121). Stanford's essay on the poem does an admirable job of discussing these issues of gender with an eye on the racial nuances.

22. See, for example, Mary Helen Washington, "'Taming All That Anger Down': Rage and Silence in Gwendolyn Brooks's *Maud Martha*."

23. Particularly telling is Washington's observation that one of the news articles about Brooks's winning the Pulitzer Prize devoted more attention to her nine-year-old son's poetry than her own (*Invented Lives* xv).

24. Jimoh, for example, proposes that Brooks's "compassionate" satire "is conveyed through [her] mocking use of high reaching" and "purposefully overdone" language (177). Similarly, Tate sees satire in the fact that the poem's "verbal complexity," "erudite diction," and "elaborate techniques" are, in her view, "peculiarly inappropriate for describing" the passivity of Annie's circumscribed existence (141, 148).

25. This argument was made most famously by Hughes in his essay "The Negro Artist and the Racial Mountain."

26. Dunbar, who was most well-known during his lifetime for his dialect poetry, in fact felt painfully constricted by his predominantly white audience's lack of interest in his ostensibly more traditional work in "standard" English (James Weldon Johnson, *Book* 34–37). Elizabeth Alexander makes the point that both Dunbar and Brown blur the boundaries between the "vernacular" (or the "folk") and the "literary" (12, 21), indicating that the two earlier poets drew no ideological bright line between the two categories.

27. I am not arguing here that Brooks's language made a 180-degree shift between *A Street in Bronzeville* and *Annie Allen*, because her first book's more sophisticated poems speak in a voice that is unmistakably similar to the voice used in many poems in the first and last sections of the second book.

28. See chapter 4 for a fuller discussion of black aesthetics in the New Negro Renaissance context.

29. Indeed, it may be appropriate for us to recall here that Brooks's first book might not have been nearly as racially marked as it ended up, but for the suggestion of an editor at Knopf, the publisher to whom she sent the original manuscript. In a letter rejecting the manuscript but offering to consider a revised version, the editor, Emily Morrison, wrote that she "especially liked the 'Negro' poems, and asked that Gwendolyn approach Knopf again when she had a full collection in which the racial poems predominated" (Kent 62).

30. Keith Leonard's discussion of Brooks as a poet in the African American "bardic tradition" recognizes that "her virtuoso use of Anglo-American poetic

techniques" was, combined with her use of African American vernacular language and culture, a signal element of her pursuit and portrayal of "cultural self-definition" and, paradoxically, of her resistance to Anglo-American cultural hegemony (see 18, 118–120). However, where Leonard constructs the forms and conventions inherited from the English tradition as "fetters" that have constrained Brooks and other African American bardic poets, I argue that Brooks approached Anglo-American formal structures instead as tools that could serve her poetic goals.

31. Madhubuti/Lee, in his preface to Brooks's autobiography, described her recourse to "traditional" (that is, European-derived) forms as detrimental to her writing: "The early years reaped with self awareness—there is no denying this— even though at times the force of her poetic song is strained in iambic pentameter, European sonnets and English ballads. Conditioned!" (Lee, "Gwendolyn" 14).

32. Mullen offers such a critique of the way the oral is privileged at the expense of more visual, script-oriented aspects of African American literature in her essay "African Signs and Spirit Writing." This study follows Mullen's lead in attempting to right that critical imbalance, without at all discounting the importance of oral forms and qualities in the work of African American poets.

33. Brooks explained to her editor at Harper, in response to feedback about the "preciousness" and "artificiality" of the manuscript that became *Annie Allen*, that she "tried very hard, especially in ['The Anniad'] . . . , to say exactly what [she] meant, instead of approximately." She expressed surprise "that this reaching toward a more careful language should strike anyone as 'a trick and shock device'" (Kent 77).

34. Brooks's biographer, George Kent, points out that as early as 1937, Brooks was writing poems that reflected her internal conflict between the desire for love, which placed certain demands upon her as a woman, and the desire for fame, which called for time spent in devotion to her craft (50–51).

35. My unusual verb is derived from the last lines of *Annie Allen*: "We are lost, must / Wizard a track through our own screaming weed" (140).

36. Chapter 5 of Leonard's *Fettered Genius* makes a related, if different, argument about Brooks's portrayal of heroism as an internal "sovereignty" in *Annie Allen* and *A Street in Bronzeville*.

37. Tracey Walters remarks that, appropriately for the scale of an epic, "Annie Allen is 'any' oppressed woman anywhere" (357). Without losing sight of Annie's specifically American, urban, and black location, I agree with Walters that Annie is able to serve a broad symbolic function.

38. In "the sonnet-ballad," the speaker, Annie, construes her beloved's military service in WWII as analogous to infidelity, in that it creates a similarly irrevocable transformation of the romantic relationship:

Some day the war will end, but, oh, I knew
When he went walking grandly out that door
That my sweet love would have to be untrue.

Would have to be untrue. Would have to court
Coquettish death, whose impudent and strange
Possessive arms and beauty (of a sort)
Can make a hard man hesitate—and change. (*Blacks* 112)

Brooks has also written powerfully about how war changes men in her sonnet series "gay chaps at the bar," in *A Street in Bronzeville*.

39. Rarely are these stanzas, and the appearance of Annie's lover, in particular, discussed in the criticism, suggesting a kind of scholarly consensus that it would be impolite—if not incorrect—to note that Brooks, quite unjudgmentally, involves her heroine in an extramarital affair. But Brooks quite coolly and matter-of-factly discussed the subject of black married women's potential for taking lovers in her 1951 essay, "Why Negro Women Leave Home." Published in the March issue of *Negro Digest*, Brooks explains dispassionately that their experiences in the work world during the war and thereafter made black women less likely to stay in marriages that subjected them to consistent disrespect and intimidation, especially those in which the husband sees fit to make the wife cower and beg him for money to take care of herself, the house, or the children. It was such indignities, rather than a husband's own infidelities, that would motivate her to walk out on him. Brooks wrote: "The number of Negro women who leave because of the simple fact that their husbands are associating romantically with 'other women' dwindles from year to year, as the women develop more interest in world, cultural, and club interests and, increasingly, as they acquire freedom and surplus romantic attachments of their own" (27).

40. A local Chicago paper, interviewing the poet upon the acceptance of her first teaching job (at Chicago's Columbia College) in 1963, naively asked how it was that a "Pulitzer Prize–winning poet and a truly great Chicagoan" had never taught in the thirteen years since earning that national recognition. Brooks straightforwardly responded that "no one ever asked me before. . . . I guess because I have three strikes on me. I am a woman. I am a Negro. And I have no college degree." Her biographer notes the paper's "gracious" refusal to see how these facts could be "strikes" against Brooks ("except in the minds of small men"), but astutely recognizes that "institutional racism . . . had, of course, done the dirty work," leaving "the individual liberal or bigot"—such as this reporter—free to be surprised and even dismayed to learn of the impact of racial discrimination upon such a well-known figure as she was" (Kent 168). Compare Brooks's response here to the one quoted in footnote 4 of this chapter.

41. See Stephanie Shaw, *What a Woman Ought to Be and to Do* (1996). In her introduction, she cautions that, while "American women—and especially African American women—faced many barriers during their lives that prevented them from living as freely and as fully as they wanted," nonetheless "it is imperative to understand the objective reality of racism and sexism" as distinct from these women's "subjective experiences," which "often transcended their being oppressed" (5).

42. Interestingly, Phyllis McGinley, one of the critics who loved the "techni-

cally dazzling" "sophistication" of "The Anniad," dismissed poems like "Benvenuti's" as works in which Brooks "is being a clever if somewhat trite social critic"
and advised her to "forget . . . her social conscience" when writing (177).

43. For an overview of the varieties of modernism, in which Brooks's multiple
modernist influences come into view with productive clarity, see the introduction
to "First-Generation Modernisms" in *The New Anthology of American Poetry*, vol. 2,
edited by Steven Gould Axelrod et al., pp. 3–8.

2. EXPANDING THE SUBJECT

1. Sanchez's title will be hereinafter referred to simply as *Lions*.

2. Salaam approvingly notes Sanchez's ability to shift seamlessly between
African American blues forms and Japanese forms like haiku and tanka. He continues: "Sanchez's . . . syncretic grafting of afrocentric musical forms and musical
content onto . . . foreign poetic forms is the essence of Black postmodernism—
the Black, cross-discipline, multi-cultural appropriation of all existing forms to innovatively produce new forms which reflect and contemporarize not only a Black
aesthetic but which also offer example[s] and paradigms that others may use to
express themselves" (77). Note that Salaam is concerned not only with the fact
of formal innovation, but also with its function, its recyclability (a term which
connects Sanchez's aesthetics with those of Harryette Mullen, whose work is the
subject of the following chapter).

3. I would like to thank my colleague Carter Mathes for pointing to the connection between my phrase "expanding the subject" and the reconfiguration of
black subjectivity Sanchez attempts through her poetic innovations.

4. See Dwight McBride's essay "Can the Queen Speak?" for a thorough discussion of the silences in the antiracist discourse of African American intellectuals around black gays and lesbians and their concerns.

5. See Cheryl L. Cole's "Containing AIDS: Magic Johnson and Post-Reagan
America":

> Mainstream media routinely characterized AIDS as evidence of immoral
> behaviors and lifestyles that denoted identity categories: homosexuals,
> intravenous drug users, and prostitutes. Moreover, the meanings and values
> already attributed to these stigmatized groups shaped the media coverage
> and popular reception of AIDS. . . . Not surprisingly, prostitutes, intravenous
> drug users, and, most prominently, homosexuals, were represented as threats
> to the general public rather than communities threatened by a devastating
> crisis. In general, the person with AIDS was represented as an "AIDS victim"
> who was portrayed as guilty, diseased, contagious, isolated, threatening, and
> deteriorating. (415)

Not surprisingly, perhaps, one response to constructions of AIDS as a "black disease" has been the circulation among black people of a variety of conspiracy theo-

ries to explain the impact of AIDS in Africa, such as those that blame AIDS on "'whites' who want to contain black population growth; 'white doctors' who inject patients with AIDS when they go for tests; the CIA and pharmaceutical companies who want to create markets for drugs in Africa; [and] the use of Africans as guinea pigs for scientific experiments with AIDS drugs" (Robins 653–54).

6. See, for example, Giddings, *When and Where* (82–85). See also Dwight McBride's important essay "Straight Black Studies," especially pp. 70–71.

7. As David Román points out, however, the fact of Johnson's HIV-positive status did not mean the end of homophobia among African Americans; for example, he notes that "Johnson's own assurance on the Arsenio Hall Show that same week that he was 'far from homosexual' was met with cheers of heterosexist, if not homophobic, complicity" (204).

8. See also Stefanie Dunning's *Queer in Black and White*. Noting that her work contests "the idea that to be queer is to be outside the black community," Dunning adds, "We can trace this notion in the contemporary moment most notably to the Black Arts Movement" and its "nationalist ethos" (4).

9. See, for example, LeRoi Jones's essay "American Sexual Reference." See also Timothy S. Chin's "'Bullers' and 'Battymen'" for a useful discussion of the construction of homosexuality among people of African descent as an "unnatural," "foreign" condition introduced into black cultures via European (neo)colonial regimes.

10. The murder of fifteen-year-old Lawrence King by a junior-high-school classmate is just one recent example of an antigay hate crime to receive sustained national media attention. See Cathcart, "Boy's Killing, Labeled a Hate Crime, Stuns a Town."

11. The myth that African Americans (and Latinos) are *especially* homophobic manifested itself prominently in the backlash against black people from the gay community after Proposition 8 was voted into law in California in November 2008. The surge in African American and Latino voters associated with Obama's popularity was conflated with the number of votes by which Prop 8 was passed and blamed for the defeat suffered by proponents of gay marriage. The widely respected numbers analyst and blogger Nate Silver refuted the accusations against the African American community on his blog, *FiveThirtyEight*, noting that the vote was not split along a racial divide, but a generational one. See also the *Times* article by Jesse McKinley and Kirk Johnson, revealing the significant role that the Mormon Church (not even head quartered in the state of California) played in securing a victory for Prop 8.

12. In a review essay for *Black Issues Book Review*, legal and gender studies scholar Toni Lester commends Sanchez for having "faced up to the impact of HIV in a way few others in our communities have managed to do" (49). She continues:

Fortunately, . . . Sanchez and others have taken on the challenge of chronicling the story that lies beyond the numbers [comprising HIV/AIDS statistics]. One important part of the story has to do with the shock, fear and sometimes shame that people feel when they learn they have HIV/AIDS. Black writers of fiction, nonfiction, and poetry have been at the forefront in helping our community handle these deeply personal and social issues resulting from the epidemic. (49)

13. As an example of active repression of the subject, Sanchez told one interviewer that a "big-time black politician started calling me on my private line to ask me to stop talking about [the cause of her brother's death] in public because white people were saying that AIDS came from Africa and that I was perpetuating that myth" ("Sonia Sanchez: Joy" 152).

14. Elisabeth Frost discusses Sanchez's participation in the BAM in terms of a negotiation between promoting racial solidarity and developing a black feminist "avant-gardism" in her welcome study, *The Feminist Avant-Garde in American Poetry*.

15. See, for example, "The Aesthetics of Rap," an article by Dara Cook for *Black Issues Book Review*, on Sanchez's celebration of rappers like Tupac Shakur, Rakim, and Mos Def, the last of whom was photographed with Sanchez for the cover of the March/April 2000 issue in which the article appeared.

16. Dr. Frenzella Elaine De Lancey's work as founder and editor of *BMa* is both a testament to Sanchez's importance and an intervention in an otherwise dismal record of critical attention to Sanchez's work. Of the approximately thirty-four critical assessments of Sanchez's poetry listed in the MLA database as of November 2008 (including general treatments for reference books, but not including the numerous interviews she has published), about half appear in *BMa*. The only other publications of which I am aware that are named for or dedicated primarily to the work of an African American writer are the *Langston Hughes Review* and the *Richard Wright Newsletter*.

17. The final appearance of the word "faggot" in any of her books occurs in "To All Brothers: From All Sisters," in *Homegirls and Handgrenades* (34); her first reference to "homophobia" appears in "On the Occasion of Essence's Twenty-fifth Anniversary," in *Wounded in the House of a Friend* (19). For poems that include gays and lesbians among the groups of people she hails as allies and envisions in the future she is working to create, see "Morning Song and Evening Walk," "For Sweet Honey in the Rock," and "Aaaayeee Babo (Praise God)," in *Shake Loose My Skin* (143–56).

18. See, for example, the Centers for Disease Control and Prevention's "Fact Sheet: HIV/AIDS among African Americans."

19. Madhubuti is quoting himself here, from a book he published in 1991, titled *Black Men: Obsolete, Single, Dangerous?*; thus, his recognition of the issue of AIDS well predates the anthology's 2007 publication.

20. Michael Warner, in *The Trouble with Normal*, notes that "AIDS activists learned quickly that effective prevention cannot be based on shame and a refusal

to comprehend; it requires collective efforts at honest discussion, a realism about desire and a respect for pleasure" (51). In other words, to prevent AIDS from spreading, you cannot ostracize and stigmatize the people you are trying to help.

21. See Stephen Henderson's introduction to *Understanding the New Black Poetry*, in which he discusses, among other things, "the poem as 'score'"; the clarifying discussion of Henderson's work in relation to more recent scholarship on orality in African American literature in Aldon Nielsen's *Black Chant* (9–10), and Meta DuEwa Jones's invaluable essay on the interrelationship of visual and aural strategies in work by African American poets (including Sanchez), "Jazz Prosodies."

22. The poem does not function as a play, or even a closet drama, in any conventional sense, largely because even when the speakers are addressing one another—which is largely *not* the case—their stanzas are monologues, not dialogues, are narrative or emotional exposition, not speech in furtherance of the action that propels a play.

23. The relationship Sanchez draws between the individual and the collective in *Lions*, while innovating the epic, also participates in the *"tradition* of African American elegies" that Marcellus Blount traces back to Paul Laurence Dunbar (241; emphasis in original). We might say, then, that like the male poets Blount discusses, Sanchez creates an elegy that imagines "how individual utterance might illustrate communal values and how the individual comes to stand for a specific community" via "meditations on the dead [that] enact an emotional and ideological relationship to the living" (241).

24. Like the traditional epic poem, *Roots* is a lengthy narrative with deep national significance. Published in 1976, this 700-page, part-factual, part-imaginative account of Haley's family history sold a few million copies within a couple of years. The book begins in 1767 with the capture of a young man by slavers, follows him from western Africa through the Middle Passage and into U.S. slavery, then traces his descendents over seven generations down to Haley himself.

25. More recently, Major Jackson also paid tribute to Brooks's influence by writing a long poem in rhyme royal stanzas, "Letter to Brooks," in his 2006 book, *Hoops*. Jackson's poem, however, is located squarely in the realm of the lyric and thus does not extend Brooks's reformulation of the epic as *Lions* does.

26. See pp. 37–41 herein.

27. Ironically, Brooks was famously hard on herself, during the latter half of her career, for not writing poems that appealed as readily to nonliterary (as distinguished from nonliterate) black audiences as did those of the younger BAM poets like Lee (Madhubuti), Jones (Baraka), and, indeed, Sanchez.

28. For a discussion of the problematic black nationalist ideology underpinning such narratives, see McBride, "Can the Queen Speak?" (215–16).

29. For an essay discussing the mutual recognition of shared (black) aesthetics between BAM poets, particularly Sanchez, and hip-hop artists who write politically informed, lyrically demanding raps, like Mos Def, see "The Aesthetics of Rap," by Dara Cook.

30. Karla Holloway's *Moorings and Metaphors* treats the signal importance of the ancestral figure in novels like Gloria Naylor's *Mama Day*, Toni Cade Bambara's *The Salt Eaters*, and Paule Marshall's *Praisesong for the Widow*. Like those, Sanchez's text "features the presence of a mediating ancestor." Holloway explains that "sometimes the presence is meditative and instructive, sometimes . . . meditative and condemnatory, [and] sometimes . . . meditative and silent," but in each case, "the ancestral presence constitutes the posture of (re)membrance" (115).

31. The usefulness and prevalence of indirection as a strategy used by African American writers to circumvent or assuage particular audiences is suggested by, for example, Gates's discussion of signifying in *The Signifying Monkey*, Houston Baker's discussion of "the mastery of form" in *Modernism and the Harlem Renaissance*, and, of course, Mae Henderson's discussion of polyvocality in "Speaking in Tongues."

32. McBride's essay "Can the Queen Speak?" provides a vital discussion of the problem of challenging the heterosexism of antiracist discourse via the rhetoric of that discourse. As he puts it, the problem with "the substitution of heterosexist race logic with a homo-positive or homo-inclusive race logic" is that "the common denominator of both positions is the persistence of race as the privileged category in discussions of black identity" (218). As long as approaches to antiracism refuse to recognize that "if I am thinking about race, I should already be thinking about gender, class, and sexuality," it will continue to marginalize black gays and lesbians (224).

3. COMPLICATING THE SUBJECT

1. Harryette Mullen, *Muse & Drudge* (1). Future references to this work will be given parenthetically within the text.

2. "Kinky Quatrains" is the title Mullen gives her short essay on the poetics of *Muse & Drudge* for the anthology *Ecstatic Occasions, Expedient Forms*. She discusses there her interest in giving the quatrain form a "texture" that would be "quirky, irregular, and sensuously kinky" (165–66).

3. The majority of the readings of *Muse & Drudge*, as well as the line of questioning in most interviews with Mullen on the subject of this book, place it in the context of "experimental" American poetics and a Steinian tradition. See, for example, Frost; Cynthia Hogue (in the introduction to her "Interview" with Mullen, published in *Postmodern Culture*); and Mitchum Huehls. Certainly, given the relationship of Mullen's earlier books *Trimmings* and *S*PeRM**K*T* to Gertrude Stein's *Tender Buttons*, it is logical to read *Muse & Drudge* for an ongoing engagement with Stein and others of Stein's literary heirs. My work suggests, however, that the extent of that engagement in *Muse & Drudge* may be overestimated, or at least overemphasized, in ways that obscure Mullen's other literary inheritances and relationships—particularly those involving African American poetry and poetics, which historically has not figured in accounts of American avant-garde writing to nearly the degree that accuracy would call for.

4. See Gates, *The Signifying Monkey*, for an outline of the distinction between these two types of signification (xxvi–xxvii).

5. For a provocative reading of *Tree Tall Woman* and Mullen's even earlier work (collected for the first time very recently in *Blues Baby*) that argues that they are in fact quite similar to Mullen's most recent collection of new poetry, *Sleeping with the Dictionary*, see Alan Gilbert's essay "The Costs of Style: Harryette Mullen and *Freestyle*" in his book *Another Future*.

6. For a discussion of the supposed split between "blackness" and "innovation"—noting that it appears not to hold for black music the way it does for black writing—see Mullen, "Conversation." Mullen talks about her decision even to design the cover of *Muse & Drudge* in a way that would "signal" that it is "a black book" in her interview with Elisabeth Frost ("An Interview" 417).

7. For instance, Paul Hoover, in his often instructive essay on linguistic doubleness, asserts that "while the organization and style of the poems are postmodern, the content is grounded in black experience" (76). His "while" syntactically sets postmodern stylistics apart from blackness, in a binary logic Mullen is at great pains to dismantle, as I shall discuss further.

8. Geoffrey Jacques offers a critique of modernist scholar Michael North for falling into this way of thinking about the relationship between African American culture and early twentieth-century modernism; indeed Jacques's book proposes to answer the question: "What happens if we think of African American culture not as 'raw material' but as a codeterminate agent of the modernist project?" (6).

9. See my introduction for a complication of this proposition.

10. Angela Davis's book *Blues Legacies and Black Feminism* argues in great detail for the importance of the blues to black women's subjectivity, for precisely these reasons.

11. See note 2 to this chapter.

12. Citing Daphne Duval Harrison's work, Davis lists the following themes as typical of black women's blues: "advice to other women; alcohol; betrayal or abandonment; broken or failed love affairs; death; departure; dilemma of staying with man or returning to family; disease and afflictions; erotica; hell; homosexuality; infidelity; injustice; jail and serving time; loss of lover; love; men; mistreatment; murder; other woman; poverty; promiscuity; sadness; sex; suicide; supernatural; trains; traveling; unfaithfulness; vengeance; weariness, depression, and disillusionment; weight loss"—but, tellingly, not "children, domestic life, husband, and marriage" (13).

13. Jones/Baraka writes that "this intensely personal nature of blues-singing is also the result of what can be called the Negro's 'American experience'" (*Blues* 66). He compares the blues to traditional African songs, the latter of which focused more on the "social unit." The blues focus on the individual's life, he argues, "is a manifestation of the whole Western concept of man's life" (66), and thus derived specifically from the black experience of living in a Western society like the U.S.

14. See Tony Bolden's instructive elaboration of this point in his study *Afro-Blue* (42–43).

15. See Mullen's discussions of these compositional patterns in her interviews with Frost ("An Interview" 413) and Bedient ("Solo" 662), for example.

16. See Mullen's interview with Cynthia Hogue ("Interview" para. 3). I know from experience how confusing it is for a child in elementary school to discover that being accused of "talking proper" is an insult, from the perspective of her peers, when her parents have been stressing proper use of the language for as long as she can remember.

17. Compare Eric Weil's discussion of "the 'I' that means 'We' voice," in his essay "Personal and Public," for examples of how other African American poets have rendered their autobiographical or first-person persona speakers as collective racial speakers.

18. For an analysis of what Cat Moses names the "blues chorus"—a "dominant voice . . . affirmed by the blues and signifying offered by other women characters"—in Toni Morrison's novel *The Bluest Eye*, see her essay "The Blues Aesthetic in Toni Morrison's *The Bluest Eye*." My borrowing of her term does not bring with it the idea of a "dominant voice," but rather draws upon the idea of women's voices as mutually affirming one another via performances of "blues and signifying" (633).

19. It is worth reiterating here that, although Sanchez was writing *Does Your House Have Lions?* over a period of years that overlapped to some degree with Mullen's writing of *Muse & Drudge*, Sanchez's poem was not completed and published until two years later than Mullen's. The connection I am pointing to is thus not one of genealogy (in either direction), but one of similar aesthetic concerns and, broadly speaking, similar strategies for responding to those concerns.

20. See, for example, Mullen, "An Interview" 405.

21. See Susan Stanford Friedman's argument that the epic, like other long poem forms, "ha[s] assumed the authority of the dominant cultural discourses" (15).

22. See Frost's discussion of the blending of Sappho and Sapphire in this stanza (157).

23. See, for example, Evelyn Brooks Higginbotham's *Righteous Discontent*, for an influential study of the vastly underestimated importance of women's work in the Black Baptist Church from the post-Reconstruction period through World War I.

24. Mullen "recycles" a number of lines from the Bible, hymns and spirituals, and broadly religious discourse, and this aspect of her language play puts her work in a long tradition of African American writing that engages what Fahamisha Patricia Brown calls "traditional church"—specifically, "vernacular performance styles of worship common among African American evangelical Protestant congregations," especially the sermon (45). See chapter 3 of Brown's study for a helpful discussion of this vernacular register in African American poetry. While Brown's examples are mostly from a fairly serious, poignant vein of poetry, I would point to a work like Paul Laurence Dunbar's "An Ante-Bellum Sermon" as one whose

hilarious use of religious vernacular to make barely coded political statements is more clearly akin to Mullen's playfully pointed writing.

25. Racism, in the service of maintaining the institution of slavery, demanded that black women's subjective experiences of the transatlantic slave trade and the condition of enslavement go unacknowledged, or certainly unrecorded. Similarly, the nearly complete disappearance of Sappho's work is not attributable simply to the passage of time; rather, sexist reactions to her gender, generally and in relation to expressions of bisexual eroticism inscribed in her poems, ensured that her writing would have a far slimmer chance of surviving than that of her male contemporaries (W. R. Johnson xvi–xvii).

26. Mullen discusses her relationship, as a poet whose work is not typically formal, to the quatrain, "a ubiquitously familiar traditional form," in her essay "Kinky Quatrains" (165–66). For a fascinating overview of the transition of the traditional English and Scottish ballads from spoken and sung pieces into literature, most influentially by way of the collections of Francis James Child, see the opening section of Paula McDowell's essay "The Manufacture and Lingua-Facture of 'Ballad-Making'" (151–55).

27. Tony Bolden's overview of the blues acknowledges the normativity of the three-line, twelve-bar blues stanza: "Many standard definitions of blues music begin by referring to an aab pattern in which twelve bars are divided into four sections that consist of three lines. The first line is repeated (often with some variation), and the last line rhymes with the first" (39).

28. The ballad "Barbara Allen," for example, tells the story of a young man who is dying of love for Barbara Allen. A deathbed scene unfolds, the young woman refuses his love, but after his death feels such remorse that she follows him to the grave—literally buried by his side, where the rose growing from his grave intertwines with the briar growing from hers. By contrast, consider the way "Me and My Gin" (a blues song recorded by Bessie Smith that Mullen samples in the third quatrain of *Muse & Drudge*) comes at the theme of drinking from different angles, not to tell a sequential story, but to variously illustrate the same basic point that she loves and depends on her gin. See Angela Davis, *Blues* 310–11.

29. This phrase appears in at least one blues song, "You Don't Know My Mind," attributed to Doc Watson, and quoted by Langston Hughes in his autobiography *The Big Sea*: "You don't know my mind / When you see me laughing I'm laughing to keep from cryin'" (238).

30. See Hazel Carby's "'It Jus Be's Dat Way Sometime'" (232).

31. Mullen says of her own household, when she was growing up: "We were one of those religious families who thought, 'Ooh, this is the devil's music!' I had to really develop my appreciation later in life" ("An Interview" 409).

32. See Meta DuEwa Jones's *The Muse Is Music* 157–62.

33. My attention strictly to the music-related references in these lines by no means exhausts their meanings, which are as multiple as any others I have unpacked more fully.

34. A turn-of-the-twentieth-century novel that dramatizes—and, ultimately, argues against—this social condition is Pauline Hopkins's *Contending Forces.*

35. Jones/Baraka understands call-and-response as an African inheritance; moreover, and interestingly in this context, he notes that it has a structural relationship to the "twelve-bar, three-line" blues stanza (*Blues* 46, 70).

36. Mullen has talked about the fact that she grew up associating the Spanish language with black people, because of one of her elementary school teachers—a Panamanian man who was black and bilingual ("Solo" 652). I like to imagine that the insight this stanza provides also allows us to hear, in the previously considered lines "somebody's anybody's / yo-yo fulani" (*Muse* 40), a faint reference to the name of a popular dancer and performer of the 1970s and 1980s, Lola Falana, whose father was Cuban.

37. As Mitchum Huehls has noted, the end of the line is loosely anagrammatic of the beginning—"Patel hotel" and "hot plate" (24). That this was a particularly apt bit of wordplay is borne out in the fact that an American travel guide was published recently bearing the title *Cheap Motels and a Hot Plate.*

38. According to a BBC News article, the "'Patel hotel' phenomenon, as it is popularly known," refers to the fact that approximately "60% of mid-sized motel and hotel properties, all over the US, are owned by the people of Indian origin. Of this nearly one-third have the surname Patel—a popular one among Indian Guajaratis" (Dublish). The 1992 release *Mississippi Masala*, a feature film directed by Mira Nair, tells the story of a troubled romance between a black businessman and the daughter of Indian immigrants from East Africa who owned and operated a roadside motel.

39. See Mullen's intervention on the question of African literacy and oral societies in "African Signs and Spirit Writing."

40. Sanchez first published haiku in her third book, *Love Poems* (1973), but had by then been writing them already for years. She included haiku in nearly every subsequent collection, though she did not call them "blues haiku" until her 1998 volume *Like the Singing Coming off the Drums*; nonetheless, even the earliest of them exhibit qualities that would earn that description retrospectively.

41. Mullen attributes these references and discusses her reasons for using them in her interview with Cal Bedient ("Solo" 662, 666).

42. I should note, perhaps, that not *only* black women have confronted the type of dilemma I describe in this paragraph—the madonna/whore complex describes the archetype in broader (if Christian) terms—but the imperatives of sexual respectability have particular, and particularly intense, implications for African American women, as I discuss in chapter 2.

43. The definition appears under the word "bruckins," for which "Ethiopian breakdown" is one of a few synonyms (Cassidy and Le Page).

44. I have not devoted much space in this chapter to stanzas like this one that *center on* anagrams, aurally grounded lists, "nonsense" words, and so forth (as opposed to stanzas that employ those devices secondarily, in the service of juxta-

posing allusions), in part because that aspect of the text has been outlined quite usefully by Huehls and Frost.

45. "Mama's Baby, Papa's Maybe," Hortense Spillers's unparalleled essay on race, gender, and sexuality within the system of New World slavery, begins with an oft-quoted list of archetypes assigned to black women that informs my reading of *Muse & Drudge*. It bears repeating here:

> Let's face it. I am a marked woman, but not everybody knows my name.
> "Peaches" and "Brown Sugar," "Sapphire" and "Earth Mother," "Aunty,"
> "Granny," God's "Holy Fool," a "Miss Ebony First," or "Black Woman
> at the Podium": I describe a locus of confounded identities, a meeting
> ground of investments and privations in the national treasury of rhetori-
> cal wealth. My country needs me, and if I were not here, I would have to be
> invented. (203)

46. See also, for example, Mullen, "An Interview" 417; Mullen, "Interview" para. 28.

47. See Mullen, "Solo" 668.

48. See Mullen, "An Interview" 416–17.

4. PROTEST/POETRY

1. See James Weldon Johnson, *Book* 47; Cullen, *Caroling* xiii; Kerlin 158; and Fauset 66.

2. Unlike Spencer, the other two writers identified, Braithwaite and Yerby, both made explicit choices to exclude African American themes and characters from their works and not to discourage readers from assuming that they were white authors. The text I have quoted (and the characterization of Spencer, Braithwaite, and Yerby as writers who "write like whites") is unchanged in the anthology's 1992 revised version (A. P. Davis, et al., *The New Cavalcade* xxi).

3. See, for example, Felipe Smith's discussion in *American Body Politics* (171–72).

4. I am gesturing here towards the tiny poem "Anne Spencer's Table," by Langston Hughes, who in 1927 came to Lynchburg to read his poetry at Spencer's invitation, passing the visit as a guest in her home. He used the metaphor of her "unsharpened pencil" to entreat her to write more of the things he was certain she might produce (*Collected* 128). As I will develop in this chapter, Spencer had rea-sons to leave unwritten some things that Hughes, as a highly mobile man without responsibility for a family, might have felt empowered to take up.

5. Fascinatingly, Arthur P. Davis was the coeditor of the first volume to reprint "White Things," *The New Negro Renaissance*, released in 1975, just four years after *Cavalcade*. In the later anthology, three of Spencer's poems ("The Wife-Woman," "At the Carnival," and "Before the Feast of Shushan") appear under the heading

"The Genteel School: 'We Are Like You . . .'" and subheading "Raceless Litera-ture," while "White Things" is placed in the "Protest Literature" section.

6. I join scholars like J. Martin Favor who prefer to call this period the "New Negro Renaissance," rather than the "Harlem Renaissance," in part because of the misplaced geographical emphasis on Harlem—and, by extension, to other northern urban centers—accorded by the latter term. As Sterling Brown noted in a 1974 interview, the misnomer tended to skew the scholarship on the era toward a shorter period and more limited group of writers than is accurate. He criticized Nathan Huggins's then-recent study *Harlem Renaissance* specifically for omitting Anne Spencer, as an example of this problem ("Let Me" 809–10).

7. See, for comparison, Greene 52.

8. Greene gives an overview of Spencer's childhood in Bramwell, West Vir-ginia, where she and her mother went to live after her parents separated. Her mother, who worked as head cook at the town's only hotel, insisted upon placing the young Annie with one of the three black families in the otherwise all-white town, rather than letting the girl grow up among her cousins in the mining camps just outside Bramwell. Between the ages of five and eleven, Spencer had only one playmate—a young white girl—but spent the large part of her time "run-ning through the grass, collecting wild flowers, listening to the sounds of the ani-mals, and sitting on the river bank alone, just thinking and looking and listening" (Greene 11, 15, 21).

9. In *Women of the Harlem Renaissance*, Wall analyzes the "acidly," yet poi-gnantly written essay by Marita Bonner, describing the card parties that were supposed to occupy her brain and the impossibility of making a quick trip from Washington, D.C., to New York without the chaperone "propriety" required (4, 8–10); Hull, in *Color, Sex, and Poetry*, outlines the differential effects of the influ-ential Alain Locke's misogyny upon the young male writers he supported and the women writers he most often did not (7–11).

10. Erlene Stetson discusses the implications of writing in the era of the "Cult of True Negro Womanhood," specifically with regard to Spencer, in her essay "Anne Spencer" (402–03).

11. Honey's introduction to *Shadowed Dreams* (especially in the second edi-tion) discusses how metaphors building on natural imagery functioned as cov-ers "for describing their oppression in ways subversive of white male power yet indirect enough not to offend that very group" (xli). Greene's contextualizing and interpretive work with regard to Spencer's poetry is similarly illuminating for and important to my project.

12. Though describing herself as an "avid . . . housewife," Spencer nonetheless insisted: "I never washed or ironed a shirt for him [her husband, Edward]; I'm not a housekeeper" (Greene 45). Tracing and analyzing the complicated class posi-tionality Spencer occupied is another project well worth undertaking.

13. See, for example, Charita Ford's discussion of "Letter to My Sister" (11)

and Wall's characterization of "Lady, Lady," as a poem that "protests the exploitation of black women's labor" (*Women* 18).

14. Sterling Brown, who first met Spencer when he worked for a few early years of his academic career at the Virginia Theological Sanctuary and College in Lynchburg, wrote a poem called "To a Certain Lady, in Her Garden (For Anne Spencer)." The penultimate stanza speaks to what Spencer later jokingly referred to as "me and my dirty dress" (Greene 73): "Surely I think I shall remember this, / You in your old, rough dress, bedaubed with clay, / Your smudgy face parading happiness, / Life's puzzle solved" (Brown, *Collected* 117–18).

15. See Honey, xxxiii–xxxiv. Specifically as to Spencer, consider also the discussion of her work by British scholar Richard J. Gray, whose recent *History of American Literature* places her once again in the company of William Braithwaite. Gray describes both as writers who sought to keep poetry and politics separate: "Spencer . . . similarly preferred non-racial themes and traditional lyric forms. She could find, she confessed, 'no civilised articulation' for the things she hated, such as racial prejudice. So, using elaborate rhythmic patterns, highly wrought language and densely woven imagery, she explored the personal but also universal subjects of life and time ('Substitution' [1927]), love and peace ('For Jim, Easter Eve' [1949]), nature and beauty ('Lines to a Nasturtium' [1926])" (527). Fascinatingly, his next line posits that "Countee Cullen is a slightly more complicated case" (527). I submit that Spencer's is just as complex a case as Cullen's, if not more so, for the gendered and geographical reasons this chapter explores.

16. Compare Hughes's short lyric "My People" (published in *Caroling Dusk* under the title "Poem"), which draws upon a similar logic in comparing the "night" and "stars" to the "faces" and "eyes" of African American people (Cullen 150).

17. See, for example, Paula Giddings, chapter 5 (*When* 85–94); Hazel Carby (*Reconstructing* 111–18).

18. See "Lynching Statistics by Year and Race," <http://www.law.umkc.edu/faculty/projects/ftrials/shipp/lynchingyear.html>.

19. For example, in a 2002 essay, Christine Gerhardt advocated bringing postcolonial theory into conversation with ecocriticsm on the grounds that the former analytical lens offers "critical tools that help to explore the ways in which black literature addresses intersections between racial oppression and the exploitation of nature" (516). Ecopoetics and ecocriticism are discussed in more detail in chapter 5.

20. See Greene for the most complete published gathering of Spencer's extant poems (appendix); on her friendship with Bess Alexander (106); and on her epistolary poem (indeed, "verse letter") to and friendship with Hughes (75). Greene also discusses the vandalism of her garden cottage (called "Edankraal") in her later years, which resulted in the destruction of many unpublished poems she had written over the years (162, 175).

21. See Spencer Papers, Box 17, in the folder "Love and Gardens." The draft es-

say is undated; the only thing of which I can be certain, at this point, is that it was written before her eyesight began to decline—which Greene dates at around 1972 (162–63)—as evidenced by the quality of her handwriting. I quote from this draft in the next paragraph.

22. The version of this poem that appears in Greene's appendix contains a substantially different first quatrain than that which appears in the Cullen anthology, based on revisions Spencer made in 1974, during her work with Greene on her biography (Greene 100). I have chosen to focus on the text as originally published.

23. The laws Spencer offers as possibly containing the prohibition against poetry like Johnson's are telling: the Supreme Court's Dred Scott Decision (1857) ruled that African Americans were not citizens of the U.S.; the Monroe Doctrine (1823) informed the European colonial powers that the Americas were off-limits to their imperial ambitions; and Marque and Reprisal letters authorize private citizens to undertake otherwise illegal seizures of property or personnel in nations deemed enemies of the U.S. Spencer thus implies that Johnson's style of love poetry—signaling African American self-determination—constitutes a threat to the nation.

24. See, for example, Gray 527.

25. Having famously stated in his "Forethought" to *The Souls of Black Folk* that "the problem of the twentieth century is the problem of the color line," Du Bois begins the first chapter of his landmark study by revealing the unspoken question that liberal white people of the day, he asserts, secretly desired to have answered: "How does it feel to be a problem?" (359, 363).

5. BLACK AND GREEN

1. June Jordan, too, outlines the issue in a moving essay, "The Difficult Miracle of Black Poetry in America or Something Like a Sonnet for Phillis Wheatley." She recounts her experience as the final judge of a Minnesota-based poetry contest, in which all sixteen finalists employed a lexicon that was "accurate to the specific Minnesota daily life of those white poets"—and distinctly *not* reflective of the danger, racist violence, and poverty that characterized her "own Black life" (72). Jordan writes:

> I did not and I would not presume to impose my urgencies upon white poets writing in America. But . . . the *difficult* miracle of Black poetry in America, is that . . . we are frequently dismissed as "political" or "topical" or "sloganeering" and "crude" and "insignificant" because, like Phillis Wheatley, we have persisted for freedom. We will write against [apartheid] South Africa and we will seldom pen a poem about wild geese flying over Prague, or grizzlies at the rain barrel under the dwarf willow trees. (72; emphasis in original)

Jordan very powerfully identifies the dynamic at stake here—all the more powerfully, perhaps, because the essay is defending Wheatley from those who would find fault with her for writing poems about Christianity, Greek mythology, American generals, death, and, yes, nature, rather than the great injustice of her enslavement.

2. Keorapetse Kgositsile, a South African activist who became a poet and participant in the Black Arts Movement while in exile in the U.S., puts it this way: "Need I remind / Anyone again that / Armed struggle / Is an act of love" (62).

3. Jennifer DeVere Brody, using contemporary critical race theory to analyze the problematic racial classifications operative in Victorian England, "argues that purity is impossible and, in fact, every mention of the related term, *hybrid*, only confirms a strategic taxonomy that constructs purity as a prior (fictive) ground" (11–12). This conceptual framework is applicable not only to distinctions between black and white racial categories, but to other attempts to "separate and distinguish (binary) categories" (12)—such as the dichotomization of politics and aesthetics.

4. Of the handful of books (monographs and essay collections) published in the last several years and devoted entirely to ecopoetry, ecocriticism, and/or nature writing that I consulted in writing this essay, I found only two African American poets treated at length: Nathaniel Mackey in Jed Rasula's *This Compost* and Derek Walcott in George Handley's *New World Poetics* and in Roy Osamu Kamada's "Postcolonial Romanticisms." The omission of African Americans from nature poetry anthologies over the years is so striking, it motivated Camille Dungy to put together an entire anthology devoted to nature poems by black poets, *Black Nature: Four Centuries of African American Nature Poetry*, which was published in 2009.

5. African American poets Julie Patton, Tracie Morris, Tyrone Williams, and LaTasha N. Nevada Diggs, for example, are represented (in poetry and in prose) in recent eco-oriented publications of the avant-garde community, while a different group of innovative African American poets, including Douglas Kearney, C. S. Giscombe, and Roberson himself, are to be found in the *Black Nature* anthology.

6. Indeed, the dichotomy is belied by the work of some of the most celebrated Romantic nature poets—such as William Wordsworth and Percy Shelley—who also penned passionately political poems. See, for example, Wordsworth's "The World Is Too Much with Us" and Shelley's "England in 1819."

7. See, for example, Bryson 5; Gilcrest 3; Skinner 6–7.

8. For example, Christopher Arigo elaborates upon Skinner's mission statement for the journal *ecopoetics*—"dedicated to exploring creative-critical edges between writing (with an emphasis on poetry) and ecology (the theory and praxis of deliberate earthlings)"—in ways that align "ecopoetics," proscriptively or in practice, with the poetic avant-garde. Repeating the oft-noted fact that *oikos*, the Greek root of "eco," means "house," Arigo argues, "A good ecopoem then is a *house made founded on the tension between the cutting edge of innovation and ecological thinking*" (1–3; emphasis in original). He continues:

> Ecopoetics does not necessarily mean nature poetry. . . . In fact, much of the ecopoetry being written seems to take place more in the realm of the innovative, as opposed to more mainstream poetries. Perhaps this is because innovative poetries are loci of resistance to mainstream poetic practices (and values) which presumably reflect larger social paradigms. Thus innovative practices and ecological thinking/being/feeling combine to produce a site of resistance, of politics, of political resistance. (3)

Similarly, Marcella Durand's frequently referenced talk-cum-essay, "The Ecology of Poetry," argues: "Ecopoetics showcases a more experimental ecological poetry, one that begins to take into itself ecological processes, as well as ecological concerns. . . . [T]his fusion of matter with perception, observation with process, concentration to transmission . . . would most decisively turn what can seem nostalgic remnants of 'nature' poetry into a more dynamic, affective and pertinent poetry" (58–59).

9. I should point out that I myself am sympathetic to many of the claims Arigo, Durand, and others are making—indeed, my reading of Roberson's work shares some of these values, to a certain degree. However, it is not just ironic, but instructive, to recognize in the positions of the heirs to Language poetry some of the same types of strategies and postures embraced by BAM poets and theorists, in the context of racial, rather than environmental politics. It underscores the accuracy of Erica Hunt's analysis in "Notes for an Oppositional Poetics" of the underlying connections between the purportedly divergent Language poetry and BAM avant-gardes.

10. The words I borrow here come from an essay in which Hart is similarly (but on different grounds) making the case for seeing Language poet Larry Eigner as a nature poet. Hart's assertion is apt, even though I must point out that Roberson has declined to identify his work as "postmodernism" (Roberson, "Down" 680). Indeed, relative emphasis on language is an important point of divergence between the two poets' aesthetics. According to Hart, it is Eigner's focus on "the materiality of language [that] brings nature and language together on the page in a manner that . . . e challenges the distinction between the inside and outside of the text that causes the polarization of nature and writing" (315–16). By contrast, Roberson claims a broader set of imperatives. In response to Crown's question whether he sees his work under the banner of "African American postmodernism," Roberson explicitly rejects the aspect of "play" associated with the term, and elaborates: "I wouldn't call it postmodernism. It's just any means possible to sing. . . . Folks [innovative African American poets] have different ways of getting it done, or making it pretty, or finding that one point in the chaos that you can carry with you downstream. We're not just going to do form and nothing else, or just language and nothing else" ("Down" 680).

11. Moreover, as Christine Gerhardt writes, "The ideology that stigmatized blacks as 'beastly' creatures to be mastered not only served as a justification of

slavery but was systematically institutionalized through slavery's various oppressive practices" (522–23).

12. To clarify, I do not mean to suggest that all African American writing about Africa is necessarily Afro-Romantic, even when one or both of the motivations I identified are involved.

13. Buell offers a concise overview of his "five-dimensional phenomenology of subjective place-attachment" in *The Future of Environmental Criticism*. Most significant for my discussion here are the three spatial dimensions he describes: (1) the "concentric circles" that mark our emotional homebase; (2) the "archipelago" composed of one's past homes, far-flung workplaces, or other locales where we feel or have felt rooted; and (3) the places to which one becomes attached purely through imagining them (72–73). As we will see, Roberson's poem "kenai lake alaska" brings all three types of spaces together.

14. Hillman's poetic statement, "Twelve Writings toward a Poetics of Alchemy, Dread, Inconsistency, Betweenness, and California Geological Syntax," appears in Claudia Rankine and Juliana Spahr's wonderful anthology *American Women Poets in the 21st Century*, which provides a selection of poetry, a poetic statement, and a critical essay for each of the ten poets included.

15. Oelschlaeger writes about the cosmos as the postmodernist's wilderness. He proposes that contemplation of cosmology and the universe could have a very different outcome than the reification of the self/other and culture/nature binaries that resulted from the Romantics' meditations upon European wildernesses. Provocatively, he writes:

> Today, stretching back into time with our instruments of technology, we reawaken the profound longing in all human beings for the ground of being. Ironically, with these instruments we discover not being but the reality of Becoming. We now hear the Cosmic Hiss, the Beginning of Time, and we intuit, as profoundly modern humans, the finitude of our being. We understand that only in this universe could carbon-based finitude such as us come into existence. We are not the privileged children fashioned in the image of God but coordinate interfaces of the historical process of nature. We do not impose value upon a valueless cosmos; rather, we are sensitive registers of values created through the unfolding of time. (336)

Rather than being the lords or dominators of the cosmos, we come to see that "we are no more than reflections of cosmic process" (336). From this view, Roberson's interest in the cosmological in his poetry is entirely logical, perhaps inevitable. But see my discussion in chapter 6 of Will Alexander's poetic meditations upon the cosmos for a very different (African-based) way of imagining one's position in the vastness of the universe—an alternative that might be an equally or more useful lens for reading Roberson's take on the space surrounding the earth.

16. Kathleen Crown has described Roberson's use of repetition as his "stut-

ters," arguing persuasively that they allow him to concretize the "historical intervals"—that is, "the breaks and gaps in our historical consciousness"—and to "register the traumatic experiences of racism" ("Reading" 196–97). The term "stammer" has been differently but relatedly deployed to describe the graphic device of a "long unbroken black line" that cuts across the page in much of Nathaniel Mackey's poetry (and Roberson's as well): first, in Brent Hayes Edwards's "Notes on Poetics Regarding Nathaniel Mackey's *Song*," and then revisited by Matthew A. Lavery in "The Ontogeny and Phylogeny of Mackey's *Song of the Andoumboulou.*"

17. The predominantly male pantheon of Romantic nature poets traditionally (and troublingly) gendered the earth and "Mother Nature" herself as feminine, playing into familiar Western dichotomies: "The usual sexual dynamic in romantic nature poetry assumes, therefore, a speaking male subject who explores his relation to a mute and female nature" (McNew 60). Roberson undercuts this norm in that the naturalized female figure has a voice in his poem. Feminist scholarship in recent decades has worked to uncover the significance of this tradition, both for the poetry of the Romantic era and contemporary neoromantic poetry, ecopoetry, and ecopoetics. See, for example, *Romanticism and Feminism*, edited by Anne Mellor; Janet McNew's essay, "Mary Oliver and the Tradition of Romantic Nature Poetry"; Buell's brief overview of the field of ecofeminism (108–112); and essays in the "Ecopoetics" special feature, edited by Harriet Tarlo, in the feminist journal on women's writing, *HOW2*.

18. Roberson's unpublished lecture is available on audio at the Poetry Foundation Website.

19. Christine Gerhardt's essay, "The Greening of African-American Landscapes," supports the argument that a contemporary African American writer might represent the identification of himself or herself with the environment in ways that draw powerfully and positively upon the negative historical construction of black people as "wild beasts" who required domination (516–17, 522–23). While I think Roberson's work, in general, gestures to a different type of identification than Gerhardt means to suggest, her work is nonetheless useful in pointing toward the significance of race in his rejection of an idea of nature as that which humankind must take care of—the benevolent counterpart of the idea of nature as that which humankind must conquer.

20. For Russo, an ecopoetics "operates through an awareness of language as a framing device, which accompanies a more basic awareness of the potential abuse of 'nature' as a framing device that identifies and isolates an 'other' onto which is cast human fears, ideals, desires, etc.—sometimes as the 'voice of nature' (3).

6. WILL ALEXANDER'S SURREALIST NATURE

1. Remarkably, his outsider status extends even to the context in which his presence would seem most likely. Franklin Rosemont and Robin D. G. Kelley coedited a rich anthology titled *Black, Brown, and Beige*, published in 2009, which

seeks to make visible the engagement of black writers and artists with surrealism over the past eighty years (which is to say, almost since its beginning). The anthology collects work not only by the fifty people of African descent who explicitly considered themselves surrealists, but also their forerunners and even individuals not affiliated with surrealism but whose work "qualifie[s] as objectively surrealist" (2). Alexander is not represented in the anthology—though a single volume from his oeuvre, the 1995 poetry collection *The Stratospheric Canticles*, is listed in its bibliography.

2. Gregson Davis, in his wonderfully instructive study, *Aimé Césaire*, is among the many critics who cite Andre Breton's enthusiastic praise for Césaire's *Cahier d'un retour au pays natal* (*Notebook of a Return to the Native Land*, as it is commonly known in English—or, "Journal of a Homecoming," as Davis translates it). Breton famously deemed the poem "the greatest lyric monument of our time" (Davis 20).

3. In an interview, Will Alexander draws attention to the fact that "Kemet," a name for ancient Egypt, "actually means 'black soil'" ("Will" 15). I use it here suggestively, but also as a way of marking the common interest of Césaire and Alexander in ancient Egyptian mythology and cosmology—of which more later.

4. Or in Will Alexander's own terms: "Words are capable of universal poetics; and I mean by universal, possessing the power of pyretic plasticity. In consequence, the language of botany, or medicine, or law, takes on a transmogrified dictation, where their particulars blend into a higher poetic service, in which they cease to know themselves as they were, thereby embarking upon a startling, unprecedented existence" ("Poetry" 173).

5. Andrew Joron, in "The Missing Body," and Charles Borkhuis, in "Writing from Inside Language," are both engaged in theorizing "the possibilities of an encounter between late Surrealism and Language poetry" in which the two traditions are constructed as equally important contributors to "the second wave of response against the modernist ego-centered lyric" (Joron, "Body" 52, 53).

6. The stream of surrealism associated with Latin American poetry, particularly with the work of Octavio Paz (which emphasizes the element of the sacred in surrealism), is also relevant to an overall understanding of Alexander's poetics, but is beyond the scope of this chapter. See, as a starting point for scholarship in English, Lloyd King's essay "Surrealism and the Sacred in the Aesthetic Credo of Octavio Paz."

7. A. James Arnold argues in *Modernism and Negritude* that Césaire's reading of the precursors of surrealism, together with the "irrationalist" ethnography of Africanist Leo Frobenius, directed Césaire toward "a pervasive antirealist attitude" that made him appreciate surrealist poetics in the late 1930s and, after his wartime encounter with Breton in Martinique, led him to embrace "surrealist ideology" as well, "graft[ing]" it onto his conception of négritude (12, 89).

8. Will Alexander points also to this compatibility when he notes that Breton and the other surrealists of the 1920s took a public stance "against the French Moroccan policy." He contrasts their racial politics with those of U.S. avant-garde

modernists, "like Pound or Eliot," who never "protest[ed] the lynchers in America" during that same general era ("Ambidextrous" 29).

9. In his exuberant essay "Poetry and Knowledge," Césaire devotes a whole page to a discussion of the role of poetry in "recall[ing]" us to the "original relationships that bind us to nature" and the role of the poet in "resolv[ing] . . . two of the most anguishing antinomies that exist: the antinomy of one and other, the antinomy of Self and World" (236, 237). The "world" is figured in this discussion in terms of "the azure sky" and "a golden spark in nature's light" (237).

10. In an interview, Marcella Durand prompts Alexander: "You've said you don't travel much physically, but you're a great mental traveler." He responds:

> The imagination has to ignite the process, wherever the base is. That said, I find that because the mind goes at such a rate, I can almost—as the old metaphysicians talked about—go directly to Mauritania or to Haiti, or Canada, or Detroit, or wherever I've been to and then relate it to the idea of the supraplane and the physical plane. All of those levels partake of one single substance. . . . I can go there instantaneously. [Giles] Deleuze talks about that—traveling from your chair. And it works because if I had to travel as fast as my mind was working, I couldn't do it. ("Will" 13)

11. Cheikh Anta Diop, whom Will Alexander cites on occasion, notes that the prevalence of the belief in the coexistence of a visible and an invisible world was one of the factors that made it relatively easy for the Muslim faith to take hold on the continent: "A third cause for the success of Islam in Africa seems to reside in a certain metaphysical relationship between African beliefs and the 'Muslim tradition.' In the latter there is to be found an invisible world, a doppelganger of the visible one . . . indeed an exact replica of it, but the initiate alone can see it" (165). Diop goes on to argue that "this conception of a dual world is to be found, in various forms, in the beliefs of Africans to such a point . . . they feel completely comfortable in Islam" (165–66).

12. As Will Alexander puts it: "When you're dealing with the surreal, when it organically vibrates—this is what Césaire said about surrealism—it's perfectly conjunctive with my understanding of an African world view. It deals with the visible and the invisible" ("Hauling" 404).

13. Writing about Jayne Cortez, another important African American surrealist poet, T. J. Anderson III notes:

> The manner in which Cortez uses language may appear exotic to readers grounded in the tradition of European surrealism, but she has more in common with Caribbean poets like Aimé Césaire and Léon Damas than their European counterparts. What Cortez shares with Césaire and Damas is a poetics that originates from a distinctly African and African American realism

in which the power and creation of nature plays an integral part in everyday existence. (120)

Anderson's observation, made in passing, about the role of nature in a black, African American surrealism initially motivated me to pursue this line of thinking with regard to Alexander.

14. My suspicion is that "chance" in this passage is a typographical error—that it should read "change"—but the emphasis on "shifts" and "transmuting" signifies that change is Alexander's focus here, in any case.

15. See, for comparison, Geoffrey Jacques, *A Change in the Weather* (3–4).

16. He writes that, as a black speaker of Dutch, English, or Spanish, for example, "I merely reflect the language of my enslavers, who have distorted my African totality, my inscrutable matrix lamp, my natural Ashanti upheaval. By carrying these languages, I do not express through them the conviction of a patriot, forever beholden to their Euro-historic objectives, artificially imposed upon my African reflex and world view. These languages merely exist as veneers" ("Singing" 149–50).

17. The Miles Davis/Gil Evans recording, *Sketches of Spain*, includes a track titled "Solea" that draws upon this musical tradition. Alexander's enthusiasm for jazz virtually ensures his familiarity with this tune. See Nielsen, "Will Alexander's Transmundane" 414.

18. The importance of the Sun God, Ra, to ancient Egyptian religion is well known (and recalled for African Americans in the name chosen for himself by the innovative jazz musician Sun-Ra). But, according to John Shields's research on the poet Phillis Wheatley, the "practice of sun worship," a "fetishistic" religion that Wheatley recalls her mother engaging in, was emphasized to such an extent that it had become indelible in her consciousness, even at the age of seven—which Wheatley is believed to have been when she made the Middle Passage journey (241–42).

19. For example, Alexander makes this point in his interview with Marcella Durand ("Will" 15, 18) and in his essay "My Interior Vita" (371).

20. In this sense, Alexander's book offers an alternative for the postmodern sublime not considered by Christopher Arigo's formulation of the "Revised Sublime." See Arigo 3–10.

21. Auriga, Bellatrix, and Canis Major are glossed in the poem as stars or constellations that together seem to suggest the entire scope of the heavens, as seen from earth, through their respective positions in the northern sky, on the celestial equator, and in the southern sky.

22. I am thinking particularly about Butler's *Parable of the Sower* and *Parable of the Talents*, the first two novels of what was to have been a trilogy that is partly about a new religion established by the character Lauren Olamina. This religion, Earthseed, literalizes the idea of heaven by decreeing that the goal and

purpose of humankind must be to develop the means of long-term extraterrestrial existence—that is, "to take root among the stars" (Butler 84).

23. See chapter 4. Spencer's language appears in a letter to James Weldon Johnson, archived in the Johnson Papers (emphasis in original).

24. For example, we see this thematic concern in the very title of William Andrews's study *To Tell a Free Story*.

25. For a succinct discussion of Kaufman's family background that addresses both the self-perpetuated rumors and the substantiated evidence of his heritage, see Smethurst, 366–67.

26. See, for example, Nielsen, "Will Alexander's 'Transmundane Specific'" 411; Mullen, "Collective" 423.

27. Two sources that helped me form a picture of the rich artistic landscape of Black L.A. during the 1960s were James Smethurst's *The Black Arts Movement* (see chapter 5) and Daniel Widener's "Writing Watts."

BIBLIOGRAPHY

Abrams, M. H. "The Correspondent Breeze: A Romantic Metaphor." Abrams, *English* 37–54.

———, ed. *English Romantic Poets: Modern Essays in Criticism*. New York: Oxford UP, 1975.

———. *A Glossary of Literary Terms*. Boston: Thompson Wadsworth, 2005.

Adamson, Joni, Mei Mei Evans, and Rachel Stein, eds. *The Environmental Justice Reader: Politics, Poetics, and Pedagogy*. Tucson: U of Arizona P, 2002.

Alexander, Elizabeth. *Power and Possibility: Essays, Reviews, and Interviews*. Ann Arbor: U of Michigan P, 2007.

Alexander, Will. "Above a Marred Poetic Zodiac and Its Confines." Alexander, *Singing* 135–40.

———. "Alchemical Dada: An Interview with Will Alexander." Interview by Grant Jenkins. Alexander, *Singing* 247–79.

———. "Alchemy as Poetic Kindling." Alexander, *Singing* 163–69.

———. "The Ambidextrous Surreal: An Interview with Will Alexander." Interview by Grant Jenkins. *Rain Taxi* 11.2 (Summer 2006): 28–30.

———. "The Caribbean: Language as Translucent Imminence." Alexander, *Singing* 141–45.

———. *Exobiology as Goddess*. Santa Clara, CA: Manifest P, 2004.

———. "The Footnotes Exploded." Alexander, *Singing* 121–25.

———. "Hauling Up Gold from the Abyss: An Interview with Will Alexander." Interview by Harryette Mullen. *Callaloo* 22.2 (1999): 391–408.

———. "The Impact of a Living Being." Alexander, *Singing* 89–95.

———. "My Interior Vita." *Callaloo* 22.2 (1999): 370–73.

———. "Nathaniel Mackey: 'An Ashen Finesse.'" *Callaloo* 23.2 (2000): 700–02.

———. "A New Liberty of Expression." *Tripwire: A Journal of Poetics* 5 (Fall 2001): 67–68.

———. "Poetry: Alchemical Anguish and Fire." Alexander, *Singing* 173–74.

———. "Re-emergence from the Catacombs." Introduction. *Electric Church*. By K. Curtis Lyle. Venice, CA: Beyond Baroque, 2003. 1–4.

———. "Singing in Magnetic Hoofbeat." Alexander, *Singing* 149–54.

———. *Singing in Magnetic Hoofbeat: Essays, Prose Texts, Interviews, and a Lecture, 1991–2007*. Ed. Taylor Brady. 1990?–2008. Typescript. Collection of the author.

———. "Will Alexander: A Profound Investigation." Interview by Marcella Durand. *The Poetry Project Newsletter* (Feb./Mar. 2005): 13+.

Anderson, T. J., III. *Notes to Make the Sound Come Right: Four Innovators of Jazz Poetry.* Fayetteville: U of Arkansas P, 2004.

Annie Allen, review. *Booklist* (1 Nov. 1949): 79.

Annie Allen, review. *New Yorker* (17 Dec. 1949): 130.

Andrews, William. *To Tell a Free Story: The First Century of Afro-American Autobiography, 1760–1865.* Champaign: U of Illinois P, 1988.

Arigo, Christopher. "Notes toward an Ecopoetics: Revising the Postmodern Sublime and Juliana Spahr's *This Connection of Everyone with Lungs*." *HOW2* 3.2 (2008). Website.

Arnold, A. James. *Modernism and Negritude: The Poetry and Poetics of Aimé Césaire.* Cambridge: Harvard UP, 1981.

Asim, Jabari. "A Revival with Sonia Sanchez." *American Visions* 13.1 (Feb./Mar. 1998): 27–28.

Attridge, Derek, and Henry Staten. "Reading for the Obvious: A Conversation." *World Picture* 2 (Autumn 2008): 1–16. Website.

Axelrod, Steven Gould, Camille Roman, and Thomas Travisano, eds. *The New Anthology of American Poetry.* Vol. 2, Modernisms, 1900–1950. New Brunswick: Rutgers UP, 2005.

Baker, Houston A., Jr. *Blues, Ideology, and Afro-American Literature: A Vernacular Theory.* Chicago: U of Chicago P, 1984.

———. *Modernism and the Harlem Renaissance.* Chicago: U of Chicago P, 1987.

———. "On the Criticism of Black American Literature: One View of the Black Aesthetic." *African American Literary Theory: A Reader.* Ed. Winston Napier. New York: NYU P, 2000. 113–31.

Bakhtin, Mikhail. "Epic and Novel: Toward a Methodology for the Study of the Novel." *The Dialogic Imagination: Four Essays.* By Bakhtin. Ed. Michael Holquist. Trans. Caryl Emerson and Michael Holquist. Austin: U of Texas P, 1981. 3–40.

Baraka, Amiri. "Black Art." *Transbluesency: Selected Poems 1961–1995.* By Baraka. New York: Marsilio, 1995. 142–43.

———. "The Revolutionary Tradition in Afro-American Literature." *Daggers and Javelins: Essays, 1974–79.* By Baraka. New York: Morrow, 1984. 137–48.

Barksdale, Richard, and Keneth Kinnamon, eds. *Black Writers of America: A Comprehensive Anthology.* New York: Macmillan, 1972.

Bernstein, Michael André. *The Tale of the Tribe: Ezra Pound and the Modern Verse Epic.* Princeton: Princeton UP, 1980.

Bettridge, Joel. "'Whose Lives Are Lonely Too': Harryette Mullen Reading Us into Contingency." *Mandorla: Nueva Escritura de las Américas / New Writings from the Americas* 7 (Spring 2004): 212–26.

Blount, Marcellus. "Paul Laurence Dunbar and the African American Elegy." *African American Review* 41.2 (Summer 2007): 239–46.

Bolden, Tony. *Afro-Blue: Improvisations in African American Poetry and Culture.* Urbana: U of Illinois P, 2004.

Bontemps, Arna, ed. *American Negro Poetry.* New York: Hill & Wang/Farrar, 1974.

Borkhuis, Charles. "Writing from Inside Language: Late Surrealism and Textual Poetry in France and the United States." *Telling It Slant: Avant-Garde Poetics of the 1990s.* Eds. Mark Wallace and Steven Marks. Tuscaloosa: U of Alabama P, 2002. 237–53.

Brody, Jennifer DeVere. *Impossible Purities: Blackness, Femininity, and Victorian Culture.* Durham: Duke UP, 1998.

Brooks, Gwendolyn. *Annie Allen.* Rpt. in *Blacks.* By Brooks. 77–140.

———. *Blacks.* Chicago: Third World P, 1987.

———. "A Conversation with Gwendolyn Brooks." Interview with Studs Terkel. Wade-Gayles 3–12.

———. "A Conversation with Gwendolyn Brooks." Interview with Susan Elizabeth Howe and Jay Fox. Wade-Gayles 140–48.

———. "Gwendolyn Brooks." Interview with Roy Newquist. Wade-Gayles 26–36.

———. "Gwendolyn Brooks: Humanism and Heroism." Interview with D. H. Melhem. Wade-Gayles 149–54.

———. "An Interview with Gwendolyn Brooks." Interview with George Stavros. Wade-Gayles 37–53.

———. *Maud Martha.* Chicago: Third World P, 1993.

———. "'My People Are Black People.'" Interview with Ida Lewis. Wade-Gayles 54–66.

———. *Report from Part One.* Detroit: Broadside P, 1972.

———. *A Street in Bronzeville.* Rpt. in *Blacks.* By Brooks. 17–75.

———. "Update on Part One: An Interview with Gwendolyn Brooks." Interview with Gloria T. Hull and Posey Gallagher. Wade-Gayles 85–103.

———. "Why Negro Women Leave Home." *Negro Digest* 9.5 (Mar. 1951): 26–28.

Brown, Fahamisha Patricia. *Performing the Word: African American Poetry as Vernacular Culture.* New Brunswick: Rutgers UP, 1999.

Brown, Sterling A. "The Blues." *Phylon* 13.4 (1952): 286–92.

———. *The Collected Poems of Sterling A. Brown.* Ed. Michael S. Harper. Chicago: TriQuarterly/Another Chicago P, 1989.

———. "'Let Me Be with Ole Jazzbo': An Interview with Sterling A. Brown." *Callaloo* 14.4 (Autumn 1991): 795–815.

———, Arthur P. Davis, and Ulysses Lee, eds. *The Negro Caravan.* New York: Arno P/New York Times, 1969.

Bryson, J. Scott, ed. *Ecopoetry: A Critical Introduction.* Salt Lake City: U of Utah P, 2002.

Buell, Lawrence. *The Future of Environmental Criticism: Environmental Crisis and Literary Imagination.* Malden, MA: Blackwell, 2005.

Butler, Octavia. *Parable of the Sower.* New York: Grand Central/Hachette, 2000.

Cade, Toni. "On the Issue of Roles." *The Black Woman: An Anthology*. Ed. Cade. New York: Mentor/New American Library, 1970. 101–10.

Carby, Hazel. "'It Jus Be's Dat Way Sometime': The Sexual Politics of Women's Blues." *Radical America* 20.4 (1986): 9–24. Rpt. in *Gender and Discourse: The Power of Talk*. Ed. Alexandra Dundas Todd and Sue Fisher. Norwood, NJ: Ablex Publishing, 1988. 227–42.

———. *Reconstructing Womanhood: The Emergence of the Afro-American Woman Novelist*. New York: Oxford UP, 1987.

Cassidy, F. G., and R. B. Le Page, eds. *A Dictionary of Jamaican English*. Kingston: U of the West Indies P, 2002.

Cathcart, Rebecca. "Boy's Killing, Labeled a Hate Crime, Stuns a Town." *New York Times* 23 Feb. 2008. Website.

Caws, Mary Ann. *The Poetry of Dada and Surrealism: Aragon, Breton, Tzara, Eluard, and Desnos*. Princeton: Princeton UP, 1970.

Centers for Disease Control and Prevention. "Fact Sheet: HIV/AIDS among African Americans." *Centers for Disease Control and Prevention*. Website.

Césaire, Aimé. *Notebook of a Return to the Native Land*. By Césaire. Trans. Clayton Eshleman and Annette Smith. Berkeley: U of California P, 1983. 35–85.

———. "Poetry and Knowledge." Trans. A. James Arnold. *Toward the Open Field: Poets on the Art of Poetry, 1800–1950*. Ed. Melissa Kwasny. Middletown, CT: Wesleyan UP, 2004. 231–43.

Chin, Timothy S. "'Bullers' and 'Battymen': Contesting Homophobia in Black Popular Culture and Contemporary Caribbean Literature." *Callaloo* 20.1 (Winter 1997): 127–41.

Chinitz, David. "Literacy and Authenticity: The Blues Poems of Langston Hughes." *Callaloo* 19.1 (Winter 1996): 177–92.

Clarke, Cheryl. *"After Mecca": Women Poets and the Black Arts Movement*. New Brunswick: Rutgers UP, 2005.

———. "The Failure to Transform: Homophobia in the Black Community." *Home Girls: A Black Feminist Anthology*. Ed. Barbara Smith. New York: Kitchen Table: Women of Color P, 1983. 197–208.

Clifton, Lucille. "surely i am able to write poems." *Mercy*. Rochester: BOA Editions, 2004. 23.

Cole, Cheryl L. "Containing AIDS: Magic Johnson and Post-Reagan America." *The Greatest Taboo: Homosexuality in Black Communities*. Ed. Delroy Constantine-Simms. Los Angeles: Alyson Books, 2000. 415–40.

Cook, Dara. "The Aesthetics of Rap." *Black Issues Book Review* 2.2 (Mar.–Apr. 2000): 22–27.

Crenshaw, Kimberlé. "Mapping the Margins: Intersectionality, Identity Politics, and Violence against Women of Color." *Stanford Law Review* 43 (1991): 1241–99. Rpt. in *Critical Race Theory: The Key Writings That Formed the Movement*. Ed. Crenshaw et al. New York: New P, 1995. 357–83.

Crown, Kathleen. "'Choice Voice Noise': Soundings in Innovative African-

American Poetry." *Assembling Alternatives: Reading Postmodern Poetries Transnationally*. Ed. Romana Huk. Middletown: Wesleyan UP, 2003. 219–45.

———. "Reading the 'Lucid Interval': Race, Trauma, and Literacy in the Poetry of Ed Roberson." *Poetics Today* 21 (2000): 187–220.

Cullen, Countee, ed. *Caroling Dusk: An Anthology of Verse by Negro Poets*. New York: Harper, 1927. Rpt. as *Caroling Dusk: An Anthology of Verse by Black Poets of the Twenties*. New York: Citadel P/Carol Publishing, 1993.

———. "Heritage." *The Vintage Book of African American Poetry*. Ed. Michael S. Harper and Anthony Walton. New York: Vintage/Random, 2000. 157–61.

Cummings, Allison. "Playing Tennis with Asbestos Gloves: Women, Formalism and Subjectivity in the 1980s." *After New Formalism: Poets on Form, Narrative, and Tradition*. Ed. Annie Finch. Ashland, OR: Story Line P, 1999.

———. "Public Subjects: Race and the Critical Reception of Gwendolyn Brooks, Erica Hunt, and Harryette Mullen." *Frontiers* 26.2 (2005): 3–36.

Cusak, George. "A Cold Eye Cast Inward: Seamus Heaney's *Field Work*." *New Hibernia Review* 6.3 (2002): 53–72.

D'Aguiar, Fred. *Bloodlines*. Woodstock: Overlook P, 2001.

Damon, Maria. Introduction. "Bob Kaufman: A Special Section." Ed. Damon. *Callaloo* 25.1 (Winter 2002): 105–11.

Davis, Angela Y. *Blues Legacies and Black Feminism: Gertrude "Ma" Rainey, Bessie Smith, and Billie Holiday*. New York: Vintage/Random House, 1998.

Davis, Arthur P. "The Black and Tan Motif in the Poetry of Gwendolyn Brooks." *College Literature Association Journal* 6.2 (1962): 90–97.

———. "The New Poetry of Black Hate." Gibson, *Modern* 147–56.

———, and Michael W. Peplow, eds. *The New Negro Renaissance: An Anthology*. New York: Holt, Rinehart and Winston, 1975.

———, and Saunders Redding, eds. *Cavalcade: Negro American Writing from 1760 to the Present*. Boston: Houghton Mifflin, 1971.

———, Saunders Redding, and Joyce A. Joyce, eds. *The New Cavalcade: African American Writing from 1760 to the Present*. Washington, D.C.: Howard UP, 1992.

Davis, Gregson. *Aimé Césaire*. New York: Cambridge UP, 1997.

Dieke, Ikenna. "Alice Walker: Poesy and the Earthling Psyche." *The Furious Flowering of African American Poetry*. Ed. Joanne Gabbin. Charlottesville: U of Virginia P, 1999. 169–81.

Diop, Cheikh Anta. *Precolonial Black Africa*. Trans. Harold Salemson. Brooklyn: Lawrence Hill, 1987.

Dove, Rita. *Selected Poems*. New York: Vintage/Random, 1993.

Downes, Jeremy M. *The Female Homer: An Exploration of Women's Epic Poetry*. Newark: U of Delaware P, 2010.

Dreer, Herman, ed. *American Literature by Negro Authors*. New York: Macmillan, 1950.

Dublish, Chhavi. "America's Patel Motels." *BBC News*. Website.

Du Bois, W. E. B. "Criteria of Negro Art." *Within the Circle: An Anthology of African American Literary Criticism from the Harlem Renaissance to the Present.* Ed. Angelyn Mitchell. Durham: Duke UP, 1994. 60–68.

———. *The Souls of Black Folk.* Ed. Nathan Huggins. New York: Library of America, 1986. 357–547.

duCille, Ann. "The Occult of True Black Womanhood." *Skin Trade.* By duCille. Cambridge: Harvard UP, 1996. 81–119.

Dunbar, Paul Laurence. "An Ante-Bellum Sermon." Randall, *Black* 44–46.

Dungy, Camille, ed. *Black Nature: Four Centuries of African American Nature Poetry.* Athens: U of Georgia P, 2009.

Dunning, Stefanie K. *Queer in Black and White: Interraciality, Same Sex Desire, and Contemporary African American Culture.* Bloomington: U of Indiana P, 2009.

Durand, Marcella. "The Ecology of Poetry." *ecopoetics* 2 (Fall 2002): 58–62.

Edwards, Brent Hayes. "Aimé Césaire and the Syntax of Influence." *Research in African Literatures* 36.2 (Summer 2005): 1–18.

———. "Black Serial Poetics: An Introduction to Ed Roberson." *Callaloo* 33.3 (2010): 621–37.

———. "Notes on Poetics Regarding Nathaniel Mackey's *Song*." *Callaloo* 23.2 (2000): 572–91.

Ellison, Ralph. "Society, Morality, and the Novel." *The Living Novel: A Symposium.* Ed. Granville Hicks. New York: Macmillan, 1957. 58–91.

Eshleman, Clayton, and Annette Smith. Introduction. *The Collected Poetry.* By Aimé Césaire. Trans. Eshleman and Smith. Berkeley: U of California P, 1983 1–31.

Fauset, Jessie. "As to Books." *The Crisis* 24.2 (June 1922): 66–68.

Favor, J. Martin. *Authentic Blackness: The Folk in the New Negro Renaissance.* Durham: Duke UP, 1999.

Ferril, Thomas Hornsby. Rev. of *Annie Allen,* by Gwendolyn Brooks. *San Francisco Chronicle: This World* 13.20 (18 Sept. 1949): 18.

Ford, Charita M. "Flowering a Feminist Garden: The Writings and Poetry of Anne Spencer." *SAGE* 1 (Summer 1988): 7–14.

Ford, Karen Jackson. *Gender and the Poetics of Excess: Moments of Brocade.* Jackson: UP of Mississippi, 1997.

Foster, Edward. "Poetry and the Art of Motorcycle Maintenance." Rev. of *Voices Cast Out to Talk Us In,* by Ed Roberson. *American Book Review* 17.3 (1996): 4+.

Fowlie, Wallace. *Age of Surrealism.* Bloomington: U of Indiana P, 1960.

Friedman, Susan Stanford. "When a 'Long' Poem Is a 'Big' Poem: Self-Authorizing Strategies in Women's Twentieth-Century 'Long Poems.'" *Dwelling in Possibility: Women Poets and Critics on Poetry.* Ed. Yopie Prins and Maeera Shreiber. Ithaca: Cornell UP, 1997. 13–37.

Frischkorn, Rebecca T., and Reuben M. Rainey. *Half My World: The Garden of Anne Spencer, A History and Guide.* Lynchburg: Warwick House, 2003.

Frost, Elisabeth A. *The Feminist Avant-Garde in American Poetry.* Iowa City: U of Iowa P, 2003.

Fuller, Hoyt W. "Towards a Black Aesthetic." *Within the Circle: An Anthology of African American Literary Criticism from the Harlem Renaissance to the Present.* Ed. Angelyn Mitchell. Durham: Duke UP, 1994. 199–206.

Gabbin, Joanne V., ed. *The Furious Flowering of African American Poetry.* Charlottesville: UP of Virgina, 1999.

Gates, Henry Louis, Jr. "Preface to Blackness: Text and Pretext." *African American Literary Theory: A Reader.* Ed. Winston Napier. New York: NYU P, 2000. 147–64.

———. *The Signifying Monkey: A Theory of Afro-American Literary Criticism.* New York: Oxford UP, 1988.

Gayle, Addison, Jr. *The Black Aesthetic.* Garden City, NY: Doubleday, 1971.

———. "Cultural Strangulation: Black Literature and the White Aesthetic." *Within the Circle: An Anthology of African American Literary Criticism from the Harlem Renaissance to the Present.* Ed. Angelyn Mitchell. Durham: Duke UP, 1994. 207–12.

———. "The Function of Black Literature at the Present Time." Gayle, *Black* 407–19.

Gerhardt, Christine. "The Greening of African-American Landscapes: Where Ecocriticism Meets Post-Colonial Theory." *Mississippi Quarterly* 55 (2002): 515–33.

Gibson, Donald B., ed. *Modern Black Poets: A Collection of Critical Essays.* Englewood Cliffs, NJ: Spectrum/Prentice-Hall, 1973.

Giddings, Paula J. *Ida: A Sword among Lions: Ida B. Wells and the Campaign against Lynching.* New York: Amistad/HarperCollins, 2008.

———. *When and Where I Enter: The Impact of Black Women on Race and Sex in America.* New York: Quill/Morrow, 1984.

Gilbert, Alan. *Another Future: Poetry and Art in a Postmodern Twilight.* Middletown, CT: Wesleyan UP, 2006.

Gilcrest, David W. *Greening the Lyre: Environmental Poetics and Ethics.* Reno: U of Nevada P, 2002.

Giovanni, Nikki. "For Saundra." Randall, *Black* 321–22.

Gladman, Renee, and giovanni singleton. Introduction. *Tripwire: A Journal of Poetics* 5 (Fall 2001): 3–4.

"The Global HIV/AIDS Timeline." The Henry J. Kaiser Family Foundation. Website.

Goodman, Jenny. "Revisionary Postwar Heroism in Gwendolyn Brooks's *Annie Allen.*" Schweizer, *Approaches* 159–80.

Gray, Richard J. *A History of American Literature.* Malden, MA: Blackwell P, 2004.

Greene, J. Lee. *Time's Unfading Garden: Anne Spencer's Life and Poetry.* Baton Rouge: Louisiana State UP, 1977.

Haley, Alex. *Roots.* New York: Doubleday, 1976.

Hamilton, Edith. *Mythology: Timeless Tales of Gods and Heroes.* New York: Mentor, 1942.

Handley, George B. *New World Poetics: Nature and the Adamic Imagination of Whitman, Neruda, and Walcott.* Athens: U of Georgia P, 2007.

Harper, Phillip Brian. *Are We Not Men? Masculine Anxiety and the Problem of African-American Identity.* New York: Oxford UP, 1996.

Hart, George. "Postmodernist Nature/Poetry: The Example of Larry Eigner." *Reading under the Sign of Nature: New Essays in Ecocriticism.* Ed. John Tallmadge and Henry Harrington. Salt Lake City: U of Utah P, 2000. 315–32.

Hartman, Geoffrey H. "Nature and the Humanization of the Self in Wordsworth." Abrams, *English* 123–32.

———. "Wordsworth, Inscriptions, and Romantic Nature Poetry." *Beyond Formalism: Literary Essays, 1958–1970.* By Hartman. New Haven: Yale UP, 1970.

Hayden, Robert. "A Letter from Phillis Wheatley." *Collected Poems.* By Hayden. Ed. Frederick Glaysher. New York: Liveright, 1997. 147–48.

Hayes, Terrance, and Evie Shockley, eds. "African American Experimental Poetry Forum." *jubilat* 16 (2009): 115–54.

Henderson, Mae Gwendolyn. "Speaking in Tongues: Dialogics, Dialectics, and the Black Woman Writer's Literary Tradition." *African American Literary Theory: A Reader.* Ed. Winston Napier. New York: NYU P, 2000. 348–68.

Henderson, Stephen E. "Saturation: Progress Report on a Theory of Black Poetry." *African American Literary Theory: A Reader.* Ed. Winston Napier. New York: NYU P, 2000. 102–12.

———. *Understanding the New Black Poetry: Black Speech and Black Music as Poetic References.* New York: Morrow, 1973.

Higginbotham, Evelyn Brooks. *Righteous Discontent: The Women's Movement in the Black Baptist Church, 1880–1920.* Cambridge: Harvard UP, 1993.

Hillman, Brenda. *Cascadia.* Middletown: Wesleyan UP, 2001.

———. "Twelve Writings toward a Poetics of Alchemy, Dread, Inconsistency, Betweenness, and California Geological Syntax." *American Women Poets in the 21st Century: Where Lyric Meets Language.* Ed. Claudia Rankine and Juliana Spahr. Middletown: Wesleyan UP, 2002. 276–81.

Holloway, Karla F. C. *Codes of Conduct: Race, Ethics, and the Color of Our Character.* New Brunswick: Rutgers UP, 1995.

———. *Moorings and Metaphors: Figures of Culture and Gender in Black Women's Literature.* New Brunswick: Rutgers UP, 1992.

Honey, Maureen. *Shadowed Dreams: Women's Poetry of the Harlem Renaissance.* New Brunswick: Rutgers UP, 2006.

hooks, bell. *Ain't I a Woman: Black Women and Feminism.* Cambridge: South End P, 1981.

Hoover, Paul. "Stark Strangled Banjos: Linguistic Doubleness in the Work of David Hammons, Harryette Mullen, and Al Hibbler." *Denver Quarterly* 36.3–4 (2002): 68–82.

Hopkins, Pauline. *Contending Forces: A Romance Illustrative of Negro Life North and South.* New York: Oxford UP, 1988.

Huehls, Mitchum. "Spun Puns (and Anagrams): Exchange Economies, Subjectivity, and History in Harryette Mullen's *Muse & Drudge.*" *Contemporary Literature* 44.1 (Spring 2003): 19–46.

Hughes, Langston. *The Big Sea: An Autobiography.* New York: Hill & Wang/Farrar, 1993.

———. *The Collected Poems of Langston Hughes.* Ed. Arnold Rampersad. New York: Vintage/Random, 1994.

———. "The Negro Artist and the Racial Mountain." *The Nation* (23 June 1926): 122. Rpt. in *Within the Circle: An Anthology of African American Literary Criticism from the Harlem Renaissance to the Present.* Ed. Angelyn Mitchell. Durham: Duke UP, 1994. 55–59.

———. "Poem" [aka "My People"]. Cullen, *Caroling* 150.

———. "The Weary Blues." Hughes, *Collected* 50.

Hull, Gloria T. *Color, Sex, and Poetry: Three Women Writers of the Harlem Renaissance.* Bloomington: Indiana UP, 1987.

Humphries, Rolfe. "Verse Chronicle." Rev. of *Annie Allen*, by Gwendolyn Brooks. Wright 8.

Hunt, Erica. "(In re:) Sources of the Black Avant-Garde (or: Maps in Sand)." *Tripwire: A Journal of Poetics* 5 (Fall 2001): 35–39.

———. "Notes for an Oppositional Poetics." *The Politics of Poetic Form.* Ed. Charles Bernstein. New York: Roof, 1990. 197–212.

Iijima, Brenda. *The Eco Language Reader.* New York: Nightboat, 2010.

Jackson, Major. *Hoops.* New York: Norton, 2006.

Jacques, Geoffrey. *A Change in the Weather: Modernist Imagination, African American Imaginary.* Amherst: U of Massachusetts P, 2009.

Jenkins, Candice M. *Private Lives, Proper Relations: Regulating Black Intimacy.* Minneapolis: U of Minnesota P, 2007.

Jimoh, A. Yemisi. "Double Consciousness, Modernism, and Womanist Themes in Gwendolyn Brooks's 'The Anniad.'" *MELUS* 23.3 (1998): 167–86.

Johnson, James Weldon. Papers. Yale University Library.

———, ed. *The Book of American Negro Poetry.* San Diego: Harvest/Harcourt, 1983.

Johnson, W. R. Foreword. *Sappho's Lyre: Archaic Lyric and Women Poets of Ancient Greece.* Trans. Diane Rayor. Berkeley: U of California P, 1991. ix–xix.

Johns-Putra, Adeline. "Satirizing the Courtly Woman and Defending the Domestic Woman: Mock Epics and Women Poets in the Romantic Age." *Romanticism on the Net* 15 (August 1999). Website.

Jones, LeRoi. "American Sexual Reference: Black Male." *Home: Social Essays.* By Jones. New York: Morrow, 1966. 216–33.

———. *Blues People: Negro Music in White America.* New York: Perennial/HarperCollins, 2002.

————. "The Myth of a 'Negro Literature.'" *Home: Social Essays*. By LeRoi Jones. New York: Morrow, 1966. 105–15.

Jones, Meta DuEwa. "Jazz Prosodies: Orality and Textuality." *Callaloo* 25.4 (Fall 2002): 66–91.

————. *The Muse Is Music: Jazz Poetry from the Harlem Renaissance to Spoken Word*. Urbana: U of Illinois P, 2011.

Jordan, June. "The Difficult Miracle of Black Poetry in America or Something Like a Sonnet for Phillis Wheatley." *By Herself: Women Reclaim Poetry*. Ed. Molly McQuade. St. Paul: Graywolf P, 2000. 61–73.

Joron, Andrew. "The Missing Body." *The Cry at Zero: Selected Prose*. By Joron. Denver: Counterpath P, 2007. 51–57.

————. "Will Alexander: The New Animism." Introduction. *Singing in Magnetic Hoofbeat: Essays, Prose Texts, Interviews, and a Lecture, 1991–2007*. Ed. Taylor Brady. New York: Factory School, forthcoming.

Joyce, Joyce A., ed. *Conversations with Sonia Sanchez*. Jackson: U of Mississippi P, 2007.

————. *Ijala: Sonia Sanchez and the African Poetic Tradition*. Chicago: Third World P, 1996.

Kamada, Roy Osamu. "Postcolonial Romanticisms: Derek Walcott and the Melancholic Narrative of Landscape." Bryson, *Ecopoetry* 207–20.

Kamboureli, Smaro. *On the Edge of Genre: The Contemporary Canadian Long Poem*. Toronto: U of Toronto P, 1991.

Kaplan, Sara Clarke. "Souls at the Crossroads, Africans on the Water: The Politics of Diasporic Melancholia." *Callaloo* 30.2 (Spring 2007): 511–26.

Keizer, Arlene. *Black Subjects: Identity Formation in the Contemporary Narrative of Slavery*. Ithaca: Cornell UP, 2004.

Keller, Lynn. *Forms of Expansion: Recent Long Poems by Women*. Chicago: U of Chicago P, 1997.

Kelley, Robin D. G. *Freedom Dreams: The Black Radical Imagination*. Boston: Beacon, 2002.

Kent, George E. *A Life of Gwendolyn Brooks*. Lexington: UP of Kentucky, 1990.

Kerlin, Robert T., ed. *Negro Poets and Their Poems*. Washington, D. C.: Associated Publishers, 1923.

Kgositsile, Keorapetse. "Red Song." *If I Could Sing: Selected Poems*. By Kgositsile. Roggebaai/Plumstead, South Africa: Kwela/Snailpress, 2002. 62–64.

King, Lloyd. "Surrealism and the Sacred in the Aesthetic Credo of Octavio Paz." *Hispanic Review* 37.3 (July 1969): 383–93.

Kufrin, Joan. "The Poet: Gwendolyn Brooks." *Uncommon Women*. By Kufrin. Piscataway, NJ: New Century, 1981. 34–51.

Kunitz, Stanley. "Bronze by Gold." Rev. of *Annie Allen*, by Gwendolyn Brooks. Wright 10–14.

Lavery, Matthew A. "The Ontogeny and Phylogeny of Mackey's *Song of the Andoumboulou*." *African American Review* 38 (2004): 683–94.

Lee, Don L. "Gwendolyn Brooks: Beyond the Wordmaker—The Making of an African Poet." Brooks, *Report* 13–30.

———. "Toward a Definition: Black Poetry of the Sixties (after LeRoi Jones)." *Within the Circle: An Anthology of African American Literary Criticism from the Harlem Renaissance to the Present.* Ed. Angelyn Mitchell. Durham: Duke UP, 1994: 213–23.

Leonard, Keith D. *Fettered Genius: The African American Bardic Poet from Slavery to Civil Rights.* Charlottesville: U of Virginia P, 2006.

Lester, Toni. "The Literature of AIDS." *Black Issues Book Review* 3.4 (July–Aug. 2001): 48–51.

Locke, Alain, ed. *The New Negro.* New York: Touchstone/Simon, 1997.

Lorde, Audre. "Sexism: An American Disease in Blackface." *Sister Outsider: Essays and Speeches.* Berkeley: Crossing P, 1984. 60–65.

Lovejoy, Arthur O. "On the Discrimination of Romanticisms." Abrams, *English* 3–24.

Lubiano, Wahneema. "Black Ladies, Welfare Queens, and State Minstrels: Ideological Warfare by Narrative Means." *Race-ing Justice, En-gender-ing Power: Essays on Anita Hill, Clarence Thomas, and the Construction of Social Reality.* Ed. Toni Morrison. New York: Pantheon, 1992. 323–63.

Mackey, Nathaniel. *Discrepant Engagement: Dissonance, Cross-Culturality, and Experimental Writing.* Tuscaloosa: U of Alabama P, 1993.

Madhubuti, Haki R. *Black Men: Obsolete, Single, Dangerous? The Afrikan American Family in Transition.* Chicago: Third World Press, 1991.

———. Foreword. *Fingernails across the Chalkboard: Poetry and Prose on HIV/ AIDS from the Black Diaspora.* Ed. Randall Horton, M. L. Hunter, and Becky Thompson. Chicago: Third World P, 2007. ix–xii.

Major, Clarence. "'I Follow My Eyes': An Interview with Clarence Major." Interview with Larry McCaffery and Jerzy Kutnik. *African American Review* 28.1 (Spring 1994): 121–38. Rpt. in *Clarence Major and His Art: Portraits of an African American Postmodernist.* Ed. Bernard W. Bell. Chapel Hill: U of North Carolina P, 2001. 77–98.

Mathes, Carter. "Peering into the Maw: Larry Neal's Aesthetic Universe." Unpublished manuscript in possession of author.

Mayfield, Julian. "You Touch My Black Aesthetic and I'll Touch Yours." Gayle, *Black* 24–31.

McBride, Dwight A. "Can the Queen Speak?" *Why I Hate Abercrombie and Fitch: Essays on Race and Sexuality.* New York: New York UP, 2005. 203–25.

———. "Straight Black Studies: On African American Studies, James Baldwin, and Queer Black Studies." *Black Queer Studies: A Critical Anthology.* Ed. E. Patrick Johnson and Mae G. Henderson. Durham: Duke UP, 2005. 68–89.

McDowell, Deborah. *"The Changing Same": Black Women's Literature, Criticism, and Theory.* Bloomington: Indiana UP, 1995.

McDowell, Paula. "The Manufacture and Lingua-Facture of 'Ballad-Making':

Broadside Ballads in Long Eighteenth-Century Ballad Discourse." *The Eighteenth Century* 47.2/3 (Summer 2006): 151–78.

McGinley, Phyllis. "Poetry for Prose Readers." *New York Times* 22 Jan. 1950: 177.

McGuirk, Kevin. "'All Wi Doin': Tony Harrison, Linton Kwesi Johnson, and the Cultural Work of the Lyric in Postwar Britain." *New Definitions of Lyric: Theory, Technology, and Culture.* Ed. Mark Jeffreys. New York: Garland/Taylor and Francis, 1998. 49–75.

McHale, Brian. *The Obligation toward the Difficult Whole: Postmodernist Long Poems.* Tuscaloosa: U of Alabama P, 2004.

McKinley, Jesse, and Kirk Johnson. "Mormons Tipped Scale in Ban on Gay Marriage." *New York Times* 14 Nov. 2008: Website.

McMorris, Mark. "Sincerity and Revolt in Avant-Garde Poetry: Créolité, Surrealism, and New World Alliances." *Tripwire: A Journal of Poetics* 5 (Fall 2001): 41–56.

McNew, Janet. "Mary Oliver and the Tradition of Romantic Nature Poetry." *Contemporary Literature* 30 (1989): 59–77.

Melhem, D. H. *Gwendolyn Brooks: Poetry and the Heroic Voice.* Lexington: UP of Kentucky, 1987.

Mellor, Anne, ed. *Romanticism and Feminism.* Bloomington: Indiana UP, 1988.

Milner, Ronald. "Black Theater—Go Home!" Gayle, *Black* 306–12.

Mix, Deborah. "Tender Revisions: Harryette Mullen's *Trimmings* and *S*PeRM**K*T*." *American Literature* 77.1 (March 2005): 65–92.

Moses, Cat. "The Blues Aesthetic in Toni Morrison's *The Bluest Eye.*" *African American Review* 33.4 (Winter 1999): 623–37.

Moten, Fred. *In the Break: The Aesthetics of the Black Radical Tradition.* Minneapolis: U of Minnesota P, 2003.

Mullen, Harryette. "African Signs and Spirit Writing." *Callaloo* 19.3 (1996): 670–89.

———. *Blues Baby: Early Poems.* Lewisburg, PA: Bucknell UP, 2002.

———. "'A Collective Force of Burning Ink': Will Alexander's *Asia & Haiti.*" *Callaloo* 22.2 (1999): 417–26.

———. "A Conversation with Harryette Mullen." Interview with Farah Griffin, Michael Magee, and Kristen Gallagher. *Electronic Poetry Center* (1997). Website.

———. "'Incessant Elusives': The Oppositional Poetics of Erica Hunt and Will Alexander." *Holding Their Own: Perspectives on the Multi-Ethnic Literatures of the United States.* Ed. Dorothea Fischer-Hornung and Heike Raphael-Hernandez. Tübingen: Stauffenburg Verlag, 2000. 207–16.

———. "An Interview with Harryette Mullen." By Elisabeth A. Frost. *Contemporary Literature* 41.3 (Spring 2000): 397–421.

———. "Interview with Harryette Mullen." By Cynthia Hogue. *Postmodern Culture* 9 (January 1999). Website.

———. "Kinky Quatrains." *Ecstatic Occasions, Expedient Forms: 85 Leading Contemporary Poets Select and Comment on Their Poems.* Ed. David Lehman. Ann Arbor: U of Michigan P, 1996. 165–67.

———. *Muse & Drudge.* Philadelphia : Singing Horse P, 1995.

———. *Sleeping with the Dictionary.* Berkeley: U of California P, 2002.

———. "The Solo Mysterioso Blues: An Interview with Harryette Mullen." Interview with Calvin Bedient. *Callaloo* 19.3 (1996): 651–69.

———. Untitled essay. *Tripwire: A Journal of Poetics* 5 (Fall 2001): 11–14.

Mulokozi, Mugyabuso M. *The African Epic Controversy: Historical, Philosophical, and Aesthetic Perspectives on Epic Poetry and Performance.* Dar es Salaam: Mkuki na Nyota Publishers, 2002.

Murray, Rolland. *Our Living Manhood: Literature, Black Power, and Masculine Ideology.* Philadelphia: U of Pennsylvania P, 2007.

Neal, Larry. "And Shine Swam On." Afterword. *Black Fire: An Anthology of Afro-American Writing.* Ed. Amiri Baraka (LeRoi Jones) and Larry Neal. 1968. Baltimore: Black Classic P, 2007. 638–56.

———. "The Black Arts Movement." *Visions of a Liberated Future: Black Arts Movement Writings.* Ed. Michael Schwartz. New York: Thunder's Mouth P, 1989. 62–78.

Newman, Lance. "Marxism and Ecocriticism." *Interdisciplinary Studies in Literature and Environment* 9.2 (Summer 2002): 1–25.

Nielsen, Aldon Lynn. *Black Chant: Languages of African-American Postmodernism.* New York: Cambridge UP, 1997.

———. *Integral Music: Languages of African American Innovation.* Tuscaloosa: U of Alabama P, 2004.

———. "This Ain't No Disco." *The World in Time and Space: Towards a History of Innovative American Poetry in Our Time.* Ed. Edward Foster and Joseph Donahue. Jersey City: Talisman House, 2001. 536–46.

———. "Will Alexander's 'Transmundane Specific.'" *Callaloo* 22.2 (1999): 409–16.

Oelschlaeger, Max. *The Idea of Wilderness.* New Haven: Yale UP, 1991.

Okpewho, Isadore. *The Epic in Africa: Toward a Poetics of the Oral Performance.* New York: Columbia UP, 1979.

Ostriker, Alicia S. *Stealing the Language: The Emergence of Women's Poetry in America.* Boston: Beacon, 1987.

Ovid. *Metamorphoses.* Trans. Rolfe Humphries. Bloomington: Indiana UP, 1955.

Palmer, R. Roderick. "The Poetry of Three Revolutionists: Don L. Lee, Sonia Sanchez, and Nikki Giovanni." Gibson 135–46.

"A People at War: The War in the Pacific: Mess Attendant First Class Doris Miller." National Archives and Records Administration. Website.

"Pencil Nebula Scribbles Notes from Past." *Exploring the Universe.* 5 June 2003. National Aeronautics and Space Administration. Website.

Perloff, Marjorie. "After Language Poetry: Innovation and Its Theoretical Discontents." *Contemporary Poetics*. Ed. Louis Armand. Evanston: Northwestern UP, 2007. 15–38.

Quetchenbach, Bernard W. *Back from the Far Field: American Nature Poetry in the Late Twentieth Century*. Charlottesville: UP of Virginia, 2000.

Radar, Ralph W. "Notes on Some Structural Varieties and Variations in Dramatic 'I' Poems and Their Theoretical Implications." *Critical Essays on Robert Browning*. Ed. Mary Ellis Gibson. New York: G. K. Hall, 1992. 37–53.

Randall, Dudley, ed. *The Black Poets*. New York: Bantam, 1971.

Rasula, Jed. *This Compost: Ecological Imperatives in American Poetry*. Athens: U of Georgia P, 2002.

Rayor, Diane J. Introduction. *Sappho's Lyre: Archaic Lyric and Women Poets of Ancient Greece*. Trans. Rayor. Berkeley: U of California P, 1991. 1–20.

Redding, J. Saunders. "Cellini-like Lyrics." Rev. of *Annie Allen*, by Gwendolyn Brooks. *Saturday Review* 32.38 (17 Sept. 1949): 23+.

Redmond, Eugene B. *Drumvoices: The Mission of Afro-American Poetry: A Critical History*. Garden City, NY: Anchor/Doubleday, 1976.

Righelato, Pat. *Understanding Rita Dove*. Columbia: U of South Carolina P, 2006.

Roberson, Ed. *Atmosphere Conditions*. Los Angeles: Sun & Moon P, 2000.

——. *City Eclogue*. Berkeley: Atelos, 2006.

——. "'Down Break Drum': An Interview with Ed Roberson (Part I)." Interview with Kathleen Crown. *Callaloo* 33.3 (Summer 2010): 651–82.

——. *Etai-Eken*. Pittsburgh: U of Pittsburgh P, 1975.

——. *To See the Earth before the End of the World*. Middletown, CT: Wesleyan UP, 2010.

——. "The Structure Then the Music: An Interview with Ed Roberson." Interview with Randall Horton. *Callaloo* 33.3 (Summer 2010): 762–69.

——. Unpublished lecture. Northwestern University, November 16, 2007. Poetry Foundation. Website.

——. *Voices Cast Out to Talk Us In*. Iowa City: U of Iowa P, 1995.

——. *When Thy King Is a Boy*. Pittsburgh: U of Pittsburgh P, 1970.

Robins, Steven. "'Long Live Zackie, Long Live': AIDS Activism, Science and Citizenship after Apartheid." *Journal of Southern African Studies* 30.3 (Sept. 2004): 651–72.

Román, David. "Fierce Love and Fierce Response: Intervening in the Cultural Politics of Race, Sexuality, and AIDS." *Critical Essays: Gay and Lesbian Writers of Color*. Ed. Emmanuel S. Nelson. New York: Haworth P, 1993. 195–219.

Rosello, Mireille. Introduction. *Notebook of a Return to My Native Land / Cahier d'un retour au pays natal*. By Aimé Césaire. Trans. Rosello with Annie Pritchard. Newcastle upon Tyne, England: Bloodaxe, 1995. 9–64.

Rosemont, Franklin. "Surrealism, Poetry, and Politics." *Race Traitor* 13–14 (Summer 2001): 55–63.

Rosemont, Franklin, and Robin D. G. Kelley, eds. *Black, Brown, and Beige: Surrealist Writings from Africa and the Diaspora*. Austin: U of Texas P, 2009.

Rushdy, Ashraf H. A. *Neo-Slave Narratives: Studies in the Social Logic of a Literary Form*. New York: Oxford UP, 1999.

Russell, Sandi. *Render Me My Song: African-American Women Writers from Slavery to the Present*. New York: St. Martin's P, 1990.

Russo, Linda. "Writing Within: Notes on Ecopoetics as a Spatial Practice." *HOW2* 3.2 (2008). Website.

Salaam, Kalamu ya. "Love and Liberation: Sonia Sanchez's Literary Uses of the Personal." *BMa: The Sonia Sanchez Literary Review* 3.1 (Fall 1997): 57–120.

Sanchez, Sonia. "'As Poets, As Activists': An Interview with Sonia Sanchez." Interview with David Reich. Joyce, *Conversations* 80–93.

———. *A Blues Book for Blue Black Magical Women*. Detroit: Broadside P, 1974.

———. *Does Your House Have Lions?* Boston: Beacon, 1997.

———. "Form and Responsibility." *A Formal Feeling Comes: Poems in Form by Contemporary Women*. Ed. Annie Finch. Brownsville, OR: Story Line P, 1997. 195–97.

———. "Form and Spirit: A Conversation with Sonia Sanchez." Interview with Annie Finch. Joyce, *Conversations* 27–46.

———. *Home Coming*. Detroit: Broadside P, 1969.

———. *Homegirls and Handgrenades*. Buffalo: White Pine Press, 2007.

———. "Interview with Sonia Sanchez." Interview with Larvester Gaither. Joyce, *Conversations* 47–61.

———. "An Interview with Sonia Sanchez." Interview with Sascha Feinstein. *Innovative Women Poets: An Anthology of Contemporary Poetry and Interviews*. Ed. Elisabeth A. Frost and Cynthia Hogue. Iowa City: U of Iowa P, 2006. 277–92.

———. *I've Been a Woman: New and Selected Poems*. Chicago: Third World Press, 1993.

———. *Love Poems*. New York: Third P, 1973.

———. *Shake Loose My Skin: New and Selected Poems*. Boston: Beacon P, 1999.

———. "Sonia Sanchez: An Interview." Interview with Herbert Leibowitz. Joyce, *Conversations* 6–16.

———. "Sonia Sanchez: The Joy of Writing Poetry." Interview with Kadija Sesay. Joyce, *Conversations* 144–54.

———. *We A BaddDDD People*. Detroit: Broadside P, 1970.

———. *Wounded in the House of a Friend*. Boston: Beacon P, 1995.

Schenck, Celeste M. "Feminism and Deconstruction: Re-Constructing the Elegy." *Tulsa Studies in Women's Literature* 5.1 (Spring 1986): 13–27.

Schultz, Elizabeth. "Natural and Unnatural Circumstances in Langston Hughes' *Not Without Laughter*." *Callaloo* 25.4 (Autumn 2002): 1176–87.

Schweizer, Bernard, ed. *Approaches to the Anglo and American Female Epic, 1621–1982*. Burlington, VT: Ashgate, 2006.

Shaw, Stephanie J. *What a Woman Ought to Be and to Do: Black Professional Women Workers during the Jim Crow Era.* Chicago: U of Chicago P, 1996.

Shelley, Percy Bysshe. "England in 1819." *The Norton Anthology of Poetry.* Ed. Alexander W. Allison, et al. New York: Norton, 1983. 620.

Shields, John. "Wheatley's Struggle for Freedom in Her Poetry and Prose." *The Collected Works of Phillis Wheatley.* By Phillis Wheatley. New York: Oxford UP, 1988. 229–70.

Shockley, Evie. "Post–Black-Aesthetic Poetry: Postscripts and Postmarks." *Mixed Blood* No. 2 (2007): 50–60.

Silver, Nate. "Prop 8 Myths." 11 Nov. 2008. *FiveThirtyEight: Politics Done Right* (blog). Website.

Simpson, Megan. "Will in the Wilderness: Language and Ecology in Will Alexander's *Stratospheric Canticles.*" *Interdisciplinary Studies in Literature and Environment* 15.2 (2008): 117–35.

Skinner, Jonathan. Editor's Statement. *ecopoetics* 1 (Winter 2001–2002): 5–8.

Slaymaker, William. "Ecoing the Other(s): The Call of Global Green and Black African Responses." *PMLA* 116 (2001): 129–44.

Smethurst, James Edward. *The Black Arts Movement: Literary Nationalism in the 1960s and 1970s.* Chapel Hill: U of North Carolina P, 2005.

Smith, Barbara. "Toward a Black Feminist Criticism." *African American Literary Theory: A Reader.* Ed. Winston Napier. New York: New York UP, 2000. 132–46.

Smith, David Lionel. "The Black Arts Movement and Its Critics." *American Literary History* 3.1 (Spring 1991): 93–110.

Smith, Felipe. *American Body Politics: Race, Gender, and Black Literary Renaissance.* Athens: U of Georgia P, 1998.

Smith, Valerie. "Black Feminist Theory and the Representation of the 'Other.'" *Changing Our Own Words: Essays on Criticism, Theory, and Writing by Black Women.* Ed. Cheryl A. Wall. New Brunswick: Rutgers UP, 1989.

Spady, James G. "The Centrality of Black Language in the Discourse Strategies and Poetic Force of Sonia Sanchez and Rap Artists." *BMa: The Sonia Sanchez Literary Review* 6.1 (Fall 2000): 47–72.

Spencer, Anne. "Before the Feast of Shushan." Johnson, *Book* 213–15.

———. "Lady, Lady." Locke, *New* 148.

———. "Letter to My Sister." Greene, *Time's* 194.

———. "Lines to a Nasturtium." Cullen, *Caroling* 52–53.

———. Papers. Special Collections. University of Virginia Library.

———. Rev. of *An Autumn Love Cycle,* by Georgia Douglas Johnson. *The Crisis* 36.3 (Mar. 1929): 87.

———. "Substitution." Cullen, *Caroling* 48.

Spillers, Hortense. *Black, White, and in Color: Essays on American Literature and Culture.* Chicago: U of Chicago P, 2003.

Stanford, Ann Folwell. "An Epic with a Difference: Sexual Politics in Gwendolyn Brooks's 'The Anniad.'" *American Literature* 67.2 (1995): 283–301.

Stetson, Erlene. "Anne Spencer." *CLA Journal* 21.3 (Mar. 1978): 400–09.

Strand, Mark, and Eavan Boland. *The Making of a Poem: A Norton Anthology of Poetic Forms.* New York: Norton, 2000.

Tate, Claudia. "Anger So Flat: Gwendolyn Brooks's *Annie Allen.*" *A Life Distilled: Gwendolyn Brooks, Her Poetry and Fiction.* Ed. Maria K. Mootry and Gary Smith. Urbana: U of Illinois P, 1987. 140–52.

Taylor, Henry. "An Essential Sanity." Wright 254–75.

Thomas, Lorenzo. *Extraordinary Measures: Afrocentric Modernism and Twentieth-Century American Poetry.* Tuscaloosa: U of Alabama P, 2000.

———. "Kindred: Origins of the Black Avant-Garde." *Tripwire: A Journal of Poetics* 5 (Fall 2001): 57–64.

Vint, Sherryl. "'Only by Experience': Embodiment and the Limitations of Realism in Neo-Slave Narratives." *Science Fiction Studies* 34.2 (2007): 241–61.

Wachman, Gay. "A Collection of Shouts." Rev. of *Does Your House Have Lions?* by Sonia Sanchez. *American Book Review* 19.6 (1998): 21+.

Wade-Gayles, Gloria, ed. *Conversations with Gwendolyn Brooks.* Jackson: UP of Mississippi, 2003.

Wagner, Vallerie. Foreword. *To Be Left with the Body.* Ed. Cheryl Clarke and Steven G. Fullwood. Los Angeles: AIDS Project Los Angeles, 2008. Website.

Wall, Cheryl. *Women of the Harlem Renaissance.* Bloomington: Indiana UP, 1995.

———. *Worrying the Line: Black Women Writers, Lineage, and Literary Tradition.* Chapel Hill: U of North Carolina P, 2005.

Walters, Tracey L. "Gwendolyn Brooks' 'The Anniad' and the Indeterminacy of Genre." *College Language Association Journal* 44.3 (2001): 350–66.

Warner, Michael. *The Trouble with Normal: Sex, Politics, and the Ethics of Queer Life.* New York: Free P/Simon & Schuster, 1999.

Washington, Mary Helen. *Invented Lives: Narratives of Black Women 1860–1960.* Garden City, NY: Anchor/Doubleday, 1987.

———. "'Taming All That Anger Down': Rage and Silence in Gwendolyn Brooks's *Maud Martha.*" *Massachusetts Review* 2.2 (Summer 1983): 453–66.

Weil, Eric A. "Personal and Public: Three First-Person Voices in African American Poetry." Gabbin, *Furious* 223–38.

Whitman, Albery Allson. *Twasinta's Seminoles; or Rape of Florida.* African American Poetry, ProQuest. Website.

Widener, Daniel. "Writing Watts: Budd Schulberg, Black Poetry, and the Cultural War on Poverty." *Journal of Urban History* 34 (2008): 665–87.

Wimsatt, W. K. "The Structure of Romantic Nature Imagery." Abrams, *English* 25–36.

Wordsworth, William. "The World Is Too Much with Us." *The Norton Anthology of Poetry.* Ed. Alexander W. Allison, et al. New York: Norton, 1983. 559.

Wright, Stephen Caldwell, ed. *On Gwendolyn Brooks: Reliant Contemplation.* Ann Arbor: U of Michigan P, 1996.

Young, Kevin. "Visiting St. Elizabeths: Ezra Pound, Impersonation, and the Mask of the Modern Poet." *Ezra Pound and African American Modernism.* Ed. Michael Coyle. Orono, ME: Nat'l Poetry Foundation, 2001. 185–204.

Yu, Timothy. *Race and the Avant-Garde: Experimental and Asian American Poetry Since 1965.* Stanford, CA: Stanford UP, 2009.

Zeiger, Melissa F. *Beyond Consolation: Death, Sexuality, and the Changing Shapes of Elegy.* Ithaca: Cornell UP, 1997.

CONTEMPORARY NORTH AMERICAN POETRY SERIES